PRAISE FOR

The Gangs of New York

". . .[T]here has been no volume before Asbury's devoted exclusively to a history of the New York gangs . . . Mr. Asbury's book must be regarded as a distinct contribution to Americana. He has rummaged through old histories and reports and has searched the morgues of newspapers for his contribution . . . The tale is one of blood, excitement, and debauchery. . . ."
—JOHN R. CHAMBERLAIN, *New York Times*

"One of the best American books of its kind. Mr. Asbury writes in a direct and engaging manner . . . He tells the story of the New York underworld of the past century, and his narrative is excellently presented in a book adorned with amusing pictures from the weeklies and newspapers."
—EDMUND PEARSON, *The Saturday Review of Literature*

"One devours its pages eagerly as though it were thrill-laden fiction rather than fact . . . a work of immense interest whether the multifarious details of skull-cracking, blood-letting and general devilishness be minutely exact or not."
—*Booklist*

"Herbert Asbury's underworld is an underworld, and not a region of heroes. The stage and the screen will look to it in vain for the broken-hearted gentlemen who turn to crime out of a frustrated goodness, and there, practice honor among thieves, punctilio toward their victims, and eloquence upon the world at large. The book has been written by a newspaper man who does not mind denying himself of the pleasure of melodrama."
—CARL VAN DOREN, *Books (NY Herald Tribune)*

"[T]hough New York was not an exception among big cities in breeding law-breakers in its slums, the species developed there was marked by distinctive features. . . . described with point, gusto and a sense of proportion . . . "
—*Times [London] Literary Supplement*

" . . . tells the story of the more spectacular gangsters, with a quantity of picturesque detail . . ."
—MALCOLM COWLEY, *The New Republic*

"This is a fine piece of historical writing, and as full of interest to any lover of the picaresque as anyone has a right to ask."
—HERSCHEL BRICKELL, *North American Review*

THE
GANGS
OF
NEW YORK

*An Informal History
of the Underworld*

<small>By</small> <small>Herbert Asbury</small>

<small>**THUNDER'S MOUTH PRESS ★ NEW YORK**</small>

THE GANGS OF NEW YORK:
An Informal History of the Underworld

Copyright © 1927, 1928 by Alfred A. Knopf, Inc.

"Monk Eastman, Purveyor of Iniquities,"
from *Collected Fictions* by Jorge Luis Borges,
translated by Andrew Hurley, © 1998 by Maria Kodama;
translation © 1998 by Penguin Putnam Inc. Used by permission of
Viking Penguin, a division of Penguin Putnam, Inc.

Published by
Thunder's Mouth Press
An Imprint of Avalon Publishing Group Incorporated
161 William St., 16th Floor
New York, NY 10038

Published by arrangement with Alfred A. Knopf, Inc.

Library of Congress Cataloging-in-Publication Data
Asbury, Herbert, 1891–1963
The gangs of New York : an informal history of the underworld /
Herbert Asbury ; foreword by Jorge Luis Borges
p. cm.
Previously published: New York : Paragon House, 1990.
Includes bibliographical references and index.
ISBN 1-56025-275-8
1. Gangs—New York (State)—New York.
2. New York (N.Y.)—Social conditions. I. Title.
HV6439.U7 N4 2001
364.1'06'097471—dc21
2001046256

9   8   7   6   5   4   3   2

Designed by *Pauline Neuwirth, Neuwirth & Associates, Inc.*
Cover design by *Howard Grossman, 12E Design*

Printed in the United States of America
Distributed by Publishers Group West

To Orell

The Five Points in 1829

CONTENTS

LIST OF ILLUSTRATIONS

FOREWORD

MONK EASTMAN, PURVEYOR OF INIQUITIES

Jorge Luis Borges

THE TOUGHS OF ONE AMERICA

Whether profiled against a backdrop of blue-painted walls or of the sky itself, two toughs sheathed in grave black clothing dance, in boots with highstacked heels, a solemn dance—the tango of evenly matched knives—until suddenly, a carnation drops from behind an ear, for a knife has plunged into a man, whose horizontal dying brings the dance without music to its end. Resigned, the other man adjusts his hat and devotes the years of his old age to telling the story of that clean-fought duel. That, to the least and last detail, is the story of the Argentine underworld. The story of the thugs and ruffians of New York has much more speed, and much less grace.

THE TOUGHS OF ANOTHER

The story of the New York gangs (told in 1928 by Herbert Asbury in a decorous volume of some four hundred octavo pages) possesses all the confusion and cruelty of barbarian cosmologies, and much of their gigantism and ineptitude. The chaotic story takes place in the cellars of old breweries turned into Negro tenements, in a seedy, three-story New York City filled with gangs of thugs like the Swamp Angels, who would swarm out of labyrinthine sewers on marauding expeditions; gangs of cutthroats like the Daybreak Boys, who recruited precocious murderers of ten and eleven years old; brazen, solitary giants like the Plug Uglies, whose stiff bowler hats stuffed with wool and whose vast shirttails blowing in the wind of the slums might provoke a passerby's improbable smile, but who carried huge bludgeons in their right hands and long, narrow pistols; and gangs of street toughs like the Dead Rabbit gang, who entered into battle under the banner of their mascot impaled upon a pike. Its characters were men like Dandy Johnny Dolan, famed for his brilliantined forelock, the monkey-headed walking sticks he carried, and the delicate copper pick he wore on his thumb to gouge out his enemies' eyes; men like Kit Burns, who was known to bite the head off live rats; and men like blind Danny Lyons, a towheaded kid with huge dead eyes who pimped for three whores that proudly walked the streets for him. There were rows of red-light houses, such as those run by the seven New England sisters that gave all the profits from their Christmas Eves to charity; rat fights and dog fights; Chinese gambling dens; women like the oft-widowed Red Norah, who was squired about and loved by every leader of the famous Gophers, or Lizzy the Dove, who put on black when Danny Lyons was murdered and got her throat cut for it by Gentle Maggie, who took exception to Lizzy's old affair with the dead blind man; riots such as that of the savage week of 1863 when a hundred buildings were burned to the ground and the entire city was lucky to escape the flames; street brawls when a man would be as lost as if he'd drowned, for he'd be stomped to death; and thieves and horse poisoners like Yoske Nigger. The most famous hero of the story of the New York City underworld is Edward Delaney, alias William Delaney, alias Joseph Marvin, alias Joseph Morris—alias Monk Eastman, the leader of the gang of twelve hundred men.

INTRODUCTION

THIS BOOK is not a sociological treatise, and makes no pretense of offering solutions for the social, economic and criminological problems presented by the gangs. Nor does it aim to interpret and analyze the gangster in the modern "I think-he-thought" manner by conducting the reader into the innermost recesses of his mind and there observing the operation of his scant mental equipment. On the contrary, it is an attempt to chronicle the more spectacular exploits of the refractory citizen who was a dangerous nuisance in New York for almost a hundred years, with a sufficient indication of his background of vice, poverty, and political corruption to make him understandable. Happily, he has now passed from the metropolitan scene, and for nearly half a score of years has existed mainly in the lively imaginations of industrious journalists, among whom the tradition of the gangster has more lives than the proverbial cat. Nothing has ever provided more or better copy than his turbulent doings, and hopeful reporters continue to resurrect him every time there is a mysterious killing in the slum districts or among the white lights of Broadway. No matter how obviously the crime be rooted in bootlegging, dope peddling or what not, it is hailed as a new gang murder; words and phrases which have grown hoary and infirm in the service are trundled out and dusted off, and next morning shriek to a delighted populace that there is blood on the face of the moon and a new gang war impends.

But the conflict never materializes, and it is quite unlikely that it ever will again, for there are now no gangs in New York, and no gangsters in the sense that the word has come into common use. In his day the gangster flourished under the protection and manipulation of the crooked politician to whom he was an invaluable ally at election time, but his day has simply passed. Improved social, economic and educational conditions have lessened the number of recruits, and the organized gangs have been clubbed out of existence by the police, who have always been prompt to inaugurate repressive campaigns when permitted to do so by their political masters. Inspector Alexander S. Williams gave the gangs the first downward push when he enunciated and put into practice his famous dictum that "there is more law in the end of a policeman's nightstick than in a decision of the Supreme Court," and their decline continued as decency invaded politics and an enraged citizenry protested against wholesale brawling and slugging. The gangs were definitely on the run when John Purroy Mitchel was elected Mayor on a reform ticket in 1914, and his Commissioners of Police, Douglas I. McKay and Arthur Woods, completed the rout by sending to prison some three hundred gangsters, including many of the shining lights of the underworld.

It is true that there remain small groups which occasionally take in vain such mighty names as the Gophers, Hudson Dusters, and Gas Housers, but they are no more gangs than an armed rabble is an army; they are merely young hoodlums who seek to take advantage of ancient reputations. Within the past few years there have also arisen various combinations of young criminals such as the Cry Babies, Cake Eaters and the bands captained by Cowboy Tessler and Richard Reese Whittemore, all of which have been called gangs in the news stories. But while some of the old time gangs could muster as many as a thousand members, none of these recent groups comprised more than half a dozen, and none was able to operate more than a few months before it was dispersed by the police and its leaders sent to prison or the electric chair. They had nothing in common with such great brawling, thieving gangs as the Dead Rabbits, Bowery Boys, Eastmans, Gophers, and Five Pointers; they were more nearly akin to the bands of professional burglars and bank robbers who infested the metropolis soon after the Civil War. In the underworld such groups are not even known as gangs; they are called mobs, the difference being that a mob is composed of only a few men, seldom

more than six or eight, who combine for a specific series of robberies or other crimes and have no particular adhesion or loyalty
to their leader. They are gunmen and burglars, but none of their
killings and stealings have anything to do with gang rivalry or
questions of gang jurisdiction; and brawling and rough and tumble fighting is quite foreign to the nature of such genteel thugs.
Their operations lack the spectacularity of the deeds of the old
timers, and probably will continue to lack it until they have been
touched by the magic finger of legend. However, they are in fact
probably even more dangerous, in proportion to numbers, than
the redoubtable thugs who once terrorized the Bowery, Hell's
Kitchen, and the ancient Five Points, for a majority are drug
addicts, and they are very peevish and quick on the trigger.

The gangster whose reign ended with the murder of Kid
Dropper was primarily a product of his environment; poverty and
disorganization of home and community brought him into being,
and political corruption and all its attendant evils fostered his
growth. He generally began as a member of a juvenile gang, and
lack of proper direction and supervision naturally graduated him
into the ranks of the older gangsters. Thus he grew to manhood
without the slightest conception of right and wrong, with an aversion to honest labor that amounted to actual loathing, and with a
keen admiration for the man who was able to get much for nothing. Moreover, his only escape from the misery of his surround-
ings lay in excitement, and he could imagine no outlets for his
turbulent spirit save sex and fighting. And many a boy became a
gangster solely because of an overwhelming desire to emulate the
exploits of some spectacular figure of the underworld, or because
of a yearning for fame and glory which he was unable to satisfy
except by acquiring a reputation as a tough guy and a hard mug.

The basic creed of the gangster, and for that matter of any
other type of criminal, is that whatever a man has is his only so
long as he can keep it, and that the one who takes it away from
him has not done anything wrong, but has merely demonstrated
his smartness. For the most part the old time gangster was apparently very courageous, but his bravery was in truth a stolid, igno-
rant, unimaginative acceptance of whatever fate was in store for

him; it is worthy of note that the gangster invariably became a first rate soldier, for his imagination was seldom equal to the task of envisioning either himself or his victim experiencing any considerable suffering from the shock of a bullet or the slash of a knife. The cruel attitude of the gangster and his callousness at the sight of blood and pain was aptly illustrated by one of Monk Eastman's exploits when that renowned thug was bouncer at an East Side dance hall, at the outset of his career. Eastman kept the peace of the resort with a huge bludgeon, in which he carefully cut a notch every time he subdued an obstreperous customer. One night he walked up to an inoffensive old man who was drinking beer and laid his scalp open with a tremendous blow. When he was asked why he had attacked the man without provocation, Eastman replied, "Well, I had forty-nine nicks in me stick, an' I wanted to make it an even fifty."

Of course, there were exceptions, for a few gang leaders came from good families and were intelligent, as well as crafty; and some of them abandoned the underworld after brief careers and succeeded in more respectable enterprises. But in the main the gangster was a stupid roughneck born in filth and squalor and reared amid vice and corruption. He fulfilled his natural destiny.

H. A.

New York,
January 5, 1928.

CHAPTER I

THE CRADLE
OF THE GANGS

1

THE FIRST of the gangs which terrorized New York at frequent intervals for almost a century were spawned in the dismal tenements that squatted in the miasmal purlieus of the Five Points area of the Bloody Ould Sixth Ward, which comprised, roughly, the territory bounded by Broadway, Canal street, the Bowery and Park Row, formerly Chatham street. The old Five Points section now contains three of the city's principal agencies for the administration of justice—the Tombs, the Criminal Courts Building and the new County Court House—but in colonial times, and during the early years of the Republic, when the Negroes' burying ground at Broadway and Chambers street was on the outskirts of the town and the present Times Square theatrical district was a howling wilderness in which the savage Indian prowled, it was chiefly marsh or swamp land, surrounding a large lake which was called Fresh Water Pond by the English and Shellpoint, or Kalchhook, by the Dutch. Later the pond became known as the Collect, and so appears on the ancient maps. It filled the area now bounded by White, Leonard, Lafayette and Mulberry streets, most of which is occupied by the Tombs and the Criminal Courts. The original prison was erected in 1838, and although its official name was Halls of Justice, it was popularly known as the Tombs because the design of the building had been copied from that of an ancient Egyptian mausoleum illustrated and described in a book called *Stevens' Travels*, written by John L. Stevens, of Hoboken, after an extensive tour of the land of the Pharaohs.

In the center of the Collect was a small island which was much used as a place of execution and other judicial punishments. It was there that a score of Negroes were hanged, burned at the stake or broken upon the wheel after the Slave Plot of 1741, when the black men rose against their lawful masters in an attempt to burn and loot the city.[1] Later the island became a storage place for powder, and was called Magazine Island. The principal outlet of the pond was at its northern end, about where White and Center streets now intersect. The stream then took a northwesterly course, flowing along the present line of Canal street through Lispenard's Meadows to the Hudson River. Many years before the Revolution, when the palisades which had been built across the southern end of Manhattan just north of the present City Hall as a protection against the Indians were still standing, a small stone bridge was constructed over the stream at Broadway and Canal street, for the use of expeditions which penetrated the wilderness

---

[1] Good accounts of this riot, of similar troubles in 1712, and of the Doctors' Riot in 1788, can be found in Headley's *Sketches of the Great Riots*. The Doctors' Riot grew out of the robbing of graves by medical students. Most of the physicians were driven from the city, the militia was under arms for several days, and Baron Steuben and John Jay were wounded while attempting to disperse the mob. This was before the time of the gangs, and the underworld had nothing to do with any of the outbreaks.

on venturesome journeys to the small settlements in Harlem and on the upper end of the island. It was on the Collect, in 1796, that John Fitch sailed an early experimental steamboat, eleven years before the Clermont swept grandly through the waters of the Hudson. Fitch's craft was an ordinary yawl, eighteen feet long with a beam of seven feet, fitted with a crude steam engine. He had as passengers Robert Fulton, Chancellor Robert R. Livingston, and a sixteen-year-old boy, John Hutchings, who stood in the stern and steered the boat with a paddle.

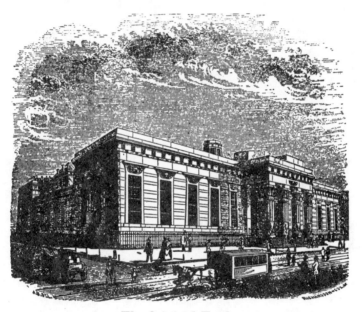

The Original Tombs

Fish abounded in the waters of the Collect, and as the Indians were dispossessed from their hunting grounds and driven northward to the main land, the pond became such a favorite resort of fishermen that conservations measures were necessary, and in 1732 a law was passed prohibiting the use of nets. During this same year Anthony Rutger obtained a grant of seventy-five acres of marsh lands lying on either side of the principal outlet stream, agreeing to drain the area within a year and throw it open to settlement. He opened a canal from the pond to the Hudson River, but dug it so deep that the waters of the Collect were appreciably lowered, and sportsmen complained that the fish were dying. Compelled to fill up the drain for thirty feet from the edge of the pond, Rutger abandoned his scheme, and no further important efforts at reclamation were made for almost seventy-five years. In 1791 the city purchased all claim to the grant from the Rutger heirs, paying about seven hundred dollars for property now worth at least that many millions.

But Rutger's attempt at drainage had reclaimed a considerable area, and as the population of the city increased, and the lower end of the island became more and more crowded, many middle and lower class families began building their homes along the borders of the pond and swamp. In 1784 these colonies had become so large and so numerous that the city authorities appointed a committee to lay out the streets in the vicinity of the Collect, and in 1796 tried unsuccessfully to induce the property holders to cooperate in a scheme to drain the pond through a forty-foot canal. In 1802 Jacob Brown, then Street Commissioner, officially recommended that the Collect be drained and filled, pointing out that it had been fouled by vast quantities of refuse, and was a menace to health. But his proposal was rejected, and nothing was done for six years.

During the winter of 1807–1808 business in New York was almost suspended because of the frightful inclemency of the weather and the unsettled condition of foreign affairs, and the poorer classes, thrown out of employment, were on the verge of starvation. In January 1808 a mob led by sailors whose ships lay idle in the harbor made a demonstration in City Hall Park, and surged through the streets displaying placards demanding bread and work. Alarmed at the temper of the mob, the city authorities made an appropriation for filling the Collect and draining the marsh lands, and the first important public improvement in the history of the city was thus begun. Great gangs of workmen levelled the hills east and west of Broadway, and the earth was dumped into the pond as the waters drained through canals which had been opened to both the Hudson and East Rivers. Several years later, when the earth had settled sufficiently, the streets which had been laid out along the swamp were extended through the site of the pond, and the entire area was thrown open to settlers. The first thoroughfare across the Collect was Collect street, which ran in almost a direct line north and south through the center of the filled-in district. In later years it was called Rynders street, in honor of Captain Isaiah Rynders, political boss of the Sixth Ward and as such the patron and protector of the Five Points gangs. For almost fifty years the thoroughfare was lined with brothels and saloons, and was one of the wickedest sections of the city. Its name was changed to Centre street when the dives were closed and the rehabilitation of the Five Points begun. In recent years the spelling has been altered to Center.

2

THE original Five Points was formed by the intersection of Cross, Anthony, Little Water, Orange and Mulberry streets, which debouched into a triangular area about an acre in extent. In the center of this area was a small park called Paradise Square, which was later surrounded by a paling fence. Eventually the fence became a community clothesline, and was generally disfigured by garments hung upon the palings to dry, while small boys, armed with brickbats and staves, stood guard. In the course of years, as the city developed and undertook new building projects, the routes of many of the Five Points streets were altered, and the physical characteristics of the entire district underwent considerable change, as did the manners and customs of its inhabitants. Anthony street was extended to Chatham Square and became the present Worth street, Orange became Baxter, and Cross bloomed anew as Park street. Little Water street vanished altogether, and Paradise Square became the southwest corner of Mulberry Park, which has been called Columbus Park since 1911. The section now known as Five Points is the intersection of Baxter, Worth and Park streets.

Paradise Square was about the only part in the city where the poor were welcome, and while the aristocrats and the wealthy merchants promenaded Broadway and City Hall Park and held

high revel in the gardens of Cherry Hill, the commoners flocked
to the Points for their recreation and their breath of fresh air. The
Square and the surrounding district thus became the Coney
Island of the period, and the resort of sailors, oystermen, laborers and small-salaried clerks. The aristocrats of the Points were
the butchers, for these gentry were then the great sports of the
city; they were hard drinkers and high-livers, demanding full-
blooded entertainment. One of their engaging diversions was
bullbaiting, a live bull being chained to a swivel ring and tor-
mented by dogs. The principal scene of this sport was Bunker
Hill, about a hundred feet north of the present line of Grand
street, near Mulberry, where the Americans erected a fort during
the Revolution and defended it valiantly against the British troops
under General Howe. After the war the Hill became a popular
duelling ground and a place for mass meetings; in more recent
times the gangs of the Five Points and the Bowery used it as a battleground. Early in the nineteenth century a Fly Market butcher
named Winship built a fence within the old fortifications, and
constructed an arena accommodating 2,000 persons. There bulls
were baited before huge throngs of butchers and their guests,
who wagered on the number of dogs the animals would gore. The
burial vault of the Bayard family, prominent in colonial times,
was on the southern end of the Hill, and when the mound was
finally levelled the bones and bodies were removed. A hermit
from the Points took possession of the vault and lived there for
many years, a terror to the children of the district. He was eventually murdered.

Dancing was the principal diversion during the early days of
the Five Points, and scores of dance houses soon appeared on the
streets surrounding Paradise Square. These places were the pre-
cursors of the modern night clubs and cabarets, although they
lacked the ornateness of the present-day jazz palaces. Curtains of
red bombazine ornamented the windows, the floors were sanded
to afford a better footing for heavy boots, and the only seats were
long benches set against the walls. From the ceilings hung lamps
or hoop chandeliers filled with candles, whale oil and tallow being
the only means of artificial illumination. Dancing was free so

long as the customer bought an occasional glass of ale, porter, or beer at the bar in one corner of the room, and when a wandering Croesus bought drinks for the house he was all but given the freedom of the Points. The dance houses generally remained open until three o'clock in the morning, but during the first few years, at least, they were operated in an orderly manner. High spirited pleasure-seekers sometimes engaged in fist fights, and occasionally a brickbat sailed through the air and cracked a skull, but the man who drew a dirk or a pistol was quickly seized by the crowd and ducked in the Collect sewer, which was all that remained of the stream that once had coursed from the pond through Canal street. Little hard liquor was drunk, but the merry-makers consumed enormous quantities of malt beverages.

The modern purveyors of hot dogs, peanuts and popcorn had their Five Points prototypes in the children and old Negro mammies who peddled mint, strawberries, radishes, and steaming hot yams, and in the Hot Corn Girls who offered piping hot roasting ears from cedar-staved buckets which hung from the hollows of their arms. Dressed in spotted calico and wrapped in a plaid shawl, but barefooted, the Hot Corn Girl appeared on the streets at dusk, and throughout the night she mingled with the crowds on the sidewalks and in the dance houses, hawking her wares and lifting her voice in song:

> Hot Corn! Hot Corn!
> Here's your lily white corn.
> All you that's got money—
> Poor me that's got none—
> Come buy my lily hot corn
> And let me go home.

The Hot Corn Girl became one of the most romantic figures of the Five Points, and her favours were eagerly sought by the young bloods of the district, who fought duels over her and celebrated her beauty and sparkling wit in song and story. The earnings of the best-looking girls were considerable, and it soon became the custom for a Five Points hero with a loathing for labor to send his

young and handsome wife into the street each night carrying a
cedar bucket filled with roasting ears, while he cruised along in
her wake and hurled brickbats at the young men who dared flirt
with her. The first hanging in the Tombs grew out of such a situation. Edward Coleman, one of the original gangsters of Paradise
Square, became enamoured of a young woman known throughout the Five Points as The Pretty Hot Corn Girl. He married her
after fierce fights with a dozen protesting suitors, and finally murdered her when her earnings failed to meet his expectations. He
was put to death in The Tombs on January 12, 1839, soon after its
completion.

3

DURING the first ten or fifteen years of its history the Five Points
was thus fairly decent and comparatively peaceful. Throughout
the greater part of this period one watchman, his head encased in
the leather helmet which gave the New York policeman his early
name of Leatherhead, was sufficient to preserve order; but it was
not long before a regiment would have been unable to cope with
the turbulent citizenry of Paradise Square, and rout the gangsters
and other criminals from their dens and burrows. The character of
the district began to change for the worse about 1820. Many of the
old tenements began to crumble or sink into the imperfectly drained
swamp, and became unsafe for occupancy; and the malarial odors
and vapors arising from the marsh lands made the whole area dangerous to health. The respectable families abandoned the clapboarded monstrosities for other parts of Manhattan Island, and
their places were taken, for the most part, by freed Negro slaves
and low-class Irish, who had swarmed into New York on the first
great wave of immigration which followed the Revolution and the
establishment of the Republic. They crowded indiscriminately
into the old rookeries of the Points, and by 1840 the district had
become the most dismal slum section in America. In the opinion
of contemporary writers it was worse than the Seven Dials and
Whitechapel districts of London.

At this time the Sixth Ward comprised about eighty-six acres, but the greater part of the land was occupied by business houses, and almost the entire population of the ward was massed about the Paradise Square section and in the area, later famous as Mulberry Bend, immediately north and slightly east of the Five Points. Thousands eked out a wretched existence in the garrets and damp cellars with which the district abounded, and the bulk of the population was in the most abject poverty, devoting itself almost exclusively to vice and crime. The Irish were overwhelmingly in the majority, a census conducted by the Five Points House of Industry about the time of the Civil War fixing the number of Irish families at 3,435, while the next in number were the Italians with 416. There were but 167 families of native American stock, and seventy-three which had recently come from England. More than 3,000 people huddled in Baxter street from Chatham to Canal, a distance of less than half a mile, and one lot in that street, twenty-five by one hundred feet, held slums which sheltered 286 persons. Around the Points and Paradise Square were 270 saloons, and several times that number of blind tigers, dance halls, houses of prostitution and green-groceries which sold more wet goods than vegetables.

"Let us go on again, and plunge into the Five Points," wrote Charles Dickens in his *American Notes*. "This is the place; these narrow ways diverging to the right and left, and reeking everywhere with dirt and filth. Such lives as are led here, bear the same fruit here as elsewhere. The coarse and bloated faces at the doors have counterparts at home and all the whole world over. Debauchery has made the very houses prematurely old. See how the rotten beams are tumbling down, and how the patched and broken windows seem to scowl dimly, like eyes that have been hurt in drunken frays. Many of these pigs live here. Do they ever wonder why their masters walk upright instead of going on all-fours, and why they talk instead of grunting?

"So far, nearly every house is a low tavern, and on the bar-room walls are colored prints of Washington and Queen Victoria, and the American Eagle. Among the pigeon-holes that hold the bottles, are pieces of plate glass and colored paper, for there is in

some sort a taste for decoration even here. And as seamen frequent these haunts, there are maritime pictures by the dozen; of
partings between sailors and their lady-loves; portraits of William
of the ballad and his black-eyed Susan; of Will Watch, the bold
smuggler; of Paul Jones, the pirate, and the like; on which the
painted eyes of Queen Victoria, and of Washington to boot, rest
in as strange companionship as on most of the scenes that are
enacted in their wondering presence.

"Open the door of one of these cramped hutches full of sleeping Negroes. Bah! They have a charcoal fire within, there is a

A Five Points Den

smell of singeing clothes or flesh, so close they gather round the
brazier; and vapours issue forth that blind and suffocate. From
every corner, as you glance about you in these dark streets, some
figure crawls half-awakened, as if the judgment hour were near at
hand, and every obscure grave were giving up its dead. Where

dogs would howl to lie men and women and boys slink off to sleep, forcing the dislodged rats to move away in quest of better lodgings. Here, too, are lanes and alleys paved with mud knee-deep; underground chambers where they dance and game; the walls bedecked with rough designs of ships, of forts, and flags, and American Eagles out of number; ruined houses, open to the street, whence through wide gaps in the walls other ruins loom upon the eye, as though the world of vice and misery had nothing else to show; hideous tenements which take their names from robbery and murder; all that is loathsome, drooping and decayed is here."

The most notorious street in early New York was Little Water, a very short thoroughfare which ran from Cross street across the base of Paradise Square to Cow Bay. The latter was so named because the site was once a small bay in the old Collect, to which farmers drove their cattle for water. During the palmy days of the Five Points district Cow Bay was a *cul de sac*, some thirty feet wide at the mouth and narrowing unevenly to a point about a hundred feet from the entrance. This dark and dismal alley, which was generally filled with filth above the shoe-tops, was lined on either side by clapboarded tenements from one to five stories in height, many of which were connected by underground passages where robberies and murders were committed and victims buried. One of the tenements was called Jacob's Ladder, because it was entered from the outside by a rickety, dangerous flight of stairs. Another rejoiced in the name of Gates of Hell. A third was known as Brick-Bat Mansion.

"If you would see Cow Bay," says a book called *Hot Corn*, published in 1854, "saturate your handkerchief with camphor, so that you can endure the horrid stench, and enter. Grope your way through the long, narrow passage—turn to the right, up the dark and dangerous stairs; be careful where you place your foot around the lower step, or in the corners of the broad stairs, for it is more than shoe-mouth deep of steaming filth. Be careful, too, or you may meet someone, perhaps a man, perhaps a woman, who in their drunken frenzy may thrust you, for the very hatred of your better clothes, or the fear that you have come to rescue them from their crazy loved dens of death, down, headlong down, those filthy stairs. Up, up, winding up, five stories high, now you are under the black smoky roof; turn to your left—take care and not upset that seething pot of butcher's offal soup that is cooking upon a little furnace at the head of the stairs—open that door—go in, if you can get in. Look: here is a Negro and his wife sitting upon the floor—where else could they sit, for there is no chair—eating their supper off the bottom of a pail. A broken brown earthen jug holds water—perhaps not all water. Another Negro and his wife occupy another corner; a third sits in the window monopolizing all the air astir. In another corner, what do we see? A Negro man and a stout, hearty, rather good-looking young white woman. Not sleeping together? No, not exactly that—there is no bed in the room—no chair—no table—no nothing—but rags, and dirt, and vermin, and degraded, rum-degraded human beings."

4

THE Old Brewery was the heart of the Five Points, and was the most celebrated tenement building in the history of the city. It was called Coulter's Brewery when it was erected in 1792 on the banks of the old Collect, and the beer brewed there was famous throughout the eastern states. It became known simply as the Old Brewery after it had been transformed into a dwelling in 1837, having become so dilapidated that it could no longer be used for its original purpose. It was five stories in height,[2] and had once been painted yellow, but time and weather soon peeled off much of the paint and ripped away many of the clapboards, so that it came to resemble nothing so much as a giant toad, with dirty, leprous warts, squatting happily in the filth and squalor of the Points. Around the building extended an alley, about three feet wide on the southern side, but on the north of irregular width,

---

[2]Prints of the Old Brewery show only three stories, but writers of the period say there were five.

gradually tapering to a point. The northern path led into a great room called the Den of Thieves, in which more than seventy-five men, women and children, black and white, made their homes, without furniture or conveniences. Many of the women were prostitutes, and entertained their visitors in the Den. On the opposite side the passageway was known as Murderers' Alley, and was all that the name implies. Many historians have confused it with another Murderers' Alley—also known as Donovan's Lane, in Baxter street not far from the Points, where the famous one-eyed pickpocket and confidence man, George Appo, son of a Chinese father and an Irish mother, lived for many years.

The cellars of the Old Brewery were divided into some twenty rooms, which had previously been used for the machinery of the brewing plant, and there were about seventy-five other chambers above-ground, arranged in double rows along Murderers' Alley and the passage leading to the Den of Thieves. During the period of its greatest renown the building housed more than 1,000 men, women and children, almost equally divided between Irish and Negroes. Most of the cellar compartments were occupied by Negroes, many of whom had white wives. In these dens were born children who lived into their teens without seeing the sun or breathing fresh air, for it was as dangerous for a resident of the Old Brewery to leave his niche as it was for an outsider to enter the building. In one basement room about fifteen feet square, not ten years before the Civil War, twenty-six people lived in the most frightful misery and squalor. Once when a murder was committed in this chamber (a little girl was stabbed to death after she had been so foolish as to show a penny she had begged) the body lay in a corner for five days before it was finally buried in a shallow grave dug in the floor by the child's mother. In 1850 an investigator found that no person of the twenty-six had been outside of the room for more than a week, except to lie in wait in the doorway for a more fortunate denizen to pass along with food. When such a person appeared he was promptly knocked on the head and his provisions stolen.

Throughout the building the most frightful living conditions prevailed. Miscegenation was an accepted fact, incest was not uncommon, and there was much sexual promiscuity; the house swarmed with thieves, murderers, pickpockets, beggars, harlots,

The Old Brewery

and degenerates of every type. Fights were of almost constant occurrence, and there was scarcely an hour of the day or night when drunken orgies were not in progress; through the flimsy, clapboarded walls could be heard the crashing thud of brickbat or iron bar, the shrieks of the unhappy victims, the wailing of starving children, and the frenzied cries of men and women, and sometimes boys and girls, writhing in the anguish of delirium tremens. Murders were frequent; it has been estimated that for almost fifteen years the Old Brewery averaged a murder a night, and the Cow Bay tenements almost as many. Few of the killers were ever punished, for unless the police came in great force they could not hope to leave the Old Brewery alive, and the inhabitants were very close-mouthed. Even if the police learned the identity of a murderer he could seldom be found, for he dived into the burrows of the Points and fled through the underground passageways. Many of the inhabitants of the Old Brewery and of the Cow Bay dens had once been men and women of some consequence, but after a

few years in the dives they sank to the level of the original inhabitants. The last of the Blennerhassetts, second son of the Harman
Blennerhassett who was associated with Aaron Burr in the great
conspiracy to found a Western Empire, is said to have died in the
Old Brewery, as did others whose families had been of equal
prominence.

The churches and welfare agencies professed great distress over conditions at the Five Points for many years, but nothing was done for the
rescue and regeneration of the district until the late 1830's, when the
Central and Spring street Presbyterian congregations sent missionaries into the area. But the population of the Points was principally Irish
and devoutly Catholic, and the missionaries were assailed as Protestant
devils and driven out by the gangsters and other criminals. In 1840 the
Broadway Tabernacle, a Congregational church, was erected in
Broadway near Anthony, now Worth street, and sporadic efforts were
made to do welfare work at the Five Points. But nothing of importance
was accomplished until 1850, when the Rev. Lewis Morris Pease and
his wife were sent into the Points by the Ladies' Home Missionary
Society of the Methodist Episcopal Church. They established their
home in a room on Cross street, near the Old Brewery, and opened a
mission.

Pease was one of the great humanitarian workers of his time,
and to his labors, more than to those of any other one man, were
due the eventual regeneration of the Five Points and the abolition
of its dens of vice and misery. But he was not long permitted to
continue his work without interruption, and within a year was dismissed by the ladies of the Missionary Society, who thereafter
made every effort to belittle his deeds. In 1854 they wrote a history of the Methodist mission at the Points, and published it in a
book called *The Old Brewery*. In it Pease's name was not mentioned; he was merely referred to in rather uncomplimentary
terms as "our first missionary." It was the ladies' idea that he
should do little except preach the Gospel and obtain converts and
members for the church, and for a few months Pease and his wife
bowed to the will of the Society. But he soon realized that the
basic troubles of the Five Points were ignorance and poverty, and
that vice and crime could not be combated successfully unless the

conditions which caused them were removed. To this end he established schools for both adults and children, and opened workrooms to which the clothing manufacturers sent materials to be made up into cheap garments under the supervision of the missionary and his wife.

The Dying Mother—A Scene in the Old Brewery

The missionary's connection with the Society ended when a group of ladies, visiting the Points to view the creatures whom their munificence was assuring places amid the glories of the hereafter, learned that he had not preached a sermon for two days. He had been too busy carting great loads of cloth from the manufacturing houses in Broadway to his Five Points workrooms. He was succeeded by the Rev. J. Luckey, a gifted evangelist. Pease and his wife refused to leave the Points, but opened an undenominational mission, and continued their efforts to bring learning and labor to Paradise Square. Out of this mission grew the Five Points House of Industry, which remains one of the fine civilizing and educational agencies of the district. Its first building was erected in 1856 in Anthony street, and in 1864 the old tenements in Cow

Bay were purchased and demolished to make way for a larger and better equipped House.

Scene in the Old Brewery

A committee consisting of Daniel Drew and others negotiated for the purchase of the Old Brewery on behalf of the Missionary Society, and in 1852 bought it for $16,000, of which the city authorities gave $1,000. The inhabitants, both human and rodent, were turned out, and on December 2, 1852, the demolition of the old rookery was begun. On January 27, 1853, Bishop Jones of the Methodist Episcopal Church laid the cornerstone of the new mission, erected on the site of the Old Brewery at a cost of $36,000. The laborers who wrecked the Old Brewery carried out several sacks filled with human bones which they had found between the walls and in the cellars, and night after night gangsters thronged the ruin searching for the treasure which rumor had it was buried there. None was found, but many holes were dug, and there was much tapping and plumbing of hidden passages and wall spaces. The destruction of the Old Brewery was accomplished amid great rejoicing, and the Rev. T. F. R. Mercein wrestled with the muse and produced a poem in honor of the occasion:

God knows it's time thy walls were going!
    Through every stone
Life-blood, as through a heart, is flowing;
    Murmurs a smother'd groan
Long years the cup of poison filling
    From leaves of gall;
Long years a darker cup distilling
    From wither'd hearts that fall!
O! this world is stern and dreary,
    Everywhere they roam;
God! hast thou never call'd the weary
    Have they in thee no home?

Foul haunt! a glorious resurrection
    Springs from thy grave!
Faith, hope and purified affection,
    Praising the "Strong to save!"
God bless the love that, like an angel,
    Flies to each call,
Till every lip hath this evangel,
    "Christ pleadeth for us all!"
Oh! this world is stern and dreary,
    Everywhere they roam;
Praise God! a voice hath called the weary,
    In thee is found a home!

CHAPTER II

EARLY GANGS OF THE BOWERY AND FIVE POINTS

1

THE ORIGINAL Five Points gangs had their genesis in the tenements, saloons, and dance halls of the Paradise Square district, but their actual organization into working units, and the consequent transformation of the area into an Alsatia of vice and crime, closely followed the opening of the cheap green-grocery speak-easies which soon sprang up around the Square and along the streets which debouched into it. The first of these speakeasies was established about 1825 by Rosanna Peers in Center street just south of Anthony, now Worth street. Piles of decaying vegetables were displayed on racks outside the store, but Rosanna provided a back room in which she sold the fiery liquor of the period at lower prices than it could be obtained in the recognized saloons. This room soon became the haunt of thugs, pickpockets, murderers, and thieves. The gang known as the Forty Thieves,

An Encounter between a Swell and a "Bowery B'hoy."
Five Points in 1827.

which appears to have been the first in New York with a definite, acknowledged leadership, is said to have been formed in Rosanna Peers' grocery store, and her back room was used as its meeting-place, and as headquarters by Edward Coleman and other eminent chieftains. There they received the reports of their henchmen, and from its dimly lit corners dispatched the gangsters on their warlike missions. The Kerryonians, composed of natives of County Kerry, Ireland, was also a product of Rosanna's enterprise. This was a small gang which seldom roamed beyond Center street and did little fighting; its members devoted themselves almost exclusively to hating the English.

The Chichesters, Roach Guards, Plug Uglies, Shirt Tails, and Dead Rabbits were organized and had their rendezvous in other grocery stores, and in time these emporiums came to be regarded as the worst dens of the Five Points, and the centers of its infamy and crime. The Shirt Tails were so called because they wore their shirts on the outside of their trousers, like Chinamen, and the expressive appellation of the Plug Uglies came from their enormous plug hats, which they stuffed with wool and leather and drew down over their ears to serve as helmets when they went into battle. The Plug Uglies were for the most part gigantic Irishmen, and included in their membership some of the toughest characters of the Five Points. Even the most ferocious of the Paradise Square eye-gougers and mayhem artists cringed when a giant Plug Ugly walked abroad looking for trouble, with a huge bludgeon in one hand, a brickbat in the other, a pistol peeping from his pocket and his tall hat jammed down over his ears and all but obscuring his fierce eyes. He was an adept at rough and tumble fighting, and wore heavy boots studded with great hobnails with which he stamped his prostrate and helpless victim.

The Dead Rabbits were originally part of the Roach Guards, organized to honor the name of a Five Points liquor seller. But internal dissension developed, and at one of the gang's stormy meetings someone threw a dead rabbit into the center of the room. One of the squabbling factions accepted it as an omen and its members withdrew, forming an independent gang and calling themselves the Dead Rabbits.[1] Sometimes they were also known as the Black Birds, and achieved great renown for their prowess as thieves and thugs. The battle uniform of the Roach Guards was a blue stripe on their pantaloons, while the Dead Rabbits adopted a red stripe, and at the head of their sluggers carried a dead rabbit impaled on a pike. The Rabbits and the Guards swore undying enmity and constantly fought each other at the Points, but in the rows with the water-front and Bowery gangs they made common cause against the enemy, as did the Plug Uglies, Shirt Tails, and Chichesters. All of the Five Point gangsters commonly fought in their undershirts.

---

[1] In the slang of the period a rabbit was a rowdy, and a dead rabbit was a very rowdy, athletic fellow.

2

THE Five Points gradually declined as an amusement center as the green groceries invaded the district and the gangs began to abuse their privileges as overlords of Paradise Square, and the Bowery became increasingly important as a place of recreation. As early as 1752, when the waters of the Collect still covered the site of the Tombs and flowed sluggishly through Canal street, the Bowery began to make some pretensions to being a street of pleasure by the opening of Sperry's Botanical Gardens, later Voxhaull's Gardens, at the upper end of the thoroughfare near Astor Place. Its claims were greatly enhanced in 1826 by the erection of the Bowery Theater on the site of the old Bull's Head Tavern, where George Washington had stopped to quench his thirst with Bowery ale on Evacuation Day in 1783. The new playhouse opened with a comedy, *The Road to Ruin,* but its first important production was in November, 1826, when Edwin Forrest played the title rôle in *Othello.* For many years it was one of the foremost theaters on the continent; its boards creaked beneath the tread of some of the greatest players of the time. It was then the largest playhouse in the city, with a seating capacity of 3,000, and was the first to be equipped with gas. The structure was burned three times between 1826 and 1838, and again caught fire some fifteen years before the Civil War, when the police, recently uniformed by order of Mayor Harper, appeared on the scene in all the glory of their new suits and glistening brass buttons. They ordered the spectators to make way for the firemen, but the Bowery gangsters jeered and laughed at them as liveried lackeys, and refused to do their bidding.

The thugs attacked with great ferocity when someone howled that the policemen were trying to imitate the English bobbies, and many were injured before they were subdued. So much ill-feeling arose because of this and similar incidents that the uniforms were called in, and for several years the police appeared on the streets with no other insignia than a star-shaped copper shield, whence came the names coppers and cops. After weathering many storms the theater was finally renamed the Thalia, and still stands in the shadow of the Third avenue elevated railroad, devoted to moving pictures and Italian stock, with occasional performances by travelling Chinese troupes.

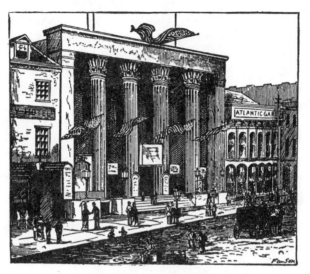

Old Bowery Theater

Several other theaters soon followed the Bowery, among them the Windsor, which became famous for its performances of *Hands Across the Sea*, and for the remarkable acting of Johnny Thompson in *On Hand*. For many years these houses presented first-class plays and were frequented by the aristocracy of the city, but in time, as the character of the street changed and the dives and gangsters made it a byword from coast to coast, they offered blood and thunder thrillers of so distinct a type that they became known as Bowery plays, and could be seen nowhere else. Among them were *The Boy Detective, Marked for Life, Neck and Neck,* and *Si Slocum*. From these productions developed the "ten, twent', thirt'" melodrama which was so popular throughout the United States until its place was taken by the moving picture. The dress circles and first balconies of the early Bowery theaters, after the first citizens had abandoned them for the playhouses farther uptown and along Broadway, were generally filled with respectable

German families from the Seventh Ward, who drank pink and yellow lemonade and noisily devoured Ridley's Old Fashioned Peppermint Kisses. But the pit and topmost galleries fairly swarmed with ragamuffins of all degrees and both sexes, who stamped and whistled and shouted "h'ist dat rag!" when the curtain failed to rise promptly on schedule time. "These places are jammed to suffocation on Sunday nights," wrote an author who visited the Bowery about the time of the Civil War. "Actresses too corrupt and dissolute to play elsewhere appear on the boards at the Bowery. Broad farces, indecent comedies, plays of highwaymen and murderers, are received with shouts by the reeking crowds which fill the low theaters. Newsboys, street-sweepers, rag-pickers, begging girls, collectors of cinders, all who can beg or steal a sixpence, fill the galleries of these corrupt places of amusement. There is not a dance hall, a free-and-easy, a concert saloon, or a vile drinking-place that presents such a view of the depravity and degradation of New York as the gallery of a Bowery theater."

A Street Sweeper

Within a few years after the erection of the first theater the Bowery was lined with playhouses, concert halls, saloons and basement dives, and huge beer gardens seating from 1,000 to 1,500 persons at long tables running lengthwise of an enormous room. As late as 1898 the Bowery had ninety-nine houses of entertainment, of which only fourteen were classed as respectable by the police, and there were six bar-rooms to a block. Now the street can muster a bare dozen theaters, devoted to burlesque, moving pictures, and Yiddish, Italian and Chinese drama. Some of the dives which dotted the Bowery before and after the Civil War have never been equalled, even by Prohibition speak-easies, for the frightful and deadly quality of their liquor. In many of the lower class places, in the early days, drinks were three cents each and no glasses or mugs were used. Barrels of fiery spirits stood on shelves behind the bar, and poured out their contents through lines of slender rubber hose. The customer, having deposited his money on the bar, took an end of the hose in his mouth, and was entitled to all he could drink without breathing. The moment he stopped for breath the watchful bartender turned off the supply, and nothing would start it again but another payment. Some of the Bowery bums became so expert at swallowing, and were able to hold their breaths for such a long period, that they could get delightfully drunk for three cents. One famous saloon, in Baxter street near the Bowery, provided and extensively advertised a rear chamber called the "velvet room." When a good customer was reduced to a nickel, he was given an extra large bowl of liquor and escorted with considerable ceremony into the "velvet room," where he was permitted to drink himself unconscious, and sleep until the effects of the potation wore off.

The most famous of the early Bowery beer halls was the Atlantic Gardens, next door to the old Bowery Theater and now a palace of the moving pictures. Upstairs and down it provided seats for more than a thousand, and two four-horse drays, working ten hours a day, were scarcely able to keep the customers supplied with beer fresh from the brewery. In this and other similar establishments there was music by pianos, harps, violins, drums and brasses; and dice, dominoes, cards, and sometimes rifles for target shooting were provided. Everything was free except the beer, which cost five cents for an enormous mug. Most of the gardens were operated by Germans, and at first were frequented by men and women of that nationality, who brought their families and spent the day quietly. Beer was served by girls from twelve to sixteen years of age, wearing short dresses and red-topped boots, which reached almost to the knees and had bells dangling from the tassels. The sale of the beverage was so profitable that the managers of the gardens bid against each other for the privilege of entertaining the large racial and political organizations, frequently paying as much as $500 to any association that would agree to hold an all-day picnic on their premises. For many years these gardens were entirely respectable, but low class thugs and hoodlums soon began to invade them, not to drink beer but to guzzle hard liquor from flasks, and in time they came to be the resorts of the gangsters and other criminals of the district, and the Bowery assumed the character which has made it one of the most renowned thoroughfares in the world.

3

THE most important gangs of the early days of the Bowery district were the Bowery Boys, the True Blue Americans, the American Guards, the O'Connell Guards, and the Atlantic Guards. Their membership was principally Irish, but they do not appear to have been as criminal or as ferocious as their brethren of the Five Points, although among them were many gifted brawlers. The True Blue Americans were amusing, but harmless. They wore stove-pipe hats and long black frock coats which reached flappingly to their ankles and buttoned close under the chin; their chief mission in life was to stand on street corners and denounce England, and gloomily predict the immediate destruction of the British Empire by fire and sword. Like most of the sons of Erin who have come to this country, they never became so thoroughly Americanized that Ireland did not remain their principal vocal interest. The other gangs were probably offshoots of the Bowery

Boys, and commonly joined the latter in their fights with the roaring denizens of Paradise Square. Their exploits earned them no place of importance in gang history.

For many years the Bowery Boys and the Dead Rabbits waged a bitter feud, and a week seldom passed in which they did not come to blows, either along the Bowery, in the Five Points section, or on the ancient battleground of Bunker Hill, north of Grand street. The greatest gang conflicts of the early nineteenth century were fought by these groups, and they continued their feud until the Draft Riots of 1863, when they combined with other gangs and criminals in an effort to sack and burn the city. In these early struggles the Bowery Boys were supported by the other gangs of the Bowery, while the Plug Uglies, the Shirt Tails, and the Chichesters rallied under the fragrant emblem of the Dead Rabbits. Sometimes the battles raged for two or three days without cessation, while the streets of the gang area were barricaded with carts and paving stones, and the gangsters blazed away at each other with musket and pistol, or engaged in close work with knives, brickbats, bludgeons, teeth, and fists. On the outskirts of the struggling mob of thugs ranged the women, their arms filled with reserve ammunition, their keen eyes watching for a break in the enemy's defense, and always ready to lend a hand or a tooth in the fray.

Often these Amazons fought in the ranks, and many of them achieved great renown as ferocious battlers. They were particularly gifted in the art of mayhem, and during the Draft Riots it was the women who inflicted the most fiendish tortures upon Negroes, soldiers, and policemen captured by the mob, slicing their flesh with butcher knives, ripping out eyes and tongues, and applying the torch after the victims had been sprayed with oil and hanged to trees. The Dead Rabbits, during the early forties, commanded the allegiance of the most noted of the female battlers, an angular vixen known as Hell-Cat Maggie, who fought alongside the gang chieftains in many of the great battles with the Bowery gangs. She is said to have filed her front teeth to points, while on her fingers she wore long artificial nails, constructed of brass. When Hell-Cat Maggie screeched her battle cry and rushed biting and clawing into the midst of a mass of opposing gangsters, even the most stout-hearted blanched and fled. No quarter was asked or given by the early gangsters; when a man fell wounded his enemies leaped joyfully upon him and kicked or stamped him to death. Frequently the police were unable to disperse the mob, and were compelled to ask the National Guard and the Regular Army for aid. The city soon became accustomed to regiments of soldiers marching in battle array through the streets to quell a gang riot. Occasionally the artillery was called out also, but generally the gangsters fled before the muskets of the infantrymen. Much of this work was done by the Twenty-seventh, later the Seventh, Regiment.

Little knowledge of the activities of most of the early Bowery gangs has survived, but the lore of the street is rich in tales of the Bowery Boys and the prowess of their mighty leaders. Sometimes this gang was called Bowery B'hoys, which is sufficient indication of its racial origin. It was probably the most celebrated gang in the history of the United States, but before the eminent Chuck Conners appeared in the late eighties and transformed the type into a bar fly and a tramp, the Bowery Boy was not a loafer except on Sundays and holidays. Nor was he a criminal, except on occasion, until the period of the Civil War. He was apt to earn his living as a butcher or apprentice mechanic, or as a bouncer in a Bowery saloon or dance cellar. But he was almost always a volunteer fireman, and therein lay much of the strength of the gang, for in the early days before the Civil War the firemen, most of them strong adherents of Tammany Hall, had much to say about the conduct of the city's government. Many of the most eminent politicians belonged to the fire brigade, and there was much rivalry between the companies, which gave their engines such names as White Ghost, Black Joke, Shad Belly, Dry Bones, Red Rover, Hay Wagon, Big Six, Yaller Gal, Bean Soup, Old Junk, and Old Maid. Such famous New York political leaders as Cornelius W. Lawrence, Zophar Mills, Samuel Willetts, William M. Wood, John J. Gorman and William M. Tweed were volunteer firemen. In still earlier days even George Washington was an ardent chaser after the fire engines, and for a short time during his residence in the metropolis was head of the New York department. Before the formation of a paid fire fighting force one of the great events of the year was the Fireman's Parade, and great crowds lined the sidewalks and cheered the red-shirted, beaver-hatted brawlers as they pulled their engines over the cobble-stones, while before them marched a brass band blaring away at *Solid Men to the Front*, a rousing tune which was a favorite for many years.

But the rivalry between the fire companies whose membership included men of substance was friendly if strenuous, while the Bowery Boy loved his fire engine almost as much as he did his girl, and considered both himself and his company disgraced if his apparatus was beaten to a conflagration. And the acme of humiliation was to roll to a fire and find that all of the fire plugs had been captured by other companies. To prevent this the Bowery Boy resorted to typically direct methods. When the fire alarm sounded he simply grabbed an empty barrel from a grocery store and hurried with it to the fire plug nearest the burning building. There he turned the barrel over the plug and sat on it, and defended it valorously against the assaults of rival firemen until his own engine arrived. If he succeeded he was a hero and his company had won a notable victory. Frequently the fight for fire plugs was so fierce that the Bowery Boys had no time to extinguish the flames.

The original Bowery Boy, who followed his chieftain in so many forays against the hated Dead Rabbits and other Five Points gangs, was a burly ruffian with his chin adorned by an Uncle Sam whisker—the type of American which is still portrayed by the English comic weeklies. On his head was a stovepipe hat, generally battered, and his trousers were tucked inside his boots, while his jaws moved constantly on a chew of tobacco as he whittled on a shingle with the huge knife which never left his possession. In later years, a little before the time of Chuck Conners, the type changed as new fashions in men's clothing appeared, and the Bowery Boy promenaded his favorite thoroughfare with his head crowned by a high beaver hat with the nap divided and brushed different ways, while his stalwart figure was encased in an elegant frock coat, and about his throat was knotted a gaudy kerchief. His pantaloons, out almost as full as the modern Oxford bags, were turned up over his heavy boots. The hair on the back of his head was clipped close and his neck and chin were shaven, while his temple locks were daintily curled and heavily anointed with bear's grease or some other powerful, evil-smelling unguent. His downfall had begun in those days, but he was still an unruly and belligerent citizen, and it was unwise to give him cause for offense.

Some of the most ferocious rough-and-tumble fighters that ever cracked a skull or gouged out an eyeball fought in the ranks of the Bowery Boys, and from their rough school emerged many celebrated brawlers and political leaders. Butcher Bill Poole, a famous gangster and ward heeler, owed allegiance to the Bowery Boys, and so did his murderer, Lew Baker, who shot him to death in Stanwix Hall in 1855.

But the greatest of the Bowery Boys, and the most imposing figure in all the history of the New York gangs, was a leader who flourished in the forties, and captained the gangsters in the most important of their punitive and marauding expeditions into the Five Points. His identity remains unknown, and there is excellent reason to believe that he may be a myth, but vasty tales of his prowess and of his valor in the fights against the Dead Rabbits and the Plug Uglies have come down through the years, gaining incident and momentum as they came. Under the simple sobriquet of Mose he has become a legendary figure of truly heroic proportions, at once the Samson, the Achilles, and the Paul Bunyan of the Bowery. And beside him, in the lore of the street, marches the diminutive figure of his faithful friend and counsellor, by name Syksey, who is said to have coined the phrase "hold de butt," an impressive plea for the remains of a dead cigar.

The present generation of Bowery riffraff knows little or nothing of the mighty Mose, and only the older men who plod that now dreary and dismal relict of a great street have heard the name. But in the days before the Civil War, when the Bowery was in its heyday and the Bowery Boy was the strutting peacock of gangland, songs were sung in honor of his great deeds, and the gangsters surged into battle shouting his name and imploring his spirit to join them and lend power to their arms. He was scarcely cold in his grave before Chanfrau had immortalized him by writing *Mose,*

The Great East Side, New York—Scenes to be Met With in a
Walk Along the Bowery—Life and Character as it is Presented
on the Gayest and Liveliest Thoroughfare in the
Great Metropolis of the Union

The Bowery B'hoy, which was first performed before a clamorous audience at the old Olympic Theater in 1849, the year of the Astor Place riot.

Mose was at least eight feet tall and broad in proportion, and his colossal bulk was crowned by a great shock of flaming ginger-colored hair, on which he wore a beaver hat measuring more than two feet from crown to brim. His hands were as large as the hams of a Virginia hog, and on those rare moments when he was in repose they dangled below his knees; it was Syksey's habit to boast pridefully that his chieftain could stand erect and scratch his knee-cap. The feet of the great captain were so large that the ordinary boot of commerce would not fit his big toe; he wore specially con-structed footgear, the soles of which were copper plates studded with nails an inch long. Woe and desolation came upon the gangs of the Five Points when the great Mose leaped into their midst and began to kick and stamp; they fled in despair and hid themselves in the innermost depths of the rookeries of Paradise Square.

The strength of the gigantic Mose was as the strength of ten men. Other Bowery Boys went into battle carrying brickbats and the ordinary stave of the time, but Mose, when accoutered for the fray, bore in one hand a great paving stone and in the other a hick-ory or oak wagon tongue. This was his bludgeon, and when it was lost in the heat of battle he simply uprooted an iron lamp-post and laid about him with great zeal. Instead of the knife affected by his followers, he pinned his faith on a butcher's cleaver. Once when the Dead Rabbits overwhelmed his gang and rushed ferociously up the Bowery to wreck the Boys' headquarters, the great Mose wrenched an oak tree out of the earth, and holding it by the upper branches, employed it as a flail, smiting the Dead Rabbits even as Samson smote the Philistines. The Five Points thugs broke and fled before him, but he pursued them into their lairs around Paradise Square and wrecked two tenements before his rage cooled. Again, he stood his ground before a hundred of the best brawlers of the Points, ripping huge paving blocks from the street and sidewalk and hurl-ing them into the midst of his enemies, inflicting frightful losses.

In his lighter moments it was the custom of this great god of the gangs to lift a horse car off the tracks and carry it a few blocks on his shoulders, laughing uproariously at the bumping the passengers received when he set it down. And so gusty was his laugh that the car trembled on its wheels, the trees swayed as though in a storm and the Bowery was filled with a rushing roar like the thunder of Niagara. Sometimes Mose unhitched the horses and himself pulled the street car the length of the Bowery at a bewildering speed; once, if the legend is to be credited, he lifted a car above his head at Chatham Square and carried it, with the horses dangling from the traces, on the palm of his hand as far as Astor Place. Again, when a sailing ship was becalmed in the East River and drifting dangerously near the treacherous rocks of Hell Gate, Mose pulled out in a rowboat, lighted his cigar, which was more than two feet long, and sent such mighty billows of smoke against the sails that the ship was saved, and plunged down the river as though driven by a hurricane. So terrific was the force of Mose's puffs, indeed, that the vessel was into the Harbor and beyond Staten Island before it would respond to the helm. Occasionally Mose amused himself by taking up a position in the center of the river and permitting no ship to pass; as fast as they appeared he blew them back. But Mose was always very much at home in the water; he often dived off at the Battery and came up on the Staten Island beach, a distance which is now traversed by ferry boats in twenty-five minutes. He could swim the Hudson River with two mighty strokes, and required but six for a complete circuit of Manhattan Island. But when he wanted to cross the East River to Brooklyn he scorned to swim the half mile or so; he simply jumped.

When Mose quenched his thirst a drayload of beer was ordered from the brewery, and during the hot summer months he went about with a great fifty gallon keg of ale dangling from his belt in lieu of a canteen. When he dined in state the butchers of the Center and Fly markets were busy for days in advance of the great event, slicing hogs and cattle and preparing the enormous roasts which the giant needs must consume to regain his strength; and his consumption of bread was so great that a report that Mose was hungry caused a flurry in the flour market. Four quarts of oysters were but an appetizer, and soup and coffee were served to him by the barrel. For dessert and light snacks he was very fond of fruit.

Historians affirm that the cherry trees of Cherry Hill and the mulberry trees of Mulberry Bend vanished because of the building up of the city, but the legend of the Bowery has it that Mose tore them up by the roots and ate the fruit; he was hungry and in no mood to wait until the cherries and mulberries could be picked.

4

THE political geniuses of Tammany Hall were quick to see the practical value of the gangsters, and to realize the advisability of providing them with meeting and hiding places, that their favor might be curried and their peculiar talents employed on election day to assure government of, by, and for Tammany. Many ward and district leaders acquired title to the green-grocery speakeasies in which the first of the Five Points gangs had been organized, while others operated saloons and dance houses along the Bowery, or took gambling houses and places of prostitution under their protection. The underworld thus became an important factor in politics, and under the manipulation of the worthy statemen the gangs of the Bowery and Five Points participated in the great series of riots which began with the spring election disturbances of 1834 and continued, with frequent outbreaks, for half a score of years. In this period occurred the Flour and Five Points riots, and the most important of the Abolition troubles, while there were at least two hundred battles between the gangs, and innumerable conflicts between volunteer fire companies.

During the summer of 1834 the opportunities for the gangs to engage in their natural employment were greatly increased by the appearance of two new political groups, the Native Americans and the Equal Rights Party. The latter was a disgruntled faction within Tammany Hall, and was vociferously in favor of equal rights for all citizens, and opposed to bank notes and the establishment of monopolies by legislation. The Native Americans deplored the election of foreigners to office, and vigorously demanded the repeal of the naturalization laws by which Tammany Hall had gained such an enormous following of Irish voters. The

Native Americans took the place of the Whigs in some of the municipal elections, and both followed the example of Tammany and hired gangsters to blackjack their opponents and act as repeaters at the polls.

The Bowery gang known as the American Guards, the members of which prided themselves on their native ancestry, was soon devotedly attached to the Native Americans party, and responded joyfully to the appeals of its ward heelers and district leaders. During the summer of 1835, about a year after the election riots, bitter enmity developed between this gang and the O'Connell Guards, which had been organized under the aegis of a Bowery liquor seller, and was the particular champion of the Irish element of Tammany Hall. These gangs came to blows on June 21, 1835, at Grand and Crosby streets on the lower East Side. The fighting spread as far as the Five Points, where the gangsters of Paradise Square took a hand and the rioting became general throughout that part of the city. The Mayor and the Sheriff called out every watchman in the city, and the force managed to stop the fighting without the aid of soldiers, although several companies were mustered and remained in their armories overnight. Dr. W. M. Caffrey, a noted surgeon, was killed by a brickbat while trying to make his way through the mob to attend a patient, and Justice Olin M. Lowndes was seriously wounded when he entered the riot area with the police.

Several minor conflicts over the Abolition movement occurred late in 1833, and the homes of many prominent Abolitionists were bombarded with stones and bricks, but for the most part the anti-slavery agitation was obscured by the excitements of the spring election, for it was the first time that a mayor had been elected by direct vote and there was fierce fighting for three days between Tammany and the Whigs before the former was finally victorious. About the middle of 1834 the feeling against the Abolitionists, which was always very strong in the metropolis, once more flared into open violence, and on July 7 mobs attacked the Chatham street Chapel and the Bowery Theater, where Edwin Forrest was playing in *Metamora* for the benefit of the manager, an Englishman named Farren. When the police drove the rioters from the playhouse they roared down to Rose street, now a dingy thoroughfare in the gloomy shadow of Brooklyn Bridge, but then an important residential street lined with pretentious mansions. There they launched an assault against the home of Lewis Tappan, a prominent Abolitionist, and smashed the doors and windows with stones. Swarming into the building, they wrecked the interior and pitched the furniture into the street, where it was arranged in huge piles and oil poured over it. In throwing out the pictures which had adorned the walls one of the gangsters came across a portrait of George Washington, and another thug tried to snatch it from his arms. But the discoverer hugged it to his breast and shouted dramatically:

"It's Washington! For God's sake don't burn Washington!"

His cry was taken up in the street, and the mob began to shout in unison:

"For God's sake don't burn Washington!"

A line was formed, and the painting of the first President was passed tenderly down the stairs and into the street, where a group of huge bullies bore it aloft to a neighboring house. There it was installed upon the verandah and carefully guarded until the end of the riot. Sporadic outbreaks occurred during the next few days, and on July 10 a mob did great damage to residences and business houses in Spring, Catherine, Thompson, and Reade streets, while another great throng, composed almost entirely of Five Points gangsters, terrorized the area around Paradise Square. The rioters there appeared to be well organized, for runners were kept passing between the different gangs, and scouts patrolled the streets to give warning of the approach of the police and soldiers. The word spread that the gang chieftains had resolved to burn and loot every house around the Five Points that did not have a candle in a window, and soon the entire Paradise Square district blazed into illumination.

Nevertheless, a dozen buildings were sacked and set on fire, and by midnight the heavens glowed with the glare of the conflagration, while a dense pall of smoke hung low over that part of the city. Five houses of prostitution were burned, and the inmates, stripped and parcelled out among the gangsters, were shamefully mistreated. St. Philip's Negro Church in Center street was destroyed, as were three houses on the opposite side of the street, and one adjoining the church. Throughout the night the screams of tortured Negroes could be heard, and an Englishman who was captured by the thugs had both eyes gouged out and his ears torn off by the frenzied rioters. But at one o'clock in the morning, when the blare of bugles told of the coming of the military, the gang chieftains dispersed their thugs, and half an hour later the Five Points was quiet except for the tramping of the troops and the wailing of the unhappy victims who mourned beside the ruins of their homes. The next night the rioters wrecked a church in Spring street and barricaded the thoroughfare with furniture, but were routed by the Twenty-Seventh Regiment of Infantry, which destroyed the fortifications and chased the mob away without firing a shot.

The worries of the city authorities were enormously increased by the great fire of December 16–17, 1835, which raged for a day and a half with the thermometer at seventeen degrees below zero, and devastated thirteen acres in the heart of the financial district. The loss was more than $20,000,000. The conflagration started at No. 25 Merchant street and swept into Pearl street and Exchange Place, burned southward almost to Broad street, eastward to the East River, and from Wall street to Coenties Slip.[2] Every building on the south side of Wall street from William street to the East River was destroyed, and the flames were not checked until Marines from the Navy Yard dynamited the Dutch Church, the Merchants' Exchange and other buildings, and created a gap which the fire could not cross. Several hundred houses were burned, and at least fifty others were wrecked and looted by criminals, who also raided the great heaps of furniture, jewelry and clothing which were piled in the streets without adequate guard. Much valuable property was recovered by the police a week later in the hovels of the Bowery

---

[2] A few blocks north of the Battery. One story of the origin of the name is: In colonial times a Dutchman, named Coen, had a sweetheart, Antye. The slip was their trysting place, and the townspeople called it Coen's and Antye's Slip. From this came Coenties

and Five Points. Many houses and stores were set on fire by the thugs, and one man who was caught applying the torch to a building at Broad and Stone streets was seized by a group of irate citizens and hanged to a tree. His body, frozen stiff, dangled for three days before the police found time to cut it down.

The fire was one of the direct causes of the panic of 1837, for the losses were so great that many banks suspended, and the insurance companies could not pay their policies in full. Consequently owners of business houses and factories were unable to obtain money with which to rebuild, and thousands who had been thrown out of employment by the disaster remained without work throughout the following summer. Early in September, 1836, flour was seven dollars a barrel, and within another month it had advanced to twelve, and commission merchants predicted that it would go to twenty before the end of the winter. Bread soon became a scarce article of diet among the poor, and in the slums of the Bowery and Five Points thousands were on the verge of actual starvation. In February, 1837, a report was circulated that there were only 4,000 barrels in the great depot at Troy, New York, instead of the customary 30,000, and the newspapers published the news with the largest headlines of the period, and in editorial articles denounced certain merchants who were said to be hoarding great quantities of flour and grain, waiting for the advance in price.

Great unrest prevailed, and many mass meetings were held, but there was no direct action until February 10, 1837, when a mob which had listened to inflammatory harangues in City Hall Park attacked the wheat and flour store of Eli Hart & Company, in Washington street between Dey and Cortlandt. Hart's watchmen retreated into the building, but neglected to bar the door, which soon gave way to the battering assault of the rioters. The mob rushed into the building and began throwing barrels of flour and sacks of wheat from the windows. Most of the casks were staved in when they struck the pavement, and the others were quickly smashed by the rioters, who had set up a sing-song shout of "here goes flour at eight dollars a barrel!" Five hundred barrels of flour and a thousand bushels of wheat in sacks had been destroyed when a large body of police appeared, supported by two companies of the National Guard. Fleeing before the muskets and nightsticks, the rioters streamed across the city and launched themselves against the store of S. H. Herrick & Company, near Coenties' Slip. There they destroyed thirty barrels of flour and a hundred bushels of wheat before they were driven away.

The next day the price of flour increased $1 a barrel.

5

ONE of the first of the political leaders to discover that the gangsters could be employed to great advantage was Captain Isaiah Rynders, Tammany boss of the Sixth Ward, king of the Five Points gangsters and head of the notorious Empire Club at No. 25 Park Row, and owner of half a dozen Paradise Square greengroceries. Captain Rynders first appeared in New York in the middle thirties, after a brief career as a gambler and pistol-and-knife fighter along the Mississippi River. He was one of the most astute politicians who ever operated in the metropolis, although he sometimes permitted his love for the Irish and his hatred of the English to upset his judgment. Eventually he became United States Marshal, and for more than twenty-five years exercised considerable power in Tammany Hall, save for several years in the fifties when he became a renegade and espoused the cause of the Native Americans. For many years Captain Rynders made his headquarters at Sweeney's House of Refreshment at No. 11 Ann street, a thoroughfare much frequented by volunteer firemen, but about 1843 he organized the Empire Club, which became the political center of the Sixth Ward and the clearing house of all gangster activities which had to do with politics. From it Rynders issued the commands and pulled the wires which kept his henchmen out of jail. With the aid of the gang chieftains and such gifted lieutenants as Dirty Face Jack, Country McCleester and Edward Z. C. Judson, better known as Ned Buntline, Captain Rynders kept the Sixth Ward under his political thumb and waxed rich and powerful. His control of the Five Points gangs was absolute, and he was frequently appealed to by the police to quell riots which the watchmen themselves could not stop.

Captain Rynders was an important figure in many of the Abolition disturbances, but his most notable exploit was performed in 1849, when he took advantage of the bitter professional jealousy between Edwin Forrest and William C. Macready, the eminent British actor, and became the principal instigator of the famous riots in Astor Place. Macready was driven from the stage of the Astor Place Opera House on May 7, 1849, by a mob which had gathered in response to fiery tirades of Captain Rynders and other agitators against the Briton, and their crafty manipulation of the racial prejudices of New York's large Irish population. Three days later, on May 10, Washington Irving, John Jacob Astor and other prominent citizens induced Macready to attempt another performance, and Captain Rynders immediately flooded the city with inflammatory handbills denouncing the English and calling upon the Americans to defend their country against foreign insult and oppression. That night a great mob of between 10,000 and 15,000 massed in Astor Place, and Macready again fled when the theater was bombarded with bricks and cobblestones and set on fire by gangsters who had been captured by the police and flung into the basement. The flames were extinguishd before much damage was done.

The police were unable to control the mob even after Macready had left the theater and escaped to New Rochelle in disguise, and the Seventh Regiment was finally called into action. The soldiers were also attacked, and after they had been forced to fall back upon the sidewalk on the east side of the Opera House, and some of their muskets snatched from their hands, they fired several volleys into the mob, killing twenty-three persons and wounding twenty-two. More than a hundred policemen and Guardsmen were injured by stones and bricks, and half a dozen of the latter were shot. Another attempt to wreck and burn the Opera House was made on the night of May 11, but the mob was cowed by additional troops and by artillery which had been planted to sweep Broadway and the Bowery. The excitement was intense for almost a week, and for several days a great crowd stood in front of the New York Hotel, where Macready had stopped, urging him to come forth and be hanged. But the actor boarded a train at New Rochelle within two hours after the rioting of May 10, and went to Boston. From there he sailed to England, and never again returned to this country.

SIN ALONG THE WATER FRONT

BEFORE THE Revolution, and for almost thirty years thereafter, the finest residential section of New York was the old Fourth Ward, lying east and south of the Five Points and including within its boundaries such famous streets as Cherry, Oliver, James, Roosevelt, Catherine, Pike, Water, and Dover. In this district, and especially in Cherry Hill, the high ground in the northeastern part of the Ward, the old families and the great merchants had their homes, and the streets were lined with fragrant cherry trees and splendid mansions. Cherry street was the heart of the fashionable district; it was on this thoroughfare, at the corner of Franklin Square, that George Washington resided when he was inaugurated President of the United States. John Hancock's home was at No. 5 Cherry street, and at No. 27 lived Captain Samuel

Chester Reid, who conceived the present plan of the American flag. The house at No. 7 Cherry street, next door to the Hancock mansion, was the first in the city to be supplied with illuminating gas. At No. 23 was a restaurant and bar-room known as The Well, a favorite resort of army and navy officers and of the captains of American privateers during the War of 1812. It was there that the beefsteak party, so popular with modern stag parties, originated.

But the wave of immigration which flowed to America soon after the Revolution forced the aristocrats northward, and by 1840 their mansions had given way to long rows of ramshackle tenements housing a miserable population steeped in vice and poverty. When the Old Brewery at the Five Points was demolished its reputation as the most squalid tenement in New York was assumed by Gotham Court, sometimes known as Sweeney's Shambles, at Nos. 36 and 38 Cherry street, although the claims of this fearsome pile were disputed by the Arch Block, which ran from Thompson to Sullivan streets between Broome and Grand. Among others the Block contained the famous dive kept by a giant Negro woman known variously as Big Sue and the Turtle. She weighed more than 350 pounds and was described by a contemporary journalist as resembling a huge black turtle standing on its hind legs.

Gotham Court comprised two rows of connected tenements, set back to back and extending for 130 feet along Cherry street in the direction of Oak street. The buildings housed more than 1,000 persons, principally Irish but with a sprinkling of Negroes and Italians. Entrance to both rows was by two alleys on the east and west sides, called Single Alley and Double Alley. The former was six feet wide and the latter nine. Double Alley was also known as Paradise Alley, and was the boyhood haunt of Edward Harrigan and William J. Scanlon, the celebrated vaudeville and music hall performers. It was this alley, also, which provided the inspiration for the famous street song, "The Sunshine of Paradise Alley":

There's a little side street such as often you meet,
  Where the boys of a Sunday night rally;
Though it's not very wide, and it's dismal beside,
  Yet they call the place Paradise Alley.
But a maiden so sweet lives in that little street,
  She's the daughter of Widow McNally;
She has bright golden hair, and the boys all declare,
She's the sunshine of Paradise Alley.

She's had offers to wed by the dozen, 'tis said,
  Still she's always refused them politely;
But of late she's been seen with young Tommy Killeen,
  Going out for a promenade nightly.
We can all guess the rest, for the boy she loves best,
  Will soon change her name from McNally;
Tho' he may change her name, she'll be known just the same,
  As the sunshine of Paradise Alley.

One of the principal sewers of that part of the city ran in a direct line beneath Gotham Court, with manholes in both Single and Double Alleys. Gangsters and other criminals who sought refuge from the police in the dismal chambers of the Court cut other openings from the cellars of the tenements, and hid themselves and their plunder on the side ledges of the sewer or in niches cut in the walls. The fearful odors and vapors which seeped into the Court made it one of the unhealthiest spots in the city. The death rate was always high, and during the cholera epidemic it reached 195 in a thousand. Of 183 children born in the Court over a period of three years sixty-one died after a few weeks of life. Infants were also frequently killed by the huge rats, some of them as large as cats, which infested the sewer and often invaded the tenements. The Board of Health condemned Gotham Court in 1871, but it was not until the middle nineties that the tenants were evicted and the buildings demolished.

Conditions such as these soon prevailed throughout the Fourth Ward, and by 1845 the whole area had become a hotbed of crime; streets over whose cobble-stones had rolled the carriages of the aristocrats were filled with dives which sheltered the members of such celebrated river gangs as the Daybreak Boys, Buckoos, Hookers, Swamp Angels, Slaughter Housers, Short Tails, Patsy Conroys, and the Border Gang. No human life was safe, and a well-dressed man venturing into the district was commonly set upon and murdered or robbed, or both, before he had gone a block. If the gangsters could not lure a prospective victim into a dive, they followed him until he passed beneath an appointed window, from which a woman dumped a bucket of ashes upon his head. As he gasped and choked, the thugs rushed him into a cellar, where they killed him and stripped the clothing from his back, afterward casting his naked body upon the sidewalk. The police would not march against the denizens of the Fourth Ward except in parties of half a dozen or more, and when their quarry sought refuge in a dive they frequently besieged the place for a week or longer until the thug was driven forth by restlessness or hunger. The principal resorts were always well garrisoned, and fully supplied with muskets, knives and pistols.

On Water street, running parallel with the East River, practically every house contained one or more dives, and some of the tenements had a saloon, dance hall, or house of prostitution on every floor. For at least twenty-five years this thoroughfare was probably the scene of more violent crime than any other street on the continent. John Allen operated his famous dance cellar and house of prostitution at No. 304 Water street, and north and south of his establishment, within a half-mile limit, were forty similar places, as well as a hundred other resorts. Kit Burns' place, Sportsmen's Hall, occupied the whole of a three-story frame house at No. 273 Water street, the lower half of which was painted a vivid and bilious green, while before the door swung a huge gilt sign. The principal room of the first floor was arranged as an amphitheater, with rough wooden benches for seats. In the center was a ring enclosed by a wooden fence about three feet high. This was the famous pit in which the huge gray rats from the wharfs were sent against terriers and sometimes, after they had been starved for several days, against each other. One of the noted gangsters who haunted Burns' place was George Leese, otherwise

A Dog Fight in Kit Burns' Rat Pit

known as Snatchem, a member of the Slaughter House gang, and, in the opinion of a contemporary journalist, "a beastly, obscene ruffian, with bulging, bulbous, watery-blue eyes, bloated face and coarse swaggering gait." This noble thug, besides plying his trade as a river pirate, was an official bloodsucker at the bare-knuckle prize fights which were frequently held in the Fourth Ward and Five Points dives. With two revolvers in his belt and a knife in his boot-top, Snatchem was an important figure at these entertainments, and when one of the pugilists began to bleed from scratches and cuts inflicted by his opponent's knuckles, it was Snatchem's office to suck the blood from the wound. He pridefully described himself as a "rough-and-tumble-stand-up-to-be-knocked-down-son-of-a-gun," and a "kicking-in-the-head-knife-in-a-dark-room fellow." Apparently he was all of that. Another attraction of Sportsmen's Hall was Kit Burns' son-in-law, known as Jack the Rat. For ten cents Jack would bite the head off a mouse, and for a quarter he would decapitate a rat.

A famous Water street resort was the Hole-in-the-Wall, at the corner of Dover street, run by One-Armed Charley Monell and his trusted lieutenants, Gallus Mag and Kate Flannery. Gallus Mag was one of the notorious characters of the Fourth Ward, a giant Englishwoman well over six feet tall, who was so called because she kept her skirt up with suspenders, or galluses. She was bouncer and general factotum of the Hole-in-the-Wall, and stalked fiercely about the dive with a pistol stuck in her belt and a huge bludgeon strapped to her wrist. She was an expert in the use of both weapons, and like the celebrated Hell-Cat Maggie of the Five Points, was an extraordinary virtuoso in the art of mayhem. It was her custom, after she had felled an obstreperous customer with her club, to clutch his ear between her teeth and so drag him to the door, amid the frenzied cheers of the onlookers. If her victim protested and struggled, she bit his ear off, and having cast the fellow into the street she carefully deposited the detached member in a jar of alcohol behind the bar, in which she kept her trophies in pickle. She was one of the most feared denizens of the water front, and the police of the period shudderingly described her as the most savage female they had ever encountered.

The dive over which Gallus Mag exercised a belligerent supervision became the most vicious resort in the city, and was finally closed by Captain Thorne of the Fourth Ward police after seven murders had been committed there in a period of less than two months. It was in the Hole-in-the-Wall that Slobbery Jim and Patsy the Barber, both desperate criminals and prominent members of the Daybreak Boys, had their famous fight. On one of their prowling expeditions along the river front Slobbery Jim and Patsy the Barber came upon a German immigrant, newly landed, walking beneath the sea wall at the Battery. They set upon him, knocked him unconscious with a club, and robbed him of twelve cents, all the money he possessed. They then cast him into the harbor, where he drowned. The thugs repaired to the Hole-in-the-Wall to divide their plunder, and Slobbery Jim pointed out that since he had hoisted the heavy German over the wall he should have at least seven and possibly eight of the twelve cents. But Patsy the Barber held out for an equal division, contending with equal logic that if he had not struck the German with a club Slobbery Jim might not have been able to push him into the water. The infuriated Slobbery

Jim promptly seized the prominent nose of Patsy the Barber between his teeth, and Patsy countered with a knife thrust between the ribs, which, however, did little damage. For more than half an hour the two thugs rolled and tumbled about the floor of the dive, unmolested either by One-Armed Charley or Gallus Mag, for it was recognized that they were not engaged in an ordinary brawl, but were desperate men fighting for a principle. Finally Slobbery Jim obtained possession of the knife and stabbed Patsy the Barber in the throat, and when the latter fell fainting from loss of blood, promptly stamped him to death with hobnailed boots. Slobbery Jim escaped, and was not again heard of until the Civil War, when he appeared as a captain in the Confederate Army.

Although Water street was the site of the most vicious dives of the Fourth Ward and the haunt of the most desperate gangsters, there was little to choose between it and other thoroughfares of the district. Cherry street, through which George Washington and John Hancock had once strolled, was the headquarters of the crimps, who operated boarding houses where sailors were robbed and murdered and from which they were shanghaied. During the late sixties an investigating committee estimated that 15,000 sailors were annually robbed of more than $2,000,000 in these places. Dan Kerrigan, a noted pugilist who fought a three-and-a-half hour bare-knuckle battle with Australian Kelly, operated a house at No. 110 Cherry street, and Mrs. Bridget Tighe, a celebrated female crimp, had a place at No. 61. Next door to Kerrigan's, at No. 110½, was the famous house kept by Tommy Hadden, the most notorious crimp of them all, who also owned a boarding house in Water street. He served two terms in state's prison for robbing and shanghaiing sailors. Both Hadden and Kit Burns had been leaders of the Dead Rabbits and other early Five Points gangs, but as they grew older they wearied of the brawling of Paradise Square and removed to the Fourth Ward, where they opened dives and waxed fat and prosperous, and became notable ornaments of the water front. However, they occasionally returned to the Points and accompanied the Rabbits and Plug Uglies on important forays.

Sailors were frequently murdered as they slept in the old Fourth Ward Hotel at Catherine and Water streets, and their bodies disposed of through trapdoors opening into underground passages which led to the docks. The first Jack-the-Ripper murder in New York is said to have occurred in this house, when an old hag known as Shakespeare was cut to pieces by a half-witted bar fly commonly called Frenchy. Shakespeare always claimed that she had come from an aristocratic family, and that in her youth she had been a celebrated actress in England. She supported her contention by reciting, in return for a bottle of swan gin, every female rôle in *Hamlet, Macbeth* and *The Merchant of Venice,* and throughout the Ward she was regarded as an authority on the drama. Through the agency of Thomas Byrnes, Chief of Police, Frenchy was released after a few years' imprisonment. He always maintained his innocence, and the belief was widespread that he had been framed, and that Shakespeare had been murdered by the original Jack the Ripper, who was then operating in London. For several years there had been much professional jealousy between Scotland Yard and the New York police, and Chief Byrnes had publicly boasted that the Ripper would have been caught had he committed his crimes in New York. He defied the English criminal to come to the United States, and soon afterward Shakespeare was killed. Many investigators believed that Jack the Ripper had accepted the challenge, and that the police had arrested Frenchy to save their professional honor. In the London killings there were various indications that Jack the Ripper was a seafarer.

Another famous sailors' house was the Pearsall & Fox Hotel, in Dover street near Water, which had a dance hall in the basement, houses of prostitution on the second and third floors, and rooms to hire on the fourth and fifth. Still another resort of this type was the Glass House at No. 18 Catherine Slip, kept by Martin Bowe, member of a celebrated Fourth Ward family. Bowe had three brothers, Jack, Jim, and Bill, all of whom were notorious shooters, cutters, and thieves. Not only did they lead other gangsters in forays upon the docks and upon ships lying in the East River, but acted as fences and disposed of the loot obtained by other gangs. One of their principal followers was Jack Madill, who was bartender at the Glass House for more than a year. He was finally sent to prison for life after he had killed his wife because she refused to help him rob a drunken sailor, or, in the expressive argot of the period, roll a lush.

The most notorious of all the Fourth Ward dives was the dance house kept by John Allen in Water street, at No. 304. Allen was a member of a pious and well-to-do family of upper New York state, and was set apart by his parents to follow in the footsteps of his brothers, two of whom became Presbyterian preachers and the third a Baptist. But about 1850 Allen became dissatisfied with the prospective rewards of a ministerial career, and abandoned his studies in Union Theological Seminary, removing with his wife to the Fourth Ward. There they opened a dance hall and house of prostitution, staffing it with twenty girls who wore low black bodices of satin, scarlet skirts and stockings, and red-topped boots with bells affixed to the ankles. One of the inmates of the Allen establishment soon after the Civil War was a daughter of the Lieutenant-Governor of a New England state. She had come to New York to seek her fortune and had been caught in the meshes of the procurers, who then abounded throughout the city and operated almost without hindrance. The dive soon became one of the principal recreational centers for the gangsters of the Fourth Ward, and Allen operated it with such shrewdness that within ten years he had banked a fortune of more than $100,000, and had become widely known as the Wickedest Man in New York, a sobriquet first applied to him by Oliver Dyer in *Packard's Monthly*. His resort became one of the worst the city has ever seen, worthy to rank alongside such notorious, but later, places as the Haymarket, McGuirk's Suicide Hall, Paresis Hall, and Billy McGlory's famous Armory Hall.

Allen had definitely left the service of the Lord when he embarked on a Fouth Ward business career, but he never entirely forgot his early training. Curiously enough, although a drunkard, a thief, a procurer, and possibly a murderer, he remained a devoutly religious man, and insisted upon surrounding his unholy occupation with a holy atmosphere. His house opened for business each afternoon at one o'clock, but on three days a week he gathered his harlots, bartenders, and musicians in the bar-room at noon and

Temptations in the Water Front Dives

there read and expounded a passage from the Scriptures. Each of the cubicles to which his women repaired with their customers was supplied with a Bible and such religious literature as Allen could obtain, and on gala nights New Testaments were given away as souvenirs. He subscribed to practically every religious paper and magazine published in the United States, and took several copies each of the *New York Observer* and *The Independent*, his favorites. He scattered them about the dance hall and bar-room, and on every table and bench reposed a hymnbook called *The Little Wanderers' Friend*, then a popular volume. Allen was always ready to lead his harlots and their customers in a religious sing-song, and it was not unusual for the house to resound with the noise of hymns. The harlots' favorite was "There is Rest for the Weary":

> There is rest for the weary,
> There is rest for you,
> On the other side of Jordan,
> In the sweet fields of Eden,
> Where the Tree of Life is blooming,
> There is rest for you.

The various magazine and newspaper articles which detailed the curious manner in which Allen operated his house attracted much attention, and the evangelical clergymen of the city determined to take advantage of the situation. The Rev. A. C. Arnold of the Howard Mission was especially indefatigable, and made frequent visits to the house, trying to induce Allen to permit an ordained preacher to conduct his meetings. Finally, on May 25, 1868, the Rev. Mr. Arnold led a detachment of six clergymen and as many devout laymen into the dangerous purlieus of Water street, and found Allen so drunk that he was unable to protest when they held a prayer meeting from midnight until four o'clock in the morning. Accounts of this meeting were published, and for several months there was a regular procession of curiosity seekers and ministers to the Water street dive, so that Allen's regular patrons were driven away and his profits dwindled. The preachers continued to hold meetings whenever Allen could be found drunk enough to give his consent, and at length they prevailed upon him to abandon his nefarious business. At midnight on August 29, 1868, the doors of the dance hall were closed for the first time in seventeen years, and the next morning this notice was posted upon the door:

THIS DANCE HOUSE IS CLOSED
NO GENTLEMEN ADMITTED UNLESS ACCOMPANIED BY THEIR
WIVES, WHO WISH TO EMPLOY MAGDALENES AS SERVANTS.

Prayer Meeting in John Allen's Dance House

The next day the Rev. Mr. Arnold announced that John Allen had been converted and reformed, and that he would never resume his former occupation. A few days later the preachers began to hold revival meetings in the dance house, and on the Sunday following Allen attended services at the Howard Mission, and the Rev. Mr. Arnold asked the congregation to pray for him, which was done. This circumstance aroused much interest, as did the public meetings, which continued daily until about the first of October. Meanwhile the ministers had prevailed upon Kit Burns to turn his rat pit over to them for services, and on September 11 meetings were also begun in Tommy Hadden's boarding house in Water street, although none were held in his Cherry street resort. Bill Slocum's gin mill in Water street was also overrun by the preachers, but Slocum, Burns, and Hadden would not attend services at the Mission, although they permitted themselves to be mentioned in prayers.

So much commotion was aroused by the Water street revival that about the middle of September a communication to the public was issued, signed by the Rev. Mr. Arnold, Dr. J. M. Ward, Rev. H. C. Fish, Rev. W. C. Van Meter, Rev. W. H. Boole, Rev. F. Browne, Oliver Dyer, Rev. Isaac M. Lee and the Rev. Mr. Huntington. This document professed to set forth the facts about the Water street preaching. It said that Allen, Burns, Slocum, and Hadden had surrendered their premises for services because they had been converted, and that they were co-operating with the preachers solely through religious motives. The communication said also that the congregations had, to a very large extent, been composed of sailors and residents of the Fourth Ward, and that some of the most wretched outcasts of the district had been present and had, in many instances, requested prayer and private religious instruction.

These things were solemnly set forth by the preachers as facts, and were accepted as such until the *New York Times*, after an extended investigation, exposed the entire scheme. The *Times* declared that there was not a religious revival in progress among the denizens of the water front, and that Slocum, Allen, and Tommy Hadden were not converted or reformed men. It was shown that the preachers and their financial backers had hired the Allen dive for one month, paying him $350 for the privilege of holding prayer meetings and other religious services, and binding him, as part of the bargain, to sing hymns and pray, and to assert that he had given the house free of charge because of his love for the preachers. The newspaper continued:

> As for the other men's reformation, that is as absolutely a piece of humbuggery as Allen's. Tommy Hadden is playing the pious with the hope of being secured from trial before the Court of General Sessions for having recently shanghaied a Brooklynite, and also in consideration of a handsome moneyed arrangement with his employers—similar to that of Allen. Kit Burn's rat pit will be opened for religious services on Monday next; but the public need not be deceived in the mat-

ter of his reformation. His motive, like that of the others, is to make money, and, be it known, he is to receive at the rate of $150 per month, for the use of his pit for an hour every day. Slocum desired prayers at the Howard Mission on Sunday last, but it is understood that he is not to be lionized because the missionaries are not willing to pay him a high enough rental for his hall. As for the general movement carried on in Water street, under the false pretense that these men have voluntarily and from purely religious motives, offered their saloons for public worship, and have, themselves, determined to reform, very little more need be said. The daily prayer meetings are nothing more than assemblages of religious people from among the higher grades of society, in what were once low dance halls. There is an unusual amount of interest displayed at these meetings, and much good, doubtless, has been accomplished thereby, but it is also a fact that there are but a few, and sometimes none, of the wretched women, or ruffianly, vicious men, of that neighborhood present. Those classes are not reached at all, and it is false to say that a revival is going on among them. The character of the audiences and the exercises are similar to that of the noon meeting at the Fulton street church.

The *New York World* gave the following account of one of the meetings in Kit Burns' rat pit:

> The Water street prayer meetings are still continued. Yesterday at noon a large crowd assembled in Kit Burns' liquor shop, very few of whom were roughs. The majority seemed to be business men and clerks, who stopped in to see what was going on, in a casual manner. In a few minutes after twelve the pit was filled up very comfortably, and Mr. Van Meter made his appearance and took up a position where he could address the crowd from the center of the pit, inside the barriers. The roughs and dry goods clerks piled themselves up as high as the roof, tier after tier, and a sickening odor came from the dogs and debris of rats' bones under the seats.
>
> Kit stood outside, cursing and damning the eyes of the missionaries for not hurrying up.
>
> Kit said, "I'm damned if some of the people that come here oughtn't to be clubbed. A fellow 'ud think they had never seen a dog-

pit before. I must be damned good looking to have so many fine fellows looking at me."

Snatchem was a prominent figure at all of the Water street revival services. His intelligence was not of a very high order, and he was easily aroused by the fiery exhortations of the preachers and the emotional appeal of the shouting and hymn-singing. He asked for prayers at every meeting, and frequently embarrassed the ministers by publicly inquiring when they would receive the barrel of water from the river Jordan, which he had been assured would wash away his sins. But he was practically abandoned to whatever fate the Devil had in store for him when, having been asked why he wanted to go to Heaven, he replied that he wanted to be an angel and bite off Gabriel's ear.

The enthusiasm of the revivalists was considerably dampened by the articles which appeared in the *Times* and the *World*, and the public began to desert the services when it became apparent that the preachers had not been wholly truthful. Eventually the campaign was abandoned, and Water street and the remainder of the Fourth Ward returned to their ways of sin. But John Allen's house never recovered from the blighting effect of the prayer meetings; the gangsters began to consider him, as he expressed it, "loose and unsound," and would not patronize his establishment. He retained his women and musicians, and after his contract with the preachers had expired tried desperately to restore his house to its former evil splendour, but within a few months he was compelled to abandon his enterprise. His last public appearance was late in December, 1868, when he and his wife, together with several of his girls, were arraigned before Justice Dowling in the Tombs Police Court, charged with robbing a seaman of $15. One of the girls, Margaret Ware, was held for immediate trial, and Allen was bound over in $300 bail for appearance in General Sessions. Allen accused Oliver Dyer of causing his arrest, and declared that it was all a "put up job."

CHAPTER IV

RIVER PIRATES

1

WHILE THE early gangsters of the Five Points and the Bowery were frequently thieves, and on occasion murderers, they were primarily brawlers and street fighters, and most of their battling was done in the open. But the thugs who infested the Fourth Ward and swarmed each night into its dives and gin-mills for their recreation and plotting, were killers and robbers first of all. They seldom engaged in gutter rows with the gangs of other districts, but when they did they usually carried the day and left their opponents maimed and bleeding upon the field, for with the possible exception of the later Whyos of Mulberry Bend they were the most ferocious criminals who ever stalked the streets of an American city. One of them was more than a match for a Dead

Rabbit, a Plug Ugly, or a Bowery Boy, and not even the legends which have so elaborated the exploits of the mighty Mose tell of a successful foray against the gangsters of the water front.

In more modern times the Hudson Dusters, as well as the Potashes, the Gophers and other gangs of Hell's Kitchen and the West Side, have gained considerable renown by their exploits on the west shore of Manhattan, but the early pirates for the most part confined their activities to the East River water front, and only one gang of importance operated along the Hudson. This was a choice collection of ruffians known as the Charlton Street Gang. They made their headquarters in a low gin-mill at the foot of Charlton street, and sallied forth each evening to steal whatever was loose upon the docks, and to rob and murder anyone who ventured into their territory. But most of the Hudson River piers were used by ocean-going steamers and sailing vessels, and the owners provided well-lighted docks and employed a small army of watchmen to guard their property. Consequently the Charlton street gangsters found the pickings very slim, and were at length driven to make a choice between regular piracy and honest labor.

Naturally, they chose piracy, and for the first year or two of their new career roamed the Hudson in rowboats, but with scant success until the spring of 1869, when they were joined by a woman known as Sadie the Goat, who proceeded to put new life into the gang. Sadie acquired her sobriquet because it was her custom, upon encountering a stranger who appeared to possess money or valuables, to duck her head and butt him in the stomach, whereupon her male companion promptly slugged the surprised victim with a slung-shot, and they then robbed him at their leisure. For several years Sadie the Goat was a favorite among the gangsters of the Fourth Ward, but she finally became embroiled in a fight with Gallus Mag and was badly worsted. She fled the ward, leaving one of her ears in Gallus Mag's pickling fluid behind the bar of the Hole-in-the-Wall, and sought refuge in the den of the Charlton Street Gang on the West Side.

Under her inspired leadership the Charlton street thugs considerably enlarged their field of operations. They stole a small sloop of excellent sailing qualities, and with the Jolly Roger flying from the masthead and Sadie the Goat pacing the deck in proud command, they sailed up and down the Hudson from the Harlem River to Poughkeepsie and beyond, robbing farmhouses and riverside mansions, terrorizing the hamlets, and occasionally holding men, women, and children for ransom. It has been said that Sadie the Goat, whose ferocity far exceeded that of her ruffianly followers, compelled several men to walk the plank in true piratical style. For several months the thugs were enormously successful, and filled their hiding-places with bales of goods, some of

Wharf Rats at Work

it of considerable value, which they disposed of gradually through the fences and junk shops along the Hudson and East Rivers. But after they had committed several murders the embattled farmers along the river began to greet their landing parties with musket and pistol fire, and by the end of the summer life had become so perilous that they abandoned their sloop. Sadie the Goat is said to have taken her share of the loot and returned to the Fourth Ward, where she made truce with Gallus Mag and acknowledged her to be queen of the water front. Gallus Mag was so touched by the abject surrender of her erstwhile rival that she dipped into her jar of trophies and returned one female ear to its original owner. Legend has it that Sadie the Goat had her ear enclosed in a locket and wore it about her throat.

In his report to the Mayor in September, 1850, Chief of Police George W. Matsell estimated that there were between four hundred and five hundred river pirates in the Fourth Ward, organized in some fifty active gangs. "The river pirates," he said, "pursue their nefarious operations with the most systematic perseverance, and manifest a shrewdness and adroitness which can only be attained by long practice. Nothing comes amiss to them. In their boats, under cover of night, they prowl around the wharves and vessels in a stream, and dexterously snatch up every piece of loose property left for a moment unguarded." Some of the thieving boats came from the Brooklyn water front, and others from the shores of Staten Island and New Jersey, and occasionally a good-sized smack lay off shore in the harbor during the night and served as a receiving ship, shifting her anchorage with the dawn and disposing of the accumulated plunder to the junkmen. But a majority of the river gangsters of whom Chief Matsell complained hailed from the dives of the Fourth Ward and, later, from the Seventh Ward and the Corlears' Hook district at the bend in the East River, north of Grand street. From the docks and ships the pirates stole everything they could lay their hands upon. They usually transferred the loot to their own containers, which prevented positive identification and made it difficult for the police to obtain conclusive evidence that the property had been stolen.

The Daybreak Boys, who had a rendezvous in a low gin mill kept by Pete Williams at Slaughter House Point, as the police called the intersection of James and Water streets, was the first of the river gangs to operate as an organized criminal unit. These thugs were so called because they generally chose the hour of dawn for their most hazardous and important enterprises, and few were the days on which the rising sun did not disclose them prowling about the docks or along the river in rowboats. Nicholas Saul and William Howlett, who were hanged in the Tombs when the former was but twenty years old and Howlett a year his junior, were the most celebrated leaders of the Daybreak Boys, although the membership of the gang included many noted criminals, among them Slobbery Jim, Sow Madden, Cow-legged Sam McCarthy and Patsy the Barber. None of these thugs was more than twenty years old when he had acquired a reputation as a murderous gangster and cutthroat, and there was scarcely a man among them who had not committed at least one murder, and innumerable robberies, before he reached his majority. Saul and Howlett joined the gang when they were sixteen and fifteen, respectively, and several others were even younger; a few were as young as ten and twelve years.

The Daybreak Boys soon became famous as the most desperate thugs of their period, ready to scuttle a ship, crack the skull of a watchman, or cut a throat without hesitation. Frequently they murdered for the sheer love of killing, without provocation or hope of gain. Saul and Howlett became captains in 1850, and under their joint leadership the gang terrorized the East River water front for two years, occasionally venturing into the more dangerous waters of the Hudson and the harbor. Both Saul and Howlett were extraordinarily adroit, and the boldness of their exploits, and the obvious prosperity of their followers, soon attracted to their banner the most vicious gangsters of the district. The police estimated that during the two years in which these heroes led the Daybreak Boys the gang stole property worth at least $100,000, and committed about twenty murders. And it is likely that they were responsible for at least twice that many killings, for a day rarely passed that one or more dead men were not found floating in the river or stretched stiff upon a lonely dock, their pockets turned inside out and fatal wounds upon their bodies. But there was seldom any evidence through which the murderer could be traced.

On the evening of August 25, 1852, a detective passing Pete Williams' dive at Slaughter House Point saw Saul and Howlett and Bill Johnson, an ineffectual member of the gang but a boon companion of the two chieftains, sitting at a table with their heads close together, taking no part in the gayety of the place. It was clear that they were plotting mischief, and as further proof Johnson was drinking heavily, as he always did when great events portended, for he was a man of small courage. An hour later the detective again passed the resort, but the three gangsters had gone, and he assumed that they had repaired to one of the dance halls much frequented by both Saul and Howlett. But instead, they had embarked in a rowboat and with greased oarlocks and muffled oars pulled to the brig William Watson, which was anchored in the East River between Oliver street and James Slip. Leaving Johnson dead drunk in the bottom of the rowboat, Saul and Howlett clambered onto the deck of the brig and made their way to the ship's cabin, where the watchman, Charles Baxter, came upon them as they tugged at the captain's sea chest, which they purposed dragging to the rail and dropping into their boat. Although Baxter was unarmed, he attacked them and fought so fiercely that the thugs lost their heads, and instead of knocking him unconscious with a club or a slug-shot, shot him through the heart.

Abandoning their attempt to plunder the vessel, Saul and Howlett hastily dropped into their rowboat and set out for shore, with Johnson still so drunk that he was unable to lend a hand at the oars. But the William Watson was lying close inshore, and the sound of the shot had been heard by a policeman on the Oliver street dock. A few minutes later he glimpsed the shadowy outlines of a rowboat gliding swiftly through the fog which had settled down upon the river during the night, and when it docked he saw Saul and Howlett drag Johnson onto the pier and half carry him into Pete Williams' dive. Several hours later, after the body of Baxter had been discovered, a squad of twenty policemen, all heavily armed, swooped down upon the resort at Slaughter House Point and captured the three gangsters after a desperate battle with a score of thugs who rallied to the defense of their captains. All three were tried and found guilty of murder, and Johnson was sent to prison for life, while Saul and Howlett were sentenced to death. On the morning of January 28, 1853, they were hanged in the courtyard of the Tombs in the presence of more than two hundred interested spectators, a hundred of whom, including Butcher Bill Poole, and Tom Hyer, the pugilist, filed past the scaffold and shook hands with the condemned thugs.

Slobbery Jim and Bill Lowrie now assumed the leadership of the Daybreak Boys, but Slobbery Jim soon fled the city to escape hanging for the murder of Patsy the Barber, and the gang declined in importance after Captain Thorne had closed the dive in Slaughter House Point. Lowrie and his sweetheart, Molly Maher, then opened The Rising States in Water street near Oliver, and tried to keep the remnants of the Daybreak Boys together, but Lowrie himself was caught in a dock robbery soon after he started his grog-shop, and was sent to prison for fifteen years. Cow-legged Sam McCarthy took his place both as leader of the gang and as lover to Molly Maher, but after a few months he abandoned both the river and the woman and cast his lot with a gang of burglars from the Five Points, who operated in the residential and manufacturing districts farther uptown.

CULVER PICTURES

The Five Points in 1859.
View taken from the Corner of Worth and Little Water St.

Meanwhile Chief Matsell and other police officials had continued their agitation for a harbor force adequate to protect the docks and shipping, in which they were joined by many prominent citizens, among them James W. Gerard, who went to London and made an exhaustive study of the London police and returned to publish a series of articles demanding that New York be given greater protection. Mr. Gerard was also a leader in the campaign which finally resulted in the police force being permanently uniformed. Not only did he urge a distinctive dress, but he had his tailor make such a uniform and himself wore it to a fancy dress ball, a circumstance which evoked much comment. But it was not until 1858 that the city authorities consented to the organization of a harbor police, and even then the force consisted of only a few men who patrolled the rivers and lower harbor in rowboats. The first boat set out on March 15, 1858, and within a few days a dozen others were cruising under command of experienced policemen, who had orders to overhaul and examine every suspicious looking craft.

With the aid of the rowboats, the police started an energetic campaign against the gangsters of the Fourth Ward, and concentrated their attack on the Daybreak Boys, who had already been demoralized by the successive misfortunes of their leaders and by the defection of Cow-legged Sam. Roundsman Blair and Patrolmen Spratt and Gilbert killed twelve of the thugs in 1858, and during that same year Detective Sergeant Edwin O'Brien arrested fifty-seven gangsters who owed allegiance to the Daybreak Boys, the Short Tails and the Border Gang. These activities soon scattered the Daybreak Boys, and by the end of 1859 the gang was practically extinct. Those members who had survived the onslaught of the police removed to the Bowery and Five Points, or to the Corlears' Hook area, where they joined various gangs. But the Swamp Angels, who made their rendezvous in the sewer under the Gotham Court tenement in Cherry street, the Hookers, and the remainder of the Fourth Ward gangs continued to give the police much trouble, and shipping men were still uncertain as to the ultimate destination of a cargo consigned to a merchant who used the East River docks. Encounters occurred nightly between the police and the gangsters, and many officers and thugs were killed and wounded. The gangs of the Brooklyn and New Jersey water fronts also began to make excursions into Manhattan waters, although for the most part the former kept pretty close to their bases, for there were plenty of opportunities for theft and murder along the Brooklyn dock. Their principal hiding-places were in the sparsely settled region between Brooklyn and Williamsburg, then called Irishtown but now populated almost entirely by Jews and Italians.

2

THE most illustrious thug who came to the attention of the police during this period was Albert E. Hicks, commonly called Hicksey, a free lance gangster and thief who lived with his wife

Albert E. Hicks

and one child at No. 129 Cedar street, not far from old Trinity Church and within two blocks of the Hudson River. Hicks spent most of his time in the dives of the Fourth Ward water front, and although a member of none of the great gangs, occasionally enlisted under the banner of a captain whose activities promised excitement and loot. On a night in March, 1860, having imbibed too deeply at a Water street dance hall, Hicks sought lodging at the house of a Cherry street crimp, trusting that his reputation would protect him. But the crimp was no respecter of persons. He put laudanum in Hicks' nightcap of rum, and in the dead of night crept into the sleeping chamber and deepened his guest's slumbers with a slung-shot. When Hicks awakened next morning he was on board the sloop E. A. Johnson, bound for Deep Creek, Virginia, for a cargo of oysters, and had been regularly shipped as a member of the crew under the name of William Johnson. Besides the shanghaied gangster, the vessel's complement comprised the master, Captain Burr, and two brothers, Smith and Oliver Watts.

The E. A. Johnson sailed out of New York harbor with Hicks lying in the forecastle trying to collect his scattered senses. Five days later the sloop was found abandoned at sea, only a few miles off Staten Island, by the schooner Telegraph of New London, Connecticut. The schooner spoke the steam tug Ceres, which towed the Johnson into the Fulton Market Slip, at the lower end of Manhattan. She had evidently collided with another vessel, for her bowsprit and cutwater had been badly damaged, and the sailors who boarded her long enough to affix a tow line reported that her decks were in the wildest confusion. After she had been tied up in the Slip, Coroner Schirmer and Captain Weed of the Second Precinct police boarded her and made an examination. They found the sails loose upon the deck, and the small boat ordinarily towed at the stern was missing. In the cabin the ceiling, floor, bunks, chairs, and table were stained with blood, as were the bedding and the ship's papers, and various articles of clothing which had been thrown about the compartment. On the floor of the cabin, and on the planking of the deck, were marks indicating that a heavy body had been dragged to the side, and the rail was splotched by blood. On the deck beneath the rail lay four human fingers and a thumb, and near them a bloody axe.

The next day Andrew Kelly and John Burke, tenants of the house in Cedar street, appeared at the police station and told Captain Weed that twenty-four hours before the sloop was brought into port Hicks had returned home with a large sum of money, and had given evasive answers when asked where he had obtained it. That night Hicks packed his household goods, and with his wife and child left the city. Patrolman Nevins traced them to a boarding-house in Providence, Rhode Island, and with the aid of the Providence police arrested the entire family. They were brought to New York, where Mrs. Hicks and her child were released, but Hicks was held for investigation because he told conflicting tales about the money.

A thorough search of the gangster's belongings disclosed a watch which was identified as having belonged to Captain Burr, and a daguerreotype which a young woman had given to Oliver Watts before the sloop sailed. Hicks denied flatly that his name was Johnson or that he had ever been on board the vessel, but was unable to explain the possession of the watch and picture. Later he was identified by John Burke as the man who had lived at Cedar street. Then a deck hand on one of the Staten Island boats identified Hicks as a man who had accosted him during the run from the Island to Manhattan, and had asked him to help count two bags of money. A web of circumstantial evidence was soon woven around Hicks, and he was transferred to the custody of Isaiah Rynders, United States Marshal, and locked up in the Tombs. In May he was tried before the United States Circuit Court, and after deliberating only seven minutes the jury found him guilty of piracy and murder on the high seas. He was sentenced to be hanged on Friday, July 13, and the Court specified that the execution take place on one of the government islands in New York Bay. Less than a week after the trial Hicks summoned the Warden of the Tombs and said that he desired to confess, and thereby ease his soul of sin. With his hands shackled behind his back and a ball and chain dragging at his ankle, the gangster paced back and forth before an audience of officials and newspaper reporters, and described in minute and gory detail the murder of Captain Burr and the two boys, Smith and Oliver Watts. The affair, he said, occurred at ten o'clock at night. He had brooded over being shanghaied, and he determined to avenge himself by murdering all hands aboard the sloop.

"I was steering," he said, "and Captain Burr and one of the Waᴛts boys were asleep in the cabin. The other Watts was on lookout at the bows. Suddenly the devil took possession of me and I determined to murder the captain and crew that very night."

Hicks lashed the steering wheel to keep the vessel on her course, and picked up a capstan bar. Creeping forward, he approached the boy who stood in the bow watching the seas as they broke over the vessel's forefoot. But his figure cast a long shadow in the moonlight which flooded the deck, and Watts turned to see who was coming. He screamed once, and then the bar descended upon his head, crushing his skull. The sound of the blow and the scream had awakened the other lad, and he came up the companion-way to learn what had happened. But meanwhile Hicks had obtained an axe, and as the boy climbed onto the deck the gangster decapitated him. Hicks then went down the companion in search of the skipper. Captain Burr, a short, thickset, but very muscular man, was aroused by the entrance of the murderous thug, and sat up in his bunk to find Hicks in the center of the cabin, leaning upon his axe. The next instant the pirate leaped forward, the blood-smeared blade glistening in the dim light cast by the swinging lantern above the Captain's pallet.

The axe crashed against Captain Burr's pillow, but the skipper rolled with the blow and tumbled upon the floor in time to save his neck. He clasped Hicks about the knees, and as the gangster plunged to the floor the Captain strove desperately to grip his throat, while Hicks struggled to bring his axe into play. The fight continued for several minutes, but at length Hicks pushed the Captain against the cabin stove, and before the latter could regain his footing the pirate drove the axe deep into the side of his head, shearing away half of his skull. Hicks then went on deck, where he found the Watts boy he had first assaulted struggling to his knees. The gangster knocked him down and then carried his body to the rail, where he hoisted the lad over the side of the sloop. But young Watts clutched at the rail, whereupon Hicks raised his axe and calmly cut off his thumb and fingers, and Watts fell into the sea. Hicks then threw the other bodies overboard, rifled the captain's money bags, and headed the vessel for shore. When the coast of Staten Island came into view he used the small boat to effect a landing, first starting the sloop out to sea.

Interior of the Cabin of the Oyster Sloop, E.A. Johnson

The conviction of Hicks and his subsequent confession caused a great stir throughout the city, and for several weeks there was a constant stream of visitors to the Tombs, where they thronged the corridors and stared for hours into the cell where Hicks lay shackled to the floor. Among the first comers was Phineas T. Barnum, the great showman, whose American Museum was then in the heyday of its popularity. Barnum asked for a private conference with the prisoner, which Hicks granted after a consultation with the Warden of the Tombs. Barnum informed the pirate that he wished to obtain a plaster cast of his head and bust for exhibition in the Museum along with the other curiosities, and after an entire day of haggling an arrangement was reached whereby Hicks agreed to pose in return for $25 in cash and two boxes of five-cent cigars. Early next morning the cast was made, and that afternoon Barnum returned to the Tombs with a new suit of clothes, which he traded to Hicks for the one the pirate was then wearing. Later Hicks complained to the Warden that Barnum had cheated him, for the new garments were shoddy and not nearly so good as his old ones.

Mrs. Hicks visited her husband at six o'clock on the evening of Thursday, July 12. Farewells having been said, the woman departed, and the Rev. Father Duranquet then entered the cell of the condemned man and remained with him until eleven o'clock, when Hicks drank a cup of tea and retired. He slept soundly, and at four o'clock next morning was awakened and told to dress. He manifested no signs of grief or penitence, but ate heartily of breakfast, and then smoked the last of the cigars which he had obtained from Barnum. He told the Warden that Barnum had asked him to return the empty boxes for display in the Museum, and the Warden agreed to see that the showman received them. A few minutes before nine o'clock Marshal Rynders, girt with the Sheriff's sword which he had borrowed for the occasion, entered the prison, attended by Sheriff Kelly and several deputies, all clad in plug hats and black frock coats. In a sonorous voice the Marshal read the death warrant, and then bade the prisoner prepare for execution, which Hicks did by arraying himself in a suit of blue cottonade, made expressly for the event. He complained that the suit did not fit, and that it had not been properly pressed, but the Warden told him there was no time for alterations.

The gangster was handcuffed and shackled with leg irons, and was then led from his cell into the main corridor of the prison, where Marshal Rynders and his party were drawn up in a solemn group to receive him. Attended by Father Duranquet and surrounded by the officials marching in hollow square with their plug hats held across their chests, Hicks was escorted with great formality through the great doors and into the street. Thousands of people who had gathered greeted his appearance with cheers, and both the prisoner and the United States Marshal bowed in acknowledgment of the ovation. For a few moments the group stood on the steps of the prison, and then around a corner into Center street swept a fife and drum corps and a string of carriages, each drawn by a team of coal black horses and driven by a coachman clad in black from head to toe. The procession halted in front of the Tombs amid flourishes and ruffles from the trumpets and drums, and Marshal Rynders, carrying his silk hat in the crook of his elbow and with his sword clanking about his heels, marched ceremoniously down the steps and ensconced himself in the front seat of the first carriage. Beside him sat Deputy Marshal Thompson, while Hicks was placed in the back seat between

Father Duranquet and Sheriff Kelly. In the second carriage were the Deputy Sheriffs, each carrying his staff of office, and in the others were policemen, gamblers, pugilists, politicians, doctors and newspaper reporters. At a signal from Marshal Rynders the drums rattled, the musicians struck up a dirge, and the carriages rolled slowly across the street along thoroughfares lined with cheering crowds to Canal street. There the steamboat Red Jacket waited to convey the hanging party to Bedloe's Island, where the Statue of Liberty now beckons with her blazing torch of freedom.

The vehicles and the fife and drum corps were dismissed when the procession arrived at the dock, and the party, augmented by more than a thousand persons who had been invited to the hanging but not for the carriage ride, went aboard the steamboat. Hicks was made comfortable in the cabin, and immediately engaged in prayer with Father Duranquet. By ten o'clock the steamboat was crowded with some 1,500 men, and a start was made for the Island. But in midstream Marshal Rynders discovered that there was plenty of time, and he determined to take his guests for a pleasure sail up the Hudson. The Red Jacket was accordingly turned about, and steamed slowly up the river as far as Hammond street, where the steamship Great Eastern, recently arrived from Europe on her maiden voyage, was anchored. Hicks was brought to the rail, and as the Red Jacket circled the Great Eastern, Marshal Rynders stationed himself on the bridge, and with his sword in one hand and a trumpet in the other, announced to the passengers of the steamship the purpose of the cruise, and the meaning of the shackles on Hicks' legs and the handcuffs on his wrists.

About 10:30 o'clock the Red Jacket again started down the Bay, arriving at Bedloe's Island half an hour later. The guests formed themselves in procession, and, preceded by Marshal Rynders, Father Duranquet, and Hicks, marched down the gangplank between lines of Marines under command of Captain John B. Hamilton, while beyond the pier a detachment of regular infantry from the garrison at Fort Hamilton awaited to escort the doomed gangster to the scene of execution. Hicks marched with his lips moving in prayer and his hands crossed on his breast, and as soon as his feet touched the soil of the Island he knelt with Father Duranquet and commended his soul to the special attention of the Almighty. He was permitted to complete his supplication, while the guests stood with bared heads, and the procession then moved forward, with Hicks in the center of a hollow square formed by the troops, while the regimental band played a dirge.

Meanwhile hundreds of boats had come from Manhattan, and from Staten Island, New Jersey, and Brooklyn, and formed a solid mass for more than a hundred feet out from shore. Beyond this fringe of small craft were many large excursion boats, gaily decorated with flags and bunting and packed to the gunwales with hilarious crowds among whom hawkers and patterers peddled hot corn, candy, and other dainties. It was estimated that at least 10,000 persons saw the execution, for the scaffold had been erected not thirty feet from the water, and the hanging was in plain view of the throng which filled the boats. Hicks stepped on the death platform promptly at 11:30 o'clock, and fifteen minutes later, after Marshal Rynders and other officials had shaken hands with him, the rope was cut and his body dropped through the trap. He struggled severely for three minutes, but thereafter exhibited no pain. The body remained suspended for half an hour, when it was cut down and carried aboard the Red Jacket, and taken back to Manhattan. Hicks was buried in Calvary Cemetery, but he was scarcely cold before the grave had been robbed by ghouls, who sold the corpse to medical students for a few dollars.

3

WHEN the police began to drive the gangs of the Fourth Ward northward along the East River, dives similar to those along Water and Cherry streets sprang up around the Corlears' Hook district, bearing such names as the Tub of Blood, Hell's Kitchen, Snug Harbor, Swain's Castle, Cat Alley, and the Lava Beds. Many celebrated thieves and gangsters frequented these resorts during the period following the Civil War, among them Skinner Meehan,

Dutch Hen, Brian Boru, Sweeney the Boy, Hop Along Peter and Jack Cody. Sweeney the Boy and Brian Boru slept in a marble yard near the Hook for twenty years, but one night Brian Boru went to sleep so drunk that he could not defend himself, and when his body was found it had been half devoured by the huge gray rats which infested the docks and frequently ranged far afield in quest of food. Hop Along Peter was a half-wit, but he was nevertheless a ferocious thug, for he flew into a furious rage whenever he saw a policeman's uniform, and became one of the most notorious cop-fighters of his time.

Patsy Conroy, who had operated with great success along the Fourth Ward water front, moved his gang bag and baggage into Corlears' Hook and soon enlisted the aid of such celebrated thugs and brawlers as Joseph Gayles, otherwise Socco the Bracer; Scotchy Lavelle; Johnny Dobbs, whose real name was Mike Kerrigan; Kid Shanahan, Pugsy Hurley, Wreck Donovan, Tom the Mick, Nigger Wallace, Beeny Kane, Piggy Noles, and a score of others. In later years Scotchy Lavelle became the proud owner of a Chinatown resort, while Johnny Dobbs achieved renown as a bank burglar. The

A Battle with River Pirates

career of Socco the Bracer, chief lieutenant of Conroy, came to a sudden end on the night of May 29, 1873. In company with Bum

Mahoney and Billy Woods he stole a small boat from the foot of Jackson street, and the three gangsters pulled down stream to Pier 27, East River, where the brig Margaret was tied up awaiting a cargo. They boarded the ship, but while ransacking a sea chest awakened the captain and the mate. A fight ensued, and the gangsters were severely beaten and driven over the side into their boat, while the skipper of the brig fired several shots to arouse the police. Patrolmen Musgrave and Kelly, patrolling the river in a rowboat, attempted to intercept the thugs, but missed them in the fog and darkness, and sculled back to the dock, under which Musgrave flashed his dark lantern. The dim light showed a boat slowly pulling out from under the pier, with Mahoney and Woods bending to the oars and Socco the Bracer standing in the stern with a cocked revolver in his hand.

Socco fired as soon as the light flashed from the lantern, but missed, and his companions dropped their oars and drew revolvers. The policemen returned the fire, and Musgrave's first shot struck Socco the Bracer below the heart. He plunged forward into the bottom of the boat, and Mahoney and Woods seized their oars and pulled rapidly into midstream, where they threw Socco the Bracer overboard to lighten the craft. But Socco, though badly hurt, was not dead, and the shock of the cold water revived him. He struggled to the rowboat and clutched the gunwale, and through the darkness the policemen could hear him begging piteously to be taken aboard. Woods suggested that they crack him on the knuckles with an oar and leave him to drown, but Mahoney was more tender-hearted, and drew the wounded gangster into the boat. But Socco died before the craft had gone fifty feet, and the disgusted Mahoney pushed him back into the river. Four days later the body came to the surface at the foot of Stanton street, within sight of the dead gangster's home.

The fate of Socco the Bracer frightened the Corlears' Hook thugs, but they soon regained their courage. Less than six months after Socco's death, on November 30, 1873, the brig Mattan filled her hold with petroleum, and during the late afternoon dropped down the East River to the Battery, where she anchored off Castle Garden, an ancient assembly hall where Jenny Lind sang and which now houses the Aquarium. Her commander and owner, Captain T. H. Connauton, expected to take a crew aboard next day and sail for Liverpool. But soon after midnight a boat containing seven masked gangsters slipped noiselessly away from the shelter of a pier at Corlears' Hook, and was rowed down to the Battery, where the thugs boarded the brig by means of a line which hād carelessly been left dangling over her bows. They started aft, but one of them stumbled over a coil of rope and fell heavily to the deck, and the mate came forward to see what had happened. He was immediately felled with a slung-shot, and then bound and gagged. The second mate was also captured, as was the steward when he ventured to poke his head above the hatchway.

Captain Connauton, his wife and their three children were asleep in the cabin, and thither the gangsters crept. They knocked, and when the skipper asked what was wanted he was told that the harbor police wished to talk to him. Captain Connauton, only half awakened, opened the door, but slammed it shut again when he saw the masked faces of the thugs peering at him, and the slung-shots and iron bars in their hands. Scarcely had the door closed when one of the gangsters fired a huge revolver, the slug ripping through a panel and wounding Captain Connauton in the leg. The skipper fell to the floor, and although Mrs. Connauton and her children strove desperately to barricade the door with furniture, the gangsters soon battered it down and swarmed into the cabin, where they told the captain that they knew he had $4,000 in cash on board and demanded that he give them the money. But Captain Connauton refused to divulge the hiding-place of his fortune, and the thugs seized Mrs. Connauton, held a pistol to her head and threatened to shoot if the money was not produced. Captain Connauton finally convinced them that he did not have as much as $4,000, and the gangsters released Mrs. Connauton when he offered to show them where they could find $45. The thugs then ransacked the cabin, and after an hour on board the brig departed with the money, a diamond ring, two watches, three gold chains, a ruby ring, and three silk dresses which Mrs. Connauton had purchased in Liverpool on her last voyage to England.

Two days after the attack on the brig the harbor police arrested Tommy Dagan and Billy Carroll, two youthful but ferocious gangsters, and they were soon convicted and sentenced to prison. But six months later the police learned that Dagan and Carroll had spent the night in a Water street dive, and that the masked men who had boarded the Mattan were members of the Patsy Conroy gang led by Denny Brady and Larry Griffin, choice thugs who were not only expert river thieves, but first-class burglars as well. When business along the water front became poor, they led a gang of masked burglars on forays against the small towns of Westchester county along the shores of Long Island Sound, and on Long Island. For two years they kept these hamlets in a chronic condition of terror, but Brady was finally convicted of robbing a house in Catskill, and Griffin and Patsy Conroy were caught in Robert Emmet's home at White Plains.

The Hook gang had also removed from the Fourth Ward to Corlears' Hook, and after Conroy had been sent to jail and his thugs scattered, became the most ferocious band of the district. This group was captained by Tommy Shay, Suds Merrick, James Coffee and Terry Le Strange, who varied their water front thievery with burglary, pocket-picking, and sneak thievery. Other noted gangsters, among them Bum Mahoney, joined the Hookers, and they made their headquarters in a dive at the foot of Stanton street, operating along the East River from Fourteenth street to the Battery. They were very successful for a short period, but late in 1874 Sam McCracken, Tommy Bonner and Johnny Gallagher, three of Merrick's prize thugs, were sent to Auburn prison for long terms after they had boarded the canal boat Thomas H. Brick, bound and gagged the captain and then looted the craft at their leisure.

With three of his best cutthroats in the hands of the police, Merrick abdicated as chieftain of the Hookers, and was succeeded by Bum Mahoney. Mahoney was only twenty-three years old, but he was one of the best known and most widely feared thugs along the river front. One of his able lieutenants was Slipsley Ward, who was sent to prison after he had clambered to the deck of a schooner at Pike street and attempted single-handed to overpower her crew of six men. Another member of the Hookers was Piggy Noles, who stole a rowboat, repainted it and then sold it to its original owner; and still another was Nigger Wallace, who came to grief when he tried to rob three men in a rowboat. Unfortunately for him, they were detectives. Mahoney also claimed the allegiance of Old Flaherty, head of a notorious family. Old Flaherty affected long white whiskers and a benevolent smile, but he was one of the most cruel thugs of the Seventh Ward. He was finally sent to the Penitentiary on Blackwell's Island for stealing, and his wife, a noted shoplifter and pickpocket, soon followed him. Meanwhile their youngest son had been sentenced to fifteen years in Sing Sing for garrotting and highway robbery, and their first-born, seeking new pastures, had acquired a ten-year sentence in the Illinois State Prison.

The police succeeded in driving the gangsters out of the Fourth Ward by the end of the Civil War, but they were not able to accomplish much against the Corlears' Hook thugs until the Steamboat Squad was organized in 1876, under command of Captain Gastlin. The steamboat Seneca was first employed, and afterward several others were added to the fleet. They cruised up and down the East and Hudson Rivers and through the harbor, their cabins crowded with policemen who set out in rowboats whenever a gangster was sighted, or when an alarm was brought to them. Later steam launches were added to the equipment of the harbor police, and eventually there developed the present Marine Division, probably the most efficient branch of the Police Department.

By 1890 most of the dives in the Water street and Corlears' Hook districts had closed for lack of patronage, and within the next ten years the police had practically cleared the water front of organized gangs, although there remained, and do to this day, individual thieves of great prowess. But until the rise of the White Hands after the World War there were no gangs worthy of mention in the same breath with the Daybreak Boys. Under the leadership of Dinny Meehan and Wild Bill Lovett the White Hands terrorized the Brooklyn Bridge and Red Hook sections of Brooklyn, on the East River, and made occasional forays against the Manhattan docks and shipping interests. However, the latter ventures were few and were never successful. Wild Bill's method was simple enough—barge and wharf owners who refused to pay tribute to the gang were beaten and stabbed, and their property burned, wrecked and looted. Lovett was killed in 1923, three years after Meehan had passed to his reward, by a jealous gangster who aspired to his crown. The gang then came under control of Peg Leg Lonergan, but Lonergan was too ambitious. He undertook a raid upon the headquarters of a South Brooklyn gang and was killed, together with two of his lieutenants. Since then the White Hands have been without a chieftain of note, and have been more or less quiescent.

CHAPTER V

THE KILLING OF BILL THE BUTCHER

1

THE MOST brazen of all the criminal elements which infested New York during the pre-Civil War period were the gamblers. They were amazingly prosperous, and were able to pay handsome sums to the political powers for protection, and so operated in open disregard of the fulminations of the reformers. Late in 1850 Jonathan H. Green, a reformed gambler who had become general executive agent of the New York Association for the Suppression of Gambling, was commissioned to survey the situation, and on February 20, 1851, presented his report at a great mass meeting in the Broadway Tabernacle, where speeches were made by Horace Greely and other prominent citizens. Green described the existence and active operation of some six thousand gambling houses, of which more than two hundred were first-class establishments catering to men of standing and sound financial substance. There were also several thousand raffling, lottery, and policy houses, policy having come into great favor as the gambling pastime of the immigrants.

A majority of the first-class houses were on Park Place, Liberty and Vesey streets, Park Row and lower Broadway, and on Barclay street, which is now largely given over to stores selling religious images and literature. Jim Bartolf's place, notorious as a skinning house, was at No. 10 Park Place, and only a few doors away Jack Wallis, a Chinaman, kept a noted establishment, once the property of French José and Jimmy Berry. Wallis won the business from them on the toss of a coin. Other famous gambling hells were Handsome Sam Suydam's and Harry Colton's in Barclay street, Hillman's in Liberty street, Pat Herne's and Orlando Moore's in lower Broadway, and Frank Stuart's in Park Place. Herne was one of the most successful of the lot, but was himself an incorrigible player, and what he won in his own establishment was quickly lost in the houses of his contemporaries. Many of the first-class resorts, as well as a great number of the policy and raffling houses, were reputed to be owned or backed by Reuben Parsons, unquestionably the gambling monarch of his time, who was widely known as the Great American Faro Banker. Parsons was a native of New England who had come to New York with several thousand dollars, intending to engage in business and continue the upright life he had led in the town of his birth. But he lost his fortune in a gambling house, and was so impressed by the ease and dispatch with which his money was taken from him that he opened a place of his own, and soon became rich. Unlike most of his fellows, Parsons dressed plainly and was unassuming in manner. He refused to associate with other gamblers, and was seldom seen publicly in any of the resorts of which he was the financial genius. And he never gambled after his first experience.

There were probably more gamblers and gambling houses in New York during the fifties and early sixties than in any other period of the city's history. "Park Row, Barclay and Vesey streets constitute the Wall street of these despicable characters," said the

New York Herald. "There is, probably, a larger business done in this line here than in London, and it is very likely that the powerful measures adopted in London and Paris to suppress this iniquitous trade will drive many of the sharpers of these capitals to this city, so that a large increase in the work of robbery and plunder, and all its accompanying vices and crimes, may be anticipated. Many of these common gamblers, compared with whom the skulking pickpocket is respectable, mingle with the leaders of fashion in this city. They saunter along Broadway in the morning, drive out on the avenue in the afternoon, lounge at the opera in the evening, and cheat in Park Row and Barclay street till five o'clock in the morning. They are the most *distingué* at the springs and watering places." The favorite gambling pastime in the resorts maintained by these elegant personages was faro, which was as popular then as poker is today. "The game of faro, another of the favorite pets of the police and of our city guardians of public morals," wrote Green in his final report, "is a game so peculiarly adapted to the taste of the American people that it may almost be styled the national game, holding the same rank with the universal Yankee nation as Rouge et Noir in France and Monte in Spain. . . . In this city the game of faro is advancing with rapid steps. A taste for its excitements is spreading among all classes of players."

All of the first-class establishments were magnificently appointed, with liveried servants to attend to the wants of the players, and, on occasion, performers from the music halls and the legitimate theaters to provide entertainment. At least a score would not have suffered by comparison with such celebrated resorts as those operated in later years by Richard Canfield and Honest John Kelly. A contemporary writer thus described one of the gilded dens of Park Row: "Mirrors of magnificent dimensions extend from the ceiling to the floor. No tawdry frescoing, but costly paintings by the first artists, adorn the walls and cover the ceiling. The richest of gold, gilt and rosewood furniture in satins and velvets abound. The dinner is served at six o'clock. Nothing in New York can equal the elegance of the table. It is spread with silver and gold plate, costly china ware and glass of exquisite cut, and the viands embrace the luxuries of the season served up in the richest style. Among the keepers of the first-class gaming houses there is a constant rivalry to excel in the matter of dinners, and the manner in which the table is spread."

2

INTO this paradise of ward-heelers, gangsters and gamblers, in the early fifties, came John Morrissey. Keen of intellect and a giant in stature and strength, Morrissey was destined to become a noted gang fighter, a professional pugilist with a victory over John C. Heenan to his credit, the owner of luxurious gambling houses in New York and Saratoga Springs, a member of the Legislature and of Congress, and, with the original Honest John Kelly, a co-leader of Tammany Hall and dispenser of its patronage. And, incidentally, although he came to New York ragged and without a cent in his pockets, Morrissey became a very rich man, with rings on his fingers and diamonds blazing from his shirt front, and his coffers piled high with gold. At one time, during the height of his career, his fortune was estimated at $700,000.

Morrissey is said to have been born in Ireland, but the first heard of him in the United States was in Troy, New York, where he tended bar and achieved great local renown as a slugger and a rough and tumble fighter. He made several brief visits to New York before he made his home permanently in the metropolis, and on one of his expeditions attempted the laudable but impossible task of wrecking the resort operated at No. 25 Park Row by Capt. Isaiah Rynders, who had temporarily deserted Tammany Hall and cast his lot with the Native American or Know Nothing Party. He had changed the name of his club from Empire to Americus, and it had become the resort of the gang leaders and bullies who fought under the Know Nothing banner. Among them were Tom Hyer, the American heavyweight champion, and Bill Poole, also called Bill the Butcher, chieftain of a gang of West Side bruisers who terrorized the area around Christopher street. Poole was commonly held to be the champion brawler and eye gouger of his time, and not even the ferocious mayhem experts of the Five Points and the Fourth Ward dared engage him in combat. Before organizing his own gang and becoming a power in politics, Poole had served an apprenticeship with the Bowery Boys.

John Morrissey

Morrissey was fearfully mauled by Poole and other Native American sluggers when he charged bellowing into the Americus Club and endeavored to lay it waste, but his strength and valor so impressed Rynders that he was put to bed in the best sleeping room of the establishment, and given medical and nursing attention until he was able to be about. He was then offered a job and a place in the front rank of the Rynders gangsters, but declined the honor, having conceived a violent dislike for Tom Hyer and Bill Poole. He went back to Troy to recuperate, but within a few weeks was again in New York doing odd jobs around the saloons and gambling houses and waiting for a chance to display his prowess. His opportunity finally came during a local election in the upper part of the city. Fearing trouble at the polls, and, indeed, hearing that Bill the Butcher had boasted that he intended to attack the place with his gangsters and destroy the ballot boxes, the honest citizens decided to fight fire with fire, knowing that they could not depend upon the police for protection. The word went out that they wished to employ a gang leader who would pit his strength against Poole and his minions.

The next morning Morrissey called upon John A. Kennedy, who later became Superintendent of Police and was brutally beaten during the Draft Riots, and arranged to organize a gang to protect the polling place and prevent Bill the Butcher from interfering. When the polls opened Morrissey was on hand with fifty of the most ferocious battlers of the Five Points, whom he had engaged at one dollar each for the duration of the fighting. He stationed his force about the building, and gave orders that once a Poole thug had been downed he was to be kept horizontal until his skull was cracked. He also let it be known that there would be no adverse criticism if Bill the Butcher's bullies were permanently maimed, and that ears and noses would be highly regarded as souvenirs of an interesting occasion. About noon a huge lumber van drawn by four horses and loaded with thirty of Poole's most courageous gangsters drove up to the polling place, and led by Bill the Butcher in person they jumped from the wagon and swarmed into the building. But they stopped short when they saw Morrissey and observed the preparations which had been made to welcome them. Poole and Morrissey met in the center of the main room and glared at each other for a moment, but Bill the Butcher realized that he had been outgeneraled, and that his thugs were outnumbered. So he turned and stalked out of the building, and, followed by his bruisers, climbed into the van and drove away. Morrissey had won a notable victory without striking a blow. However, his disappointed battlers flung a few brickbats as Poole's henchmen retreated, and three of the latter were knocked down.

When the news of Morrissey's exploit reached the ears of the Tammany leaders, they received him with open arms and gave him money with which he opened a small gambling house. With a prosperous business and money in his pocket, Morrissey now took his rightful place among the lesser powers of Tammany Hall, and became the associate and fighting companion of such notorious sluggers as Jim Turner, Lew Baker, and Yankee Sullivan, the last named a celebrated pugilist who was afterward lynched by the San Francisco Vigilantes. His real name was Ambrose. All of these men had essayed to stand up before Tom Hyer and Bill the Butcher, but had gone down before their thudding fists and stamping feet. Late in 1854 Hyer gave Yankee Sullivan an unmerciful drubbing in an oyster bar at Park Place and Broadway, and repeated the feat a few months later when they met in the professional prize ring. Naturally enough, Sullivan, Turner, and Baker saw eye to eye with Morrissey in his hatred of the Native American gladiators, and there were frequent clashes between the two groups.

Early in January, 1855, Turner and Baker went into Platt's Saloon in the basement of Wallack's Theater at Broadway and Twelfth street, where they found Hyer standing before the bar drinking a jigger of hot rum. As they passed Turner rubbed his elbow against Hyer's nose and knocked the glass from his lips, at the same time making a remark which implied that he doubted the legitimacy of Hyer's birth. Hyer remonstrated, whereupon both Turner and Baker threw off their Talmas[1] and drew pistols, which they brandished menacingly and dared Hyer to attack them. Hyer mildly suggested that he did not wish to have any trouble, and Turner, emboldened by the pugilist's attitude, fired twice, one of the balls grazing Hyer's neck. Hyer then drew his own pistol, but instead of firing at Turner discharged the weapon into the wall. When he turned he saw Turner attempting to cock his pistol for a third shot, whereupon he grabbed the Tammany gangster and hurled him to the floor with such force that the weapon was thrown from his hand. Meanwhile Baker had attacked Hyer from the rear, and was trying to brain the pugilist with the butt of his pistol, which he had been unable to cock. Hyer flung Baker on top of Turner, and when a policeman came into the room a moment later demanded that Baker be arrested. But the policeman declined to interfere in a private fight between gentlemen,

---

[1] A cape, or short full cloak, named after Talma, a French actor.

so Hyer seized Baker by the nape of the neck and dragged him up the short flight of stairs into the street, where he kicked and pummelled him unmercifully. Baker had managed to draw a knife while he lay upon the floor, and as he was carried out struggled fiercely, cutting Hyer's knuckles. But Hyer soon kicked the knife from his hand. With Baker lying senseless upon the sidewalk, Hyer went back into the saloon after Turner, but that hero had abandoned his pistol and escaped through the back door.

The encounter in Platt's caused tremendous excitement in gang and political circles, and both the Tammany and Native American bullies armed themselves and went about boasting loudly of their belligerent intentions. A few days later Bill the Butcher came upon Baker in a Canal street dive called the Gem, and gave the Tammany gangster a fearful beating, attempting, so Baker said later, to gouge out his eyes and bite off his ear. The police interfered before Baker had been completely ruined, and Poole left the saloon swearing volubly that he would yet "settle Baker's hash." Thereafter Baker went armed day and night, and seldom stirred abroad unless accompanied by Turner or by Paudeen McLaughlin, another noted Tammany battler whose disposition had been particularly murderous since his nose was chewed off during an affray at the Five Points; he was particularly adept at putting the boots to an adversary after felling him with a bludgeon or slung-shot, and was highly respected in the underworld. Encouraged by Turner and McLaughlin, Baker vowed boastfully that he would kill Poole on sight, while Poole retorted that if he ever got his hands on Baker the remains would scarcely be worth the attention of an undertaker.

Morrissey saw in the bitter enmity between Poole and Baker an opportunity to prove his frequent boast that he could defeat the Native American slugger in a rough and tumble combat with nothing barred. Physically, Poole and Morrissey were about equal, each being well over six feet tall and weighing more than two hundred pounds. Poole was probably the more ferocious, but Morrissey made up for this defect in his nature by greater science and speed. It was generally felt that a battle between the two would be worth travelling miles to see, and sportsmen made every effort to bring them together. However, they never fought. One night a few weeks after Baker had fared so badly at the hands of Poole, the latter and Morrissey came face to face in a Broadway bar-room, and Morrissey offered to bet fifty dollars that Bill the Butcher could not name a place where he would not meet him. Poole named the Christopher street pier, in the heart of the area controlled by his own gang, and Morrissey paid the bet without protest. Half an hour later he declared that Poole could not name another place, and Bill the Butcher suggested that they meet at the Amos street dock, one block north of Christopher street, at seven o'clock the next morning.

This time Morrissey accepted the challenge, against the advice of his friends, who warned him that he was venturing into dangerous territory. Accompanied by a dozen men, Morrissey drove to the dock in a carriage, and was promptly attacked by a mob of some two hundred of Poole's thugs. He fought vigorously, but they dragged him about the pier and gave him a sound beating before he was rescued by a crowd of Tammany gangsters who had been informed of the sorry plight of their hero. Poole did not appear on the scene at all, but a few days later, on the night of February 24, 1855, he and Morrissey met in Stanwix Hall, a newly opened bar-room in Broadway near Prince street across from the old Metropolitan Hotel, then a center of the city's night life. Morrissey and Mark Maguire, King of the Newsboys, were playing cards in a back room when Poole came in, but Morrissey walked into the bar-room when he heard the boastful voice of Bill the Butcher proclaiming his prowess. Approaching Poole, Morrissey spat in his face and then drew an ancient pistol, which he pointed at Poole's head and snapped three times. But the cartridge missed fire, and Morrissey begged some one in the crowd to lend him another weapon. No one complied, and Poole drew his own pistol. He was about to shoot when Maguire clutched his sleeve and said, reproachfully:

"You wouldn't kill a helpless man in cold blood, would you?"

Poole swore fiercely and flung his pistol to the floor. He then seized two huge carving knives from the free lunch counter, and hurled them onto the bar, inviting Maguire to take his choice and fight it out. But Maguire politely declined, as did Morrissey when Poole pressed the Tammany gladiator to take advantage of the offer. Poole, a professional butcher, knew all about knives, and it was common knowledge that he could throw a butcher knife through an inch of pine at twenty feet. During the altercation Baker came in, and when Morrissey saw his friend he pressed forward and would have attacked Poole with his fists and feet. But several policemen were close upon Baker's heels, and Morrissey and Poole were placed under arrest and led out of the building. Neither protested at the indignity, for apparently they had no stomach for the conflict. In the vernacular of the period, "one was afraid and the other dasn't." Once outside the bar-room, both Poole and Morrissey were released when they agreed to go home and remain there until the following morning.

Morrissey, who had been married only a few days, went at once to the house at No. 55 Hudson street, where he lived with his father-in-law, and was seen no more about the streets that evening. But half an hour after he had been discharged from the custody of the police, Poole returned to Stanwix Hall, accompanied by his brother-in-law, Charley Lozier, and a boon companion and adviser, Charley Shay. Ostensibly he came to apologize to the owner of the resort, but in reality he was looking for further trouble. Meanwhile Baker had conferred with Turner, Paudeen, and half a dozen other Tammany fighters, and they determined to do something about Bill Poole immediately. They went to the saloon about midnight, and found Poole standing at the bar with Lozier, Shay, and other friends and supporters. Paudeen, the last of the group to enter, locked the door.

Turner called for drinks, and Paudeen, moving along the bar, jostled Poole's elbow, and when Bill the Butcher glared at him Paudeen snarled:

"What are you looking at, you black-muzzled bastard?"

Clutching Poole's coat lapels, Paudeen spat three times in his face and dared him to fight. Poole calmly drew five golden eagles from his pockets and slapped them on the bar, offering to fight any man of the Tammany group who would cover his money, but remarking that Paudeen was not worth fighting. For a moment no one moved, and then Turner cried in great excitement:

"Sail in!"

He quickly flung aside his Talma, displaying a huge Colt's revolver, with a long barrel, strapped about his waist. He drew the weapon, levelled it in the hollow of his elbow and pulled the trigger. But his aim was poor and he shot himself in the arm, whereupon he screeched and fell to the floor. There he fired again, striking Poole in the leg. Bill the Butcher staggered forward under the impact of the bullet, clutching at Baker with outstretched arms. But the latter dodged, and as Poole fell heavily to the floor Baker drew a pistol and placed it against his chest.

"I guess I'll take you, anyhow," said Baker.

He fired twice, but Bill the Butcher, although one of the bullets had penetrated his heart and the other had ripped into his abdomen, slowly scrambled to his feet. For a moment he stood

The Murder of Bill the Butcher

swaying before the bar, and then he seized a huge carving knife and staggered toward Baker, screaming that he would cut his assailant's heart out. But he had gone but a few feet when he collapsed into Shay's arms, and Baker, Turner, and the others escaped through the front door, which Paudeen had unlocked. As Poole fell he flung the knife, and the blade quivered in the door jamb as Baker fled. Everyone who had been in the Hall, except

Baker, surrendered to the police within two hours, but Baker crossed the Hudson river to Jersey City, where he remained in hiding until March 10, when he boarded the brig Isabella Jewett, bound for the Canary Islands. George Law, a wealthy leader of the Native American party, put his clipper yacht Grapeshot at the disposal of the authorities, and the swift vessel was dispatched in pursuit of the brig. The Isabella Jewett was overhauled two hours out of Teneriffe, and New York policemen took Baker off and brought him in irons back to New York. He was promptly indicted, together with Turner, Morrissey, Paudeen and several others, and was thrice brought to trial. But each time the jury disagreed, and finally the authorities abandoned the prosecution and Baker was released.

Despite his wounds, Poole lived for fourteen days after the shooting, to the vast amazement of his doctors, who declared vehemently that it was unnatural for a man to linger so long with a bullet in his heart. But at last, while Tom Hyer and other Native American gladiators watched anxiously by his bedside and relayed bulletins to a sorrowful crowd in the street, Bill the Butcher died, gasping with his last breath:

"Good-bye, boys: I die a true American!"

The Native Americans gave Poole one of the most remarkable funerals ever seen in New York. More than five thousand men rode in carriages or trudged afoot behind the hearse, and half a dozen brass bands played dirges as the solemn procession passed slowly down Broadway to Whitehall street, where boats awaited to carry the cortege to Greenwood Cemetery in Brooklyn. From Bleecker street southward to the Battery, Broadway was packed solidly with thousands of silent spectators. For weeks little was discussed throughout the city but the murder of Butcher Bill and the magnificence of his funeral, and the last words of the famous gangster were widely quoted. New plays were hurriedly written for the cheaper theaters which specialized in melodrama, and the endings of current productions were changed, so that as the final curtain fell the hero could drape himself in an American flag and gasp hoarsely, "Good-bye, boys; I die a true American!" while the audience expressed its emotion in thunderous applause.

3

JOHN Morrissey retired from the professional prize ring in 1857, after he had defeated Heenan, and thereafter devoted his attention to politics and to the development of his gambling enterprises. The house which he had opened with his first earnings as a gangster was very prosperous, and by 1860 had given way to one of the most magnificent establishments in the city. It was on Broadway near Tenth street, not far north of the present Grace Protestant Episcopal Church and Wanamaker's store. "His table, attendants, cooking and company," wrote a contemporary author, "are exceeded by nothing on this side of the Atlantic." In 1867 Morrissey established a luxurious gambling house and restaurant at Saratoga Springs, which after his death came eventually into the hands of Richard Canfield, perhaps the most celebrated gambling-house owner America has ever produced. It was John Morrissey's boast that he had "never struck a foul blow or turned a card," but he does not appear to have been so particular in his political activities, for in William M. Tweed's confession, in 1877, Morrissey is mentioned as having introduced a system of repeating from Philadelphia, and as having been the paymaster of a fund of $65,000 which was distributed among the Aldermen to secure the confirmation of a Tweed henchman as City Chamberlain. Morrissey became co-leader of Tammany Hall with Honest John Kelly in the early seventies, but dropped out of sight within a few years. His active connection with the gangs ceased soon after his fight with Tom Heenan.

CHAPTER VI

THE POLICE AND DEAD RABBIT RIOTS

1

IN COMMON with the remainder of the country, New York City seethed with the clamors and excitements of the impending conflict during the ten years which preceded the Civil War. There were frequent clashes, both verbal and physical, between the Abolitionist and pro-Slavery elements of the population, while from his pulpit in Plymouth Church, Brooklyn, the Rev. Henry Ward Beecher added fuel to the flame of unrest by his thundering excoriations of the Southern owners of human flesh and souls. Many of the most prominent ministers followed Beecher's example and added their voices to the rising tide of protest, but others professed to see a more imminent source of damnation in the current theater, and trained their heaviest guns upon the celebrated dancer Sontag, who had set the town by the ears with her short skirts and the abandoned fling of her gifted feet—she is said to have been the first woman in America who, in public at least, kicked higher than her head. Enthusiastic crowds packed the playhouse wherein she appeared and followed her about the streets, while the young bloods toasted her in the taverns and serenaded her beneath the windows of her lodgings.

Pleasure seekers who were not enchanted by the ravishing Sontag flocked in great throngs to Niblo's Garden, where Adelina Patti, not yet in her teens, astounded the critics with the beauty of her voice; or to the National Theater, where a remarkable new play, called *Uncle Tom's Cabin,* opened in the early fifties and began its record-breaking run of two hundred consecutive nights. But there was scant appreciation of the elder Southern, who trod the creaking boards of Barnum's Museum and struggled painfully to develop the art which in later years was to bring him fame as *Lord Dundreary* and establish him as one of the foremost actors of the American stage. Nor did the unobtrusive arrival of Dr. James Littlefield early in 1854 bring out the brass bands and cause dancing in the streets, although he immeasurably enhanced the dignity of a barbershop at No. 413 Broadway, and was the forerunner of a profession which now counts its clients by the millions. He was the first chiropodist to practise in New York.

It was during this period, and perhaps a little earlier, that the Tammany politicians began the systematic looting of the city treasury which continued almost unchecked until the collapse of the Tweed Ring in 1870. So rapacious were the members of the Common Council of 1850 that they were aptly called the Forty Thieves, thus dragging in the muck and mire of politics the honorable name of the earliest of the great gangs of the Five Points. The Council of 1856 was similarly described, and the gangsters, obviously ashamed of the depths to which their appellation had fallen, dissolved their organization and enlisted in the ranks of the Dead Rabbits. Disclosures made by reform elements during the early fifties showed that every department of the city government was corrupt. Officials who were presumably poor men laboring in the public cause for meager salaries suddenly retired with vast fortunes in real estate, secured to them in the names of their wives, and their pockets bulging with gold, all amassed by the sale of permits, grants, franchises and leases, collections from crime centers and houses of prostitution, and the judicious awarding of contracts. In his *History of Tammany Hall,* documented by official records of the Board of Aldermen and various investigations, Gustavus Myers cites such choice morsels of graft as the deeding of 368 conveyances in one year to the Superintendent of Police, George W. Matsell, and his partner, Captain Norris; and the payment of tribute by more than a hundred men who regularly patronized the establishment operated in Greenwich street by Madame Restall, also known as Madame Killer, the notorious abortionist who committed suicide in her bathtub when Anthony Comstock raided her place. Madame Restall's house and occupation became so well known that during the last years of her life, whenever she ventured abroad in her carriage, street boys followed her and shouted "Yah! Your house is built on babies' skulls!"

The power of appointing members of the police force remained in the hands of the Aldermen and the Assistant Aldermen from 1844, when the Municipal Police force was organized, until 1853, when the Legislature intervened, and in an effort to check the rising tide of corruption formed a Board of Police Commissioners consisting of the Mayor, the Recorder and the City Judge. But the practical result was the same, whoever made the appointments; the graft was merely transferred from one group of politicians to another. It was customary for a patrolman to pay $40 to the captain in whose precinct he desired to enroll, and two or three times that amount to the statesman who appointed him. Police captains paid a minimum of $200 to their political masters, and policemen of all ranks were regularly employed as collectors of graft, and as go-betweens in arranging the questionable deals of the politicians. The entire force was bewildered and demoralized, and the few honest officials of the department could do little toward enforcing the laws and ridding the city of its swarming criminal population, for the arrest of a notorious thug was quickly followed by the appearance of an indignant ward-heeler who demanded and procured his release.

Except for the successful thrusts against the power of the river gangsters of the Fourth Ward, who were so far beyond the pale that not even the politicians dared protect them, the only important police campaign of the period was carried out against the Honeymoon gang, which in 1853 began to operate with great success in the Eighteenth Ward along the middle East Side, then a sparsely settled district inhabited principally by squatters. The police did not molest the thugs for several months, and they became extraordinarily bold. Every evening the chieftain of the Honeymooners stationed a gangster at each corner of Madison avenue and Twenty-ninth street, and these worthies maintained their positions until midnight, knocking down and robbing every well-dressed man who appeared. When George W. Walling was appointed captain of police late in 1853 and assigned to the command of the district, he found the entire area terrorized by the Honeymoon gang. To suppress them he organized the first Strong Arm Squad and inaugurated a method of attack which was used very effectively in later years. Walling had always been impressed by the fact that the gangster would seldom stand up before a policeman armed with a heavy locust club, and that there was nothing a thug feared so much as a sound thumping. So he chose half a dozen of his bravest and huskiest patrolmen, and sent them forth in the guise of citizens. They simply walked up to the gangsters and knocked them senseless before the thugs could get into action with their slung-shots, bludgeons, and brass knuckles. After a few nights of this sort of warfare the gang leader withdrew his men from their accustomed posts, but Captain Walling gave them no rest. Every patrolman in the precinct was provided with the names of the Honeymooners, and whenever one was sighted he was attacked and beaten. Within two weeks the Honeymoon gang had been dispersed, and its members had fled southward into the Five Points and the Bowery, where the police were not so rough. Captain Walling also employed the strong arm method to stop the nightly brawls between the inhabitants of two rows of tenements, known as the English and the Irish, on opposite sides of Twenty-second street between Second and Third avenues. Before his advent the denizens of these slums swarmed into the street for as many as a dozen fights an evening, and when the police entered the block at all it was in parties of three or more. But Walling massed his entire force around a corner, and when the fighting began the policemen rushed in and clubbed English and Irish indiscriminately. The brawling soon ceased and the block became comparatively safe and peaceful.

2

THE number of thugs who followed the great gang captains of the Five Points, the Bowery, and the Fourth Ward was enormously increased during the decade preceding the Civil War by the throngs of bruisers and bullies who swarmed into New York from other cities. By 1855 it was estimated that the metropolis contained at least thirty thousand men who owed allegiance to the gang leaders, and through them to the political leaders of Tammany Hall and the Know Nothing or Native American Party, who kept the political pot boiling furiously by their frantic and constant struggles for the privilege of plundering the public funds.

At every election gangs employed by the rival factions rioted at the polling places, smashing ballot boxes, slugging honest citizens who attempted to exercise the right of franchise, themselves voting early and often, and incidentally acquiring a contempt for the police and for constituted authority which was to have appalling consequences during the Draft Riots. The climax of the purely political rioting was reached in 1856, when Fernando Wood was elected to a second term as Mayor. Wood was bitterly opposed, not only by the Native Americans, who accused him of favoring the Irish and other foreign elements, but by the reformers as well, for he had shown himself a reckless and unprincipled official, and had thrown the city treasury wide open to the looting fingers of his henchmen. But he had the staunch support of all the lower strata of society, especially the saloon and gambling-house keepers, whose loyalty he had assured by preventing the enforcement of a Sunday closing law passed in 1855. He compelled every man on the police force to contribute to his campaign fund, one patrolman who at first refused to do so being kept on duty twenty-four hours without relief.

The Dead Rabbits, the largest and most powerful of the gangs, were enrolled under the Wood banner, as were most of the other bruisers of the Five Points and many of the most celebrated sluggers of the water front. The Bowery Boys and other gangs of the Bowery district were adherents of the Native Americans. The night before the election Mayor Wood issued an executive order sending a majority of the policemen off on furlough, with strict orders not to go near the polling places except to cast their votes. When the gangs began rioting they were confronted by small and ineffective detachments of patrolmen who were soon overwhelmed by sheer force of numbers and driven from the field. In the Sixth Ward, of which the Five Points was the heart, a crowd of Bowery gangsters made a surprise attack on the polling place and scattered the Dead Rabbit patrols, but the latter were quickly reinforced by thugs who swarmed from the dives and tenements of Paradise Square, and returned to the fray, armed with clubs, knives, axes, brickbats, and pistols. They soon defeated the Native American bullies, while half a dozen policemen added to the excitement by barricading themselves in a vacant house and firing an occasional shot through the windows. Throughout the day there were similar clashes in other wards, but Wood's gangsters proved the more efficient repeaters and the more ferocious battlers, and Tammany Hall carried the day, re-electing Wood with 34,860 votes to 25,209 for Isaac O. Barker, the Native American candidate. The count showed an enormous increase in the number of ballots cast over the previous election, and Wood's enemies charged that at least 10,000 of them were fraudulent. But there was no investigation.

In 1857, two years after Bill Poole had gone to his reward, New York passed through one of the most turbulent and disastrous twelve months in her history, beginning with appalling governmental corruption and ending with financial calamity, for this was the year of the great panic, and before the end of December more than a score of banks and almost a thousand business houses had failed with liabilities exceeding $120,000,000. During Fernando

Wood's second administration as Mayor the police force had become so corrupt, and its organization so chaotic and inefficient, that the Legislature again intervened and relieved the city government of all control over the department. During the spring session several bills affecting the city charter were passed, the most important of which abolished the Municipal Police and the Police Board formed by the Act of 1853, and substituted a Metropolitan Police District comprising Manhattan, Brooklyn, and the small towns on Staten Island and on the mainland north of the Harlem River, all embraced within the counties of New York, Kings, Richmond and Westchester. The Governor was empowered to appoint five Commissioners, who were in turn to name a Superintendent of Police. The first Board was composed of Simeon Draper, James Bowen, James W. Nye, Jacob Cholwell and James S. T. Stranahan, all of whom had been more or less active in the various fights waged by the reformers against the political despoilers of the city. Frederick A. Talmage, who had been Recorder during the Astor Place riots in 1849, became the first Superintendent of Police, accepting the post after several others had declined.

The new Police Board called upon Fernando Wood to disband the Municipal force and turn over all police property, but the Mayor refused, and would not submit even when the Supreme Court handed down a decision in May, 1857, affirming the constitutionality of the new law. He called upon the police force to stand by him, and when the question was put to a vote fifteen captains and eight hundred patrolmen, as well as Superintendent George W. Matsell, refused to acknowledge the authority of the Metropolitan Board, and decided to continue as members of the Municipal Police. The remaining officers and men, among them Captain George W. Walling, took the oath of allegiance to the new organization, which opened headquarters in White street and set about filling the places of the patrolmen who had remained loyal to the Mayor. Wood in turn appointed men to succeed those who had gone over to the Metropolitans. The trouble reached a crisis on June 16, when Daniel D. Conover went to City Hall to assume the office of Street Commissioner, to which he had been appointed by

Governor King. The Mayor also claimed the power of appointment, and had named Charles Devlin, to whom it was charged he had sold the office for $50,000.

When Conover appeared he was forcibly ejected from the building by the Municipal Police, and immediately obtained two warrants for the Mayor's arrest, one charging him with inciting to riot and the other accusing him of violence against Conover's person. One of the warrants was given to Captain Walling, who went alone to City Hall and was admitted to Mayor Wood's private office, where the Mayor sat behind the desk clutching his ornate staff of office. Walling explained his errand, and when the Mayor vociferously refused to be placed under arrest the Captain calmly seized him by the arm and remarked that he would take him forcibly from the building, as he would any other person subject to a warrant. But more than three hundred Municipal Police had been stationed in City Hall in anticipation of trouble, and the Mayor was rescued before Captain Walling had dragged him beyond the door of the private office. Walling was then thrown into the street. He made several attempts to re-enter, but was prevented, and was still arguing with Captain Ackerman of the Municipals when a detachment of fifty

Police Riot at City Hall

Metropolitan policemen, under command of Coroner Perry and Captain Jacob Sebring, marched through Chambers street into City Hall Park to serve the second warrant obtained by Conover.

The Metropolitans presented an imposing appearance in their frock coats and plug hats, and with their new badges glistening in the sunshine, but they were no match for the throng of Municipals who swarmed from the building and attacked them. For more than a half hour the combat raged fiercely on the steps and in the corridors of City Hall, but at length the Metropolitans were pushed from the building and fled the scene in disorder. During the battle fifty-two policemen were injured, and one, Patrolman Crofut of the Seventeenth precinct, was so terribly beaten that he was ever afterward an invalid. They were carried into the offices of Recorder James M. Smith and their wounds treated by physicians, while the Mayor and his supporters gathered in the private offices, which had been barricaded, and jubilantly congratulated each other that the sacred person of the chief executive had been saved.

While the fighting was in progress Conover called upon Sheriff Westervelt to serve the warrants, and the Sheriff was advised by his lawyers that it was clearly his duty to do so. Accompanied by Conover and his attorney and bearing his staff of office, with his sword strapped to his waist and the official plug hat on his head, the Sheriff marched with great dignity up the steps of the City Hall and into the Mayor's offices, where Wood again angrily refused to submit to arrest. Meanwhile the Seventh Regiment of the National Guard, with flags flying and drums beating, was marching down Broadway to take a boat for Boston, where the troops were to be entertained by one of the Massachusetts regiments. A hundred yards from City Hall the members of the Metropolitan Police Board met the soldiers and informed the commander, Major-General Charles Sandford, that they had come to exercise the power granted to them by the Legislature of calling upon the National Guard whenever the peace and dignity of the city were threatened. They were unanimously of the opinion that such a time had arrived.

The Seventh Regiment was thereupon marched into the Park and City Hall surrounded, after which General Sandford and his staff held a conference with Sheriff Westervelt and the Police Commissioners. Then, with his sword clanking at his heels and a platoon of infantry with fixed bayonets surrounding him, the General strode fiercely into the building, where he informed Mayor Wood that he represented the military power of the Empire State and would tolerate no further resistance. Wood glanced out of the window, and seeing the Park filled with soldiers, accepted the warrants and submitted to arrest. Within an hour he was released on nominal bail, and so far as the records show was never brought to trial, the Civil Courts holding that the Governor had no right to appoint a Street Commissioner and that Devlin was entitled to the office. Several months later the policemen who had been injured in the clash between the Metropolitans and the Municipals brought suit against Wood and received judgment of $250 each. But the Mayor never settled, and the city finally paid the claims, together with the costs of the actions.

In the early autumn the Court of Appeals affirmed the decision of the Supreme Court and upheld the constitutionality of the new law, and within a few weeks the Mayor had disbanded the Municipals. But during the summer both police forces patrolled the city, and paid more attention to their private feud than to protecting the lives and property of the citizens. Whenever a Metropolitan arrested a criminal, a Municipal came along and released him, and the thug went about his business while the policemen fought. Aldermen and magistrates who supported the Mayor spent their days in the Metropolitan police stations, and whenever a prisoner was brought in they immediately released him on his own recognizance, while officials who favored the Metropolitan Board did the same at the Municipal stations. In consequence of this situation the gangsters and other criminals ran wild throughout the city, revelling in an orgy of loot, murder and disorder. Respectable citizens were held up and robbed in broad daylight on Broadway and other principal streets, while Municipal and Metropolitan policemen belabored each other with clubs, trying to decide which had the right to interfere. Gangs of thieves and rowdies invaded and plundered stores and other business houses, and stopped the stage coaches and compelled passengers to surrender their money and jewelry, while private residences had no protection save stout locks and the valour of the householders.

The gangs of the Five Points and the Bowery, by far the most turbulent of the city's inhabitants, took advantage of the opportunity to vent their ancient grudges against each other, and engaged in almost constant rioting. Scarcely a week passed without half a dozen conflicts, and once more, as during the great riot period of 1834, the National Guard regiments stood to arms and quelled the lawless elements with bayonet and saber. The most sanguinary of these battles occurred on July 4 and 5, 1857, when the dispute between the Mayor and the Metropolitan Board was at its height and the police organization was in a condition of utter chaos. Led by the Dead Rabbits and the Plug Uglies, all of the gangs of the Five Points with the exception of the Roach Guards began their celebration of the Fourth with a raid on the building at No. 42 Bowery, occupied by the Bowery Boys and the Atlantic Guards as a club-house. There was furious fighting, but the Bowery gangsters triumphed and drove their enemies back to their dens around Paradise Square. On this day the rioting spread as far as Pearl and Chatham streets, now the northern half of Park Row, and a few Metropolitan policemen who tried to interfere were badly beaten. The Municipals said it was not their fight, and would have no hand in any attempt to suppress the trouble.

Early the next morning the Five Points gangs, reinforced by the Roach Guards, marched out of Paradise Square and attacked a resort called the Green Dragon, in Broome street near the Bowery, a favorite loafing place of the Boys and other Bowery gangs. Carrying iron bars and huge paving blocks, the Five Pointers swarmed into the establishment before the Bowery thugs could rally to its defense, and after wrecking the bar-room and ripping up the floor of the dance hall, proceeded to drink all of the liquor in the place. News of the outrage reached the Bowery Boys, and they boiled furiously out of their holes, supported by the Atlantic Guards and the other gangsters who owed allegiance to them or loyalty to the Bowery. The gangs came together at Bayard street and immediately began the most ferocious free-for-all in the history of the city.

A lone policeman, with more courage than judgment, tried to club his way through the mass of struggling men and arrest the ringleaders, but he was knocked down and his clothing stripped from his body, and he was fearfully beaten with his own nightstick. He crawled through the plunging mob to the sidewalk, and, naked except for a pair of cotton drawers, ran to the Metropolitan headquarters in White street, where he gasped out the alarm and collapsed. A squad of policemen was dispatched to stop the rioting, but when they marched bravely up Center street the gangs made common cause against them, and they were compelled to retreat after a bloody encounter in which several men were injured. However, they rallied and finally fought their way into the center of the mob, where they arrested two men who seemed to be leaders. But again they were compelled to fall back, for the gangsters forced their way into the low houses which lined the Bowery and Bayard street, and after driving out the inhabitants, swarmed to the roofs and windows, whence they pelted the Metropolitans with stones and brickbats.

When the police had marched away without their prisoners, there was a breathing spell of a few moments, but the excitement grew more intense, and the Dead Rabbits attacked with great fury after a mob of wild-eyed, screaming Five Points hussies had rushed into their midst and taunted them with cowardice. Reinforcements from the dives of Paradise Square followed close on the heels of the women, and other thugs had arrived to swell the ranks of the heroes of the Bowery. It was estimated that from eight hundred to one thousand fighters were actively engaged, all armed with bludgeons, paving stones, brickbats, axes, pitchforks, pistols and knives. And from all parts of the city had hurried several hundred thieves and thugs who were members of none of the gangs. Attracted by the prospect of loot, and knowing that if the police were there at all they would be very busy with the rioters, these men attacked the residences and stores along the Bowery, and along Bayard, Baxter, Mulberry and Elizabeth streets, so that the owners had to barricade their buildings and protect their property with muskets and pistols. "Brick-bats, stones and clubs were flying thickly around," said the *New York Times* of July 6, 1857, "and from the windows in all directions, and men ran wildly about brandishing firearms. Wounded men lay on the sidewalks and were trampled upon. Now the Rabbits would make a combined rush and force their antagonists up Bayard street to the Bowery. Then the fugitives, being reinforced, would turn on their pursuers and compel a retreat to Mulberry, Elizabeth and Baxter streets."

Early in the afternoon Police Commissioner Simeon Draper dispatched another and larger force of policemen against the mob, and they marched in close formation to the scene of the riot, although assailed at every step. They cleared the street as they advanced, and forced scores of the Dead Rabbits and Bowery Boys into the houses and up the stairs to the roofs, clubbing them at every jump. One desperate gangster who refused to surrender was knocked off the roof of a house in Baxter street, and his skull was fractured when he hit the sidewalk. His enemies promptly stamped him to death. On another roof the police captured two of the leaders of the Dead Rabbits, and although the Five Points gangsters attacked with great fury managed to march their prisoners to the police station, escorted by a detachment of cheering Bowery Boys.

But no sooner had the police departed than the gangsters renewed their battle, and the rioting went forward with greater ferocity than ever. Barricades of carts and stones were piled up in the streets, and from behind these defenses the gangsters shot and hurled bricks and used their clubs. One giant member of the Dead Rabbits walked coolly along in front of his barricade and, although fired at repeatedly, used his pistol with such deadly accuracy that he killed two Bowery thugs and wounded two others. He was finally knocked unconscious by a small boy whose brother was fighting in the ranks of the Bowery Boys. This lad crept on his stomach along the barricade, and when he was close enough slammed a huge brickbat, about as heavy as he could lift, against the skull of the Dead Rabbit.

The police continued their efforts to disperse the battling gangs, but failed, and were compelled to retreat several times with heavy losses. Early in the evening the police authorities, in despair, sent for Captain Isaiah Rynders, political boss of the Sixth

Ward and as such king of the Five Points gangsters, and implored him to stop the slaughter. But the rioters were in such a rage that they refused to obey his commands, and as he stood before their barricades haranguing them the Bowery Boys attacked and Captain Rynders was badly beaten before he could find refuge in the midst of his own henchmen. Realizing the futility of further appeal, he made his way to Metropolitan Police Headquarters and advised Commissioner Draper to call out the troops. Meanwhile the gangsters had set fire to two or three houses, and the fighting continued, while the independent thugs made life miserable for the householders who insisted on remaining in their homes within the battle area.

Commissioner Draper asked Major-General Sandford to order three regiments into action, but it was nine o'clock before the blare of bugles and the rattle of drums was heard and the soldiers, their bayonets glistening in the moonlight and the glare of the burning buildings, marched down White and Worth streets, supported by two police detachments of seventy-five men each, who ranged ahead of the troops and clubbed every gangster they could catch. Two regiments instead of three, the Eighth and the Seventy-first, had answered the call, and neither was up to full strength, but the display of force was sufficient to overawe the thugs, who abandoned the battlefield and slunk back to their dens. There was no more rioting, for the police and soldiers patrolled the district throughout the night and all the next day. During the two days' fighting eight men were killed and more than a hundred injured, of whom fifty were compelled to remain in hospitals for treatment. It is believed that many more dead and injured were carried away by their comrades, for several days after the fighting had ended it was reported that half a dozen new graves had been dug in the cellars and underground passageways of the Five Points and Paradise Square, and some of the most noted sluggers of both the Dead Rabbits and the Bowery Boys were no longer to be seen in their accustomed haunts.

On July 6 a wandering band of Bowery Boys engaged in a desperate fight with the Kerryonians in Center street, but were driven back to the Bowery and Chatham Square before the police could interfere. A few days later the excitement spread to the German settlements along the East Side, near the East River, and strong detachments of police were sent to Avenues A and B to quell outbreaks among the ambitious young hoodlums of that area, who desired to emulate the deeds of their Irish fellow citizens. For more than a week there was sporadic fighting whenever patrols of the Five Points gangsters came upon thugs from the Bowery, but the former bitterly resented the insinuations of the police and the newspapers that they were criminals. "We are requested by the Dead Rabbits," said *The Times*, "to state that the Dead Rabbit club members are not thieves, that they did not participate in the riot with the Bowery Boys, and that the fight in Mulberry street was between the Roach Guards of Mulberry street and the Atlantic Guards of the Bowery. The Dead Rabbits are sensitive on points of honor, we are assured, and wouldn't allow a thief to live on their beat, much less to be a member of their club."

3

THE situation was considerably improved when Mayor Wood finally dissolved the Municipal Police, but the Metropolitan Board experienced great difficulty in recruiting the new force to full strength. By autumn, when the financial panic began in earnest, no more than eight hundred patrolmen were available for duty throughout the district, approximately one to each eight hundred and four inhabitants. Although the actual criminal element had by this time been brought fairly well under control, and even the gangs had wearied of continual brawling, there were still frequent outbreaks of rioting and looting, which increased in numbers and seriousness as banks, factories and other business houses closed their doors and filled the city with idle men. And in November, as winter came on, mobs of hungry and unemployed, frightened at the prospect of starvation, surged violently through the streets crying for bread and work. Several threats were made against the State Arsenal, wherein huge quantities of muskets and ammunition were stored, and the building was guarded by a police detail, while troops of the United States Army were on duty day and night at the Customs House at the Battery and the Assay Office in Wall street. It was not until the financial skies had cleared and business had returned to normal that the Metropolitan Police Board was able to proceed with the reorganization of the department.

THE DRAFT
RIOTS

1

THE FIGHTING which raged through the streets of New York City from Monday to Saturday during a hot week in July, 1863, began as a protest against the Conscription Act which had been passed by Congress in March, but that phase of the struggle was soon forgotten, and thereafter the riots were an insurrection of the criminal element against the established order. The disturbances were the natural end of the ruinous road along which the city had travelled during the preceding fifteen years, and the logical result of the governmental corruption which had permitted Manhattan Island to become the Mecca of criminals from all parts of the United States and the slums of Europe. "This mob is not the people," wrote Henry J. Raymond in *The New York Times*, "nor

Civil War Draft Riot
Sacking a Drug Store in Second Avenue. ca. 1863

does it belong to the people. It is for the most part made up of the vilest elements of the city. It has not even the poor merit of being what mobs usually are—the product of mere ignorance and passion. They talk, or rather they did talk at first, of the oppressiveness of the Conscription Law; but three-fourths of those who have been actively engaged in violence have been boys and young men under twenty years of age, and not at all subject to the Conscription. Were the Conscription Law to be abrogated tomorrow, the controlling inspiration of the mob would remain the same. It comes from sources quite independent of that law, or any other law—from a malignant hate toward those in better circumstances, from a craving for plunder, from a barbarous spite

against a different race, from a disposition to bolster up the failing
fortunes of the Southern rebels. . . . The mob must be crushed at
once. . . . Give them grape and plenty of it." The *New York
Herald* at first described the rioters as "the people," and *The
World* as "the laboring men of the city," but these papers soon
adopted the viewpoint of *The Times*. From the beginning of the
riots Horace Greeley's *Tribune* advocated the employment of the
greatest possible force in suppressing the mobs.

The census of 1860, the last official count before the riots, fixed
the population of New York City, which then comprised only
Manhattan Island, at 813,669, of which a little more than half
were foreign-born. Among the aliens the Irish were overwhelmingly in the majority with a total of 203,740, while the next high-
est were the Germans, with 119,984. The Irish had settled principally in the Five Points and Mulberry Bend districts, which contained 310 persons to the acre, while the Germans were massed
along the middle East Side. The Germans caused little or no trouble during the riots; on the contrary, they organized patrols which
rendered effective aid to the police and military units. Other races
clustered in similarly national colonies, keeping to themselves,
maintaining their own languages and customs, and making no pretense at amalgamation except to become naturalized citizens at the
behest of shady politicians who voted them like sheep.

During the year ending July 1, 1860, the total number of persons actually convicted of crime in New York was 58,067. Of
these about eighty per cent. had been born in Europe. In 1862,
the year before the riots, the police arrested 82,072 men and
women, approximately one-tenth of the population, and the number of criminals in the metropolis during that year was estimated
at from 70,000 to 80,000, an increase of about 20,000 within ten
years. These figures do not take into account the keepers of the
myriad low dives and resorts, nor the political protectors of
thieves and murderers, who were themselves criminals however
much they may have been within the law. The number of rioters
actively engaged in looting, murdering and burning during the
week was variously estimated at from 50,000 to 70,000 while some
of the individual mobs which swarmed through the streets con-

tained as many as 10,000 frenzied men and women. For the most part they were the human sweepings of European cities who had been packed into ships during the forties and fifties and dumped in ever-increasing numbers upon American shores. A vast majority landed in New York and remained there, and soon found their natural levels in the great gangs of the Bowery, the Five Points and the other areas into which the gangsters had spread and become firmly entrenched. It was these gangs, swarming from their holes at the first indication of trouble, that formed the organized nuclei around which the rioters rallied.

2

THE Confederate armies under General Robert E. Lee began their northward movement early in June, and the Federal government at Washington called upon the states of New York, Pennsylvania, West Virginia and Maryland for 120,000 soldiers for emergency service until the Conscription Law could be put into operation. Seventeen New York city and Brooklyn regiments were rushed to the seat of war in Pennsylvania, and the most important city on the American continent was denuded of troops, except for some two hundred men of the Invalid Corps, a thousand members of various National Guard and Volunteer units and of companies in process of organization, and approximately seven hundred sailors, marines, and soldiers of the Twelfth and Third infantry regiments, comprising the crews of the warships anchored in the Hudson and the garrisons of the Navy Yard, Fort Hamilton, Governor's Island and other posts. These units had a few pieces of artillery, including both howitzers and field guns. But none was available during the first two days of the fighting except the regular army detachments and the Invalid Corps, composed of crippled and wounded soldiers who had been doing guard duty at arsenals, armories and munitions factories. During this period the brunt of the fighting was borne by the Metropolitan Police force, numbering 2,297 men of all ranks, of whom only 1,620 were patrolmen. In some of the fights the policemen were outnumbered at least five hundred to one, but not more than half a dozen times did they fall back before the mobs. By Tuesday night a thousand citizens, armed with nightstick and pistol, had been sworn in as Volunteer Specials, and Wednesday morning regiments of infantry and cavalry began to arrive from the battlefields of Pennsylvania. Soon between seven thousand and ten thousand troops were marching against the rioters, among them the 152nd, Fifty-second, Eleventh, Fifty-fourth and Eighty-third infantry regiments of Volunteers; the Thirteenth Cavalry, of Rochester; the Twenty-sixth infantry of the Michigan state Volunteers; the Sixty-fifth infantry of the National Guard of New York from Buffalo, and the Seventh, Old Guard, Eighteenth, Seventy-fourth and Sixty-ninth National Guard regiments, which had been recruited principally in New York and Brooklyn. A dozen batteries of artillery had also gone into action, and were pouring grape and canister into the frenzied mobs which surged through Manhattan.

A vast majority of the rioters were Irish, simply because the gangsters and the other criminal elements of the city were largely of that race. In some quarters it was declared that the riots were a Roman Catholic insurrection, the statement being based on various circumstances, one of which was the burning and looting of the Methodist Episcopal Mission at the Five Points by a mob which shouted the glories of the Pope and carried banners inscribed "Down With the Protestants!" There was, of course, no truth in the charge, for the riots, while criminal, were in no sense religious. Yet much significance was seen in the fact that no Roman Catholic property was destroyed or even threatened; that on several occasions lone Catholic priests turned back mobs plainly bent on murder and loot; and that Archbishop Hughes, although repeatedly requested by Mayor George L. Opdyke and Governor Horatio L. Seymour, refused to counsel the rioters to disband until the morning of Friday, the last day of the fighting. He then issued a proclamation, but prefaced it with such a bitter and undignified attack upon Horace Greeley of the *Tribune* that it defeated its own purpose. Later the same day the Archbishop appeared on the balcony of his residence and addressed a large crowd which had gathered in response to a pastoral letter entitled "Archbishop Hughes to the Men of New York, who are called in many of the papers rioters."

3

IN April President Lincoln issued a proclamation calling for 300,000 men, and within a month the War Department announced that the draft would begin in New York City on Saturday, July 11. The city authorities were not requested to coöperate, nor was the police force asked to provide a guard for the Provost Marshals' offices which were opened at various points in the city. The Invalid Corps, under command of Colonel Ruggles, was directed to detach men from duty at the armories and arsenals and furnish whatever protection might be required. Throughout New York, as well as in many other parts of the country, there was bitter opposition to the Conscription Act, based principally on the clause which exempted any drafted man who paid the government three hundred dollars. This operated in favor of the rich man, and made it certain that the poor would form the bulk of the conscripted army. Some of the newspapers published inflammatory articles as the time for the draft drew near, and a political organization called the Knights of the Golden Circle was very active in opposition to the law. This society was believed to have formed the nucleus of the first mob which gathered, but there is little historical support for the belief; at any rate it was quickly swept away and forgotten as the gangsters and other criminals poured out of the Five Points and other slum districts and began looting and burning. Workmen, especially the unskilled laborers, were violently opposed to the draft, for few if any of them possessed three hundred dollars, and it was obvious that if their names were drawn they would have to go to war. Several of the Provost Marshals were threatened when they went about collecting names, and only a few days before the drawing began Captain Joel B. Erhardt, Provost Marshal of the Ninth District, was attacked by several men armed with iron bars when he visited a new building at Broadway and Liberty street. He sent for aid, and for three hours confronted them with drawn pistol, but was finally compelled to retreat without the names.

Early on the morning of July 11 the police received a report that the Knights of the Golden Circle and others opposed to the new law planned to seize the Arsenal at Seventh avenue and Thirty-fifth street, and Superintendent John A. Kennedy sent Sergeant Van Orden and fifteen patrolmen to guard the property. A crowd had begun to gather when the police arrived, but soon dispersed when the patrolmen marched into the building and closed the doors. A few hours later the actual drawing of names began in the Ninth District draft office at Third avenue and Forty-sixth street, and passed off quietly, although crowds gathered outside the building and muttered ominously as the wheel was turned. On this day 1236 names were drawn, and the work was then abandoned until the following Monday, when, it was announced, 264 additional names would be chosen to complete the quota of the district.

The next day, July 12, was Sunday, and although the city appeared to be quiet, beneath the surface there was a dangerous undercurrent of fear and excitement. Groups of men gathered on the street corners, and the wide-spread discussion of the exemption clause of the Conscription Act increased in bitterness when it was rumored that several rich men whose names had already been drawn had promptly paid the government three hundred dollars each, and had been released from their military obligations. Detectives found unusual activity among the gangs. Messages were constantly being exchanged between the chieftains, and detachments of gangsters were busily engaged collecting great quantities of clubs, brickbats, paving stones and other weapons, and carrying them into the dives. That night several fires were started in the lower part of the city, and the throngs which gathered to watch the firemen were larger and more boisterous than usual. Notwithstanding these circumstances, the police authorities professed not to be alarmed, and except for retaining the guard at the Arsenal, Superintendent Kennedy made only the routine assignments for the next day.

Monday dawned hot and clear, and the sun was not two hours above the horizon before it was apparent that trouble was brewing. About six o'clock groups of both men and women marched out of the dives and slum centers of the lower half of the island, and began to assemble at various points along the middle West Side. As rapidly as these gatherings reached large proportions they moved northward along Eighth and Ninth avenues, while small detachments spread into the side streets and visited factories and large construction jobs, intimidating the laborers and compelling them to quit work and join the hurrying throng. Several employers and foremen who protested were beaten. Thus, while the respectable portion of the city's population was at breakfast, the elements of a savage mob, armed with weapons of every description, were assembling at an appointed rendezvous in a vacant lot east of Central Park, in what is now the most fashionable residential section of the city. As the lot began to fill agitators harangued

Rioters Marching Down Second Avenue

the crowd with inflammatory speeches against the draft, and about eight o'clock the huge mass surged into the street and moved southward in two columns along Fifth and Sixth avenues, brandishing their weapons and shouting defiance of the government and the police. At Forty-seventh street the columns joined, turned east and proceeded steadily toward Third avenue, and then down that broad thoroughfare to the draft office at Forty-sixth street. The strength of the mob has been variously estimated at from five thousand to fifteen thousand. An accurate idea of its size may be obtained from a statement by the son of President King of Columbia College, who timed the marchers and found that they required between twenty and twenty-five minutes to pass a given point, and filled Forty-seventh street from curb to curb.

A crowd had already begun to form in front of the Third avenue draft office, and another was milling and shouting threateningly before the office at Broadway and Twenty-ninth street. Half an hour after the mob had swept out of the Central Park rendezvous, Superintendent Kennedy dispatched sixty-nine patrolmen, commanded by Captain Speight and Sergeants Wade, Mangin, McCredie and Wolfe, to guard the Broadway office, and at the same time directed Captain Porter to send sixty men to the threatened point on Third avenue and reinforce the squad on duty there. Fifty men of the Invalid Corps also stood to arms and marched to the rescue of the latter office. At nine o'clock so many alarming reports had been received at Headquarters that the Superintendent sent the following message over the police telegraph system:

To all stations in New York and Brooklyn: Call in your reserve platoons and hold them at the station house subject to further orders.

The force under command of Captain Speight was sufficiently strong to prevent trouble at the Broadway office, and the drafting continued there without interruption until noon, when it was adjourned for twenty-four hours. But in Third avenue the mob had grown to huge proportions, and while the Provost Marshal drew from the spinning wheel the slips of paper bearing the names of those chosen in the draft, the crowd pushed and yelled and milled furiously up and down the thoroughfare, packing the avenue for half a dozen blocks on either side of Forty-sixth street. Horse cars and private carriages which attempted to make their way through the swarm of men and women were stopped, the horses unhitched and the drivers and passengers driven from the vehicles. Placards on which were inscribed "No Draft!" appeared at various points, and were paraded back and forth amid cheers. The excitement increased, and by ten o'clock the front rank of the mob pressed closely against the thin line of policemen who stood with drawn clubs and their backs to the building, waiting for the riot to burst into flame. The fire had been laid and required only the touch of a match.

This was provided by Volunteer Engine Company No. Thirty-Three, popularly known as the Black Joke, an organization of noted street brawlers. Their leader had been drawn in the draft on Saturday, and his followers had announced their intention of smashing the wheel and destroying the records. The entire company was massed in front of the building when the great crowd surged howling through the street from the vacant lot near Central Park, and as the mob became more boisterous the firemen crowded closer. Suddenly someone raised a pistol and fired into the air, and the next moment the men of the Black Joke made a concerted rush for the door. The police fought valiantly, but were soon overwhelmed, and Captain Porter ordered a retreat into the building. But they were not quick enough to close and barricade the doors, and the firemen swarmed inside and wrecked the wheel, although the Provost Marshal was able to save his documents. Behind the firemen swept the mob, yelling and brandishing firearms and clubs, and after a short but fierce struggle in the hallways the police fled into an alley and thence to Second avenue, leaving the rioters in possession of the building. They promptly applied the torch, and when other fire companies arrived the mob would not permit them to put out the fire, assaulting Chief Engineer John Decker when he tried to run hose lines into the building. The firemen were compelled to stand by and watch the destruction of the entire block from Forty-sixth to Forty-seventh streets.

Meanwhile Superintendent Kennedy had left Police Head-quarters on a tour of inspection, not knowing that the riot had grown to such proportions. Wearing ordinary citizens' clothing and carrying a light bamboo cane, he drove in a light carriage to

Burning of the Provost-Marshal's Office in Third Avenue

Forty-sixth street and Lexington avenue, where he saw the crowd surging about the burning building and columns of smoke rising high into the hot July air. He left his vehicle at the corner and walked through Forty-sixth street toward Third avenue. Halfway down the block he was recognized, and a gang of bruisers rushed upon him. Before he could defend himself he was knocked down by a man in an old army uniform. He scrambled upright and slashed his assailant across the face with his light cane, but the next instant was again beaten to the ground, where he was stamped and kicked. He managed to regain his feet, but the crowd rushed him to the edge of an embankment where street grading was being done, and flung him onto a pile of rocks at the bottom. Once more he struggled to his feet, and with the howling mob at his heels, fled across a vacant lot toward Forty-seventh street. But another gang met him, and he was mauled and pushed toward

Lexington avenue, where a huge thug hit him with a club and knocked him into a deep mudhole. Others leaped after him, but Kennedy, with his face and body bleeding from a score of wounds, splashed through the muck to Lexington avenue, where he collapsed in the arms of John Eagan, an influential citizen of the vicinity, who persuaded the mob that the Superintendent was dead. After the crowd had surged back toward the burning houses, Kennedy was loaded into a wagon and covered with old sacks, and was then driven to Police Headquarters. There a surgeon found seventy-two different bruises on his body and more than a score of cuts. He was able to take no further part in the fighting.

With Superintendent Kennedy lying unconscious in a hospital, the command of the police and responsibility for the suppression of the riots devolved entirely upon Police Commissioners John C. Bergen and Thomas C. Acton, the latter a prominent Republican politician and one of the founders of the Union League Club. The third member of the Board, James Bowen, had been appointed a Brigadier-General of Volunteers, and had gone to join his division several weeks before the riots began. Bergen took charge of the situation on Staten Island and in Brooklyn, while Acton assumed command in Manhattan. From Monday morning until Friday afternoon Acton neither slept nor removed his clothing, and except for brief tours of inspection, did not leave his office at Police Headquarters, which had been removed from White street to No. 300 Mulberry street upon the organization of the Metropolitan Police District. During this period Acton received and answered more than four thousand telegrams, and directed the disposition of both the police and the military forces, for the army officers kept in close touch with him and generally deferred to his judgment concerning troop movements.

Before leaving Police Headquarters Superintendent Kennedy had ordered detachments from various precincts, including those which had dispersed the mob before the Broadway draft office, to march to the rescue of the hard-pressed policemen who were trying to protect the building at Third avenue and Forty-sixth street. The first of these details to encounter the mob was a squad of thirteen men under command of Sergeant Ellison. They were attacked at Third avenue and Forty-fourth street, and, outnumbered more than two hundred to one, were compelled to retreat before the savage onslaught of the rioters. Sergeant Ellison was cut off from his command and his club wrested from his hand, but he knocked a gangster down and captured the man's musket, with which he cracked several skulls before he was knocked senseless by a thug armed with a club. He lay unconscious on the sidewalk while the fighting surged back and forth, and was not rescued until another detachment commanded by Sergeant Wade appeared and clubbed a passage through the mass to his body.

While the police under Sergeant Wade, and the remnant of the force with which Sergeant Ellison had gone into action, were engaging the rioters, a third detachment arrived under the command of Sergeants Mangin and Smith. But the mob was too strong even for their combined forces, and the police were retreating slowly down Third avenue, with half their number badly wounded, when Sergeant McCredie, known on the force as Fighting Mac, charged into the mêlée with fifteen men, and Sergeant Wolfe attacked from another corner with ten. McCredie took command of the entire body of police, and was able to muster forty-four clubs. With this force he turned and struck at the mob, and by hard fighting drove the rioters back to Forty-fifth street. But thousands still roared down from the north, and McCredie and his men were soon overwhelmed by a great throng which assailed them from all sides. Every policeman in the battle was disabled, and Sergeant McCredie, forced onto the steps of a house by the rioters, was dealt such a terrific blow that he hurtled through the panels of the front door. Dazed and badly hurt, he staggered to his feet and ran up the stairs to the second floor, where a young German woman secreted him between two mattresses and persuaded the mob that he had leaped from a window. The rioters set fire to the house and departed, and the young woman then hoisted McCredie to her back and carried him across lots into Lexington avenue, where a carriage took him to the police station.

Other groups of police marched against the mob while McCredie was being rescued, and were defeated in turn with great losses, the vast mass of rioters surging tumultuously up and down the street and preventing the police from concentrating for an attack in force. By one o'clock the mob had swept southward to Thirty-fifth street, where Captain Steers and a strong force of patrolmen made a desperate stand but were finally overwhelmed and fled in disorder. Meanwhile a detachment of the Invalid Corps, numbering fifty men armed with saber and musket, marched up Third avenue, and were greeted by a shower of paving stones and brickbats, which killed one of the soldiers and wounded half a dozen others. Bewildered by the unexpected attack, the commander ordered his front rank to fire with blanks, but the volley had no other effect than to further inflame the mob and leave half the troops defenseless. With a roar the great throng

Policeman Killed by Rioters

charged, and the second rank of the Invalids fired with ball cartridges, killing and wounding six men and one woman. For an instant the mob was checked, and then the rioters attacked with greater ferocity than ever. Before the troops could reload, their guns had been wrested from their hands and they were being clubbed and shot with their own weapons. Hopelessly outnumbered, the soldiers turned and fled pell mell down the street, leaving a score of dead and wounded. The mob proceeded to torture and mutilate them.

Some of the more intelligent of the rioters realized that if they could obtain firearms the police could be annihilated and the city captured and looted before effective military aid could arrive. With this in mind, they planned to seize the State Armory at Second avenue and Twenty-first street, and the plant of the Union Steam Works a block farther north, which had been transformed into a munitions factory. In each of these structures was stored about four thousand carbines and some two hundred thousand rounds of ammunition. But detectives learned of the scheme, and Captain Cameron of the Eighteenth Precinct rushed a strong detachment of police to guard each building. Sergeant Banfield and twenty men took possession of the Armory, and at two o'clock were relieved by thirty-two men of the famous Broadway Squad, under command of Sergeant Burdick and Roundsmen Ferris and Sherwood. The patrolmen were armed with carbines, besides their nightsticks and revolvers, and a man was stationed at each window to await the expected attack.

It was not long in coming. Within half an hour after the police had entered a mob estimated at ten thousand men and women swarmed before the Armory, hurling bricks and paving stones and firing pistols and muskets whenever a policeman showed his head. About four o'clock the rioters attacked, led by a giant thug who brandished a sledge-hammer, and began an assault upon the main door. Repeated blows soon smashed a panel, and a man widely known in Five Points gang circles rushed forward and started to crawl through the aperture, eager to be the first inside the building. A policeman immediately shot him through the head. For a moment the rioters fell back, but they soon came on again with renewed fury, hammering at the doors with sledges, crowbars and small tree trunks which they used as battering rams, and dealing such terrific blows that the whole building trembled.

It soon became apparent that the Armory could not be defended, and Sergeant Burdick prepared to lead his men out. It was obviously suicide to attempt a passage through the mob, and there was but one avenue of retreat which the rioters had not guarded. That was a hole in the rear wall, some twelve by eighteen inches and eighteen feet from the ground. Every man of the Broadway Squad was well over six feet tall and a giant in build, but they managed to squeeze themselves through the hole, and after clubbing a path through a small crowd which tried to intercept them, made their way to the Eighteenth Precinct station house in Twenty-second street near Third avenue. But within an hour this structure was attacked and burned, and the Broadway Squad fled to Police Headquarters in Mulberry street.

The last of the Squad had scarcely dropped through the hole and left the Armory before the doors crashed in and the triumphant mob streamed into the building. There was considerable plunder downstairs, but the bulk of the carbines and ammunition was stored in the drill room on the third floor, and thither the crowd rushed. Within a few minutes the room was jammed with excited rioters snatching guns from the racks and stuffing their pockets with cartridges. To prevent interference from the police, the mob barricaded the door of the drill room, an act which was to have frightful consequences. While the Armory was being sacked the detachments of police which had been fighting the throngs in Second and Third avenues had effected a junction, and more than a hundred men launched an attack upon the crowd which still milled about in front of the Armory. The thudding locust clubs soon cleared a pathway, and the police formed a lane four deep in front of the broken door.

Scores of the rioters rushed from the building to aid their fellows, and as fast as they tried to run the gauntlet the police clubbed them down. Several were killed by mighty blows. Meanwhile other elements of the mob, fearing that the police had come in sufficient force to recapture the Armory, fired the building in half a dozen places. The structure was of wood and very old, and within ten minutes the lower half was a mass of flames. Rioters who ran out after the fire had started were not molested

by the police unless they carried carbines or ammunition. These
were clubbed without mercy. The mob in the drill room had slight
chance of escape, for the door had been barricaded to such good
purpose that it could not be opened for some time, and when it
was finally ripped from the hinges the whole building below the
third floor was a roaring torch. A moment later the frenzied rioters began leaping from the windows, but many who did so
cracked their skulls against the pavement and were killed, while

Burning of the Second Avenue Armory

others received broken legs and arms. But not more than a score
had jumped before the floor of the drill room collapsed and the
screaming men were hurled into the flames. The number who
thus perished was never known, but after the riots had subsided

and workmen began to clear away the debris, more than fifty baskets and barrels of human bones were carted from the ruins and buried in Potter's Field.

4

WHILE the battle was raging for possession of the Armory, the great throng which had massed in Third avenue divided into smaller mobs and surged across Manhattan Island from the Hudson to the East Rivers, looting, burning, and beating every Negro who dared show himself. Three black men were hanged before nightfall on the first day of the rioting, and thereafter an average of three a day were found by the police hanging to trees and lamp-posts, their bodies slashed by knives or beaten almost to a pulp. Some were little more than charred skeletons, for the women who followed in the wake of the rioters and on occasion took part in the fierce fighting, poured oil into the knife cuts and set fire to it, and then danced beneath the blazing human torch with obscene songs and imprecations. Within three hours after the first attack on the Third avenue draft office several fine private residences in Lexington avenue near Forty-sixth street had been pillaged and set on fire, the rioters staggering out of the houses laden with clothing, furniture and other property. The Bull's Head Tavern in Forty-sixth street was burned, as was the block of buildings in Broadway between Twenty-fourth and Twenty-fifth streets. The mob which had massed before the Provost Marshal's office in Broadway at Twenty-ninth street during the morning returned early in the afternoon, and fired the structure, carrying the furniture into the streets and hacking it to pieces with hatchets and axes. Half a dozen jewelry stores and other shops in the vicinity were looted, and several hundred guns and pistols stolen from hardware stores.

One of the mobs which had detached itself from the main body of the rioters moved eastward to attack the residence of Mayor Opdyke, in First avenue, while another marched southward through Broadway to burn Police Headquarters. Small detach-

ments of police continued to engage the rioters, but a force sufficient to strike an effective blow could not be formed, and so many
mobs were roaring through the streets that a concentration
against one would only have left the others free to burn and pillage without hindrance. About two hundred patrolmen had made
their way to Headquarters, but many had been seriously wounded, and fewer than one hundred and fifty were fit for active duty.
Instead of sending them out in small detachments to harry the
rioters until military aid could be organized and sent into the
field, Commissioner Acton decided to stake everything in an
attempt to disperse the great throng which was marching against
Headquarters, for detectives who had mingled with the rioters
reported that their leaders planned, if successful in Mulberry
street, to invade the financial district and loot the banks and the
United States sub-treasury.

Every available policeman was mustered and placed under command of Inspector Daniel C. Carpenter, senior uniformed officer
of the department, who made a brief speech after Drill Officer
Copeland had formed them in front of the building. "We are going
to put down a mob," said Carpenter, "and we will take no prisoners." The savage roar of the rioters could be heard as Inspector
Carpenter and about one hundred and twenty-five men marched
through Mulberry and Bleecker streets, and as they turned into
Broadway they saw that the slowly moving mass filled the broad
thoroughfare from curb to curb, and extended northward as far
as the eye could reach. There were at least ten thousand howling
men and women, with the former in the majority, and they were all
armed with clubs, guns, pistols, crowbars and swords. At their
head marched a giant carrying an American flag, and another
who staggered beneath the burden of a huge plank on which had
been crudely lettered, "NO DRAFT!" During its progress down
Broadway the mob set fire to half a dozen houses, and a pall of
black smoke enveloped that section of the city. Storekeepers put
up their shutters and abandoned their shops, stages turned into
the side streets and were quickly emptied of drivers and passengers, and ahead of the advancing mob raced frightened Negroes,
and rumbling carts piled high with the household belongings of

citizens who had been forced from their burned and pillaged homes.

Inspector Carpenter deployed his men in four lines of skirmishers across Broadway, and the police marched steadily northward, establishing contact with the mob at Amity street just south of La Farge House, into which a hundred of the rioters had swarmed and were beating the Negro servants. For a moment the front rank of the mob halted, and then a huge thug, armed with a bludgeon, sprang forward and rushed upon Inspector Carpenter, who was marching several feet in advance of his men. But Carpenter was a fierce fighter. Instead of falling back, he ran to meet his assailant, and dodging the blow which would have cracked his skull, killed the man with his nightstick. Behind him rushed Patrolmen Doyle and Thompson, the latter capturing the flag and the former killing the rioter who bore the lettered plank. The next moment a hail of brickbats and paving stones whirled from the mob and hurtled into the ranks of the police, and a score of shots followed in rapid succession. Several of the policemen fell seriously wounded, but the remainder closed ranks and continued their steady march, their clubs rising and falling in almost perfect unison and seldom failing to find marks as they came to close quarters with the surging throng. Gradually the mob gave ground before the onslaught of the disciplined fighters, and after fifteen minutes of furious slugging the rioters broke and scattered in all directions, while the police pursued them up the side streets and clubbed them unmercifully. The pavements and sidewalks were littered with the dead and wounded, who were carried away by their comrades several hours later under cover of darkness.

Mayor Opdyke had neglected to provide a police guard for his home, but his neighbors had recognized the likelihood of an assault, and when the rioters swept into First avenue they found the house and grounds garrisoned by more than fifty citizens, armed with swords, carbines and pistols, under command of Colonel B. F. Manierre. This display of force turned back the mob without a shot being fired, and it surged across the city and joined a great crowd which had gathered in front of the Colored Orphan

Asylum, in Fifth avenue between Forty-third and Forty-fourth streets, just north of the present Public Library and now in the heart of the fashionable shopping district. The Asylum was a four-storied brick structure, with two wings of three stories each, and housed two hundred Negro children under twelve years of age, together with a staff of about fifty adults. The Superintendent, William E. Davis, barricaded the front doors when the mob began to assemble, and while the rioters attempted to force an entrance he marched the children out the back way and through the grounds into Madison avenue, whence they were driven in stages to the Twenty-second precinct station house in Forty-seventh street, between Eighth and Ninth avenues. Later they were removed to Blackwell's Island, in the East River, under military escort.

Scarcely had the children left the Asylum when the doors were ripped from their hinges and the mob streamed into the building, while smaller gangs attacked stores and residences in the vicinity, looting and setting fire to them. The rioters who had invaded the

Colored Orphan Asylum—
Fifth Avenue between 43d and 44th Streets

Asylum destroyed the furniture with hatchets and axes, and killed a little Negro girl who had been overlooked in the hurried exodus of the children, and had sought refuge under a bed. The bedding, trinkets and toys of the children were carried away, and then the mob fired the building in half a dozen places. Chief Engineer John Decker of the Fire Department, arriving with two companies, was twice knocked down when he attempted to carry hose lines into the house, but with fifteen firemen at his heels finally forced his way inside. They extinguished half a dozen fires, but were at last set upon by a great mob of rioters and thrown bodily into the street, where they were surrounded and compelled to watch the destruction of the Asylum, as well as three other buildings nearby.

For several hours the rioting was confined to the central portion of the city; none of the mobs had penetrated below Twenty-first street except the great mass which had been defeated in Broadway by Inspector Carpenter. But about the middle of the afternoon the gangsters began pouring out of the Five Points, the Bowery and the water front district, and new mobs began to assemble at various points in the lower half of the city. Then in rapid succession came reports of outrages in all parts of Manhattan south of Fifty-ninth street. The Negro settlements in the lower east and west sides were attacked, and several houses were burned or wrecked after the inhabitants had been killed or beaten. Twenty Negro families were ousted from their homes at Leonard and Baxter streets, and Crook's restaurant in Nassau street was sacked by a mob which beat the Negro waiters. Half a dozen houses in Pell street were destroyed, and a mob also invaded the notorious Arch Block in Thompson street, which seethed with a crowded population of poverty-stricken Negroes. The rioters demolished the dive kept by Big Sue, or the Turtle, and after she had been frightfully beaten by a gang of Irishwomen from the Five Points, her liquor was confiscated and served out to the howling rioters. Half drunk, they surged throughout that part of the city, burning, looting and murdering.

5

BY nightfall New York was practically in the hands of the mob, for from all quarters came reports that the small detachments of police were meeting with defeat and fleeing before the rioters; and military aid was not yet available in sufficient force to accomplish anything. Fires from a score of burning buildings pierced the darkness, and the hot stillness of the July night was made more oppressive by the columns of black smoke which hung low over the city. Early in the evening minor outbreaks were reported in Harlem and on the upper West Side, which culminated just before midnight in the burning of Postmaster Abram Wakeman's home in West Eighty-sixth street. About eight o'clock word was received at Police Headquarters that a vast mob had formed uptown and was marching down Fifth avenue with the avowed intention of hanging Horace Greeley and burning *The Tribune* building in Printing House Square, opposite City Hall Park. The mob turned east in the lower Twenties and proceeded down Third avenue to the Bowery, and thence through Chatham Square and Park Row, led by a giant thug carrying an American flag. Thousands swarmed after him, singing at the top of their voices:

We'll hang old Greeley to a sour apple tree,
We'll hang old Greeley to a sour apple tree,
We'll hang old Greeley to a sour apple tree,
    And send him straight to Hell!

Throughout the evening another crowd had been assembling in City Hall Park and Printing House Square, and when the uptown mob came streaming down Park Row an attack was immediately begun. Sergeant Devoursney attempted to defend *The Tribune* building single handed, and fought valiantly in the doorway until he was surrounded by a ring of dead and disabled gangsters, but he was finally overwhelmed and the mob rushed into the building, overrunning it and setting it on fire in half a dozen places. The editorial and mechanical forces, led by Horace Greeley, escaped down the back stairways, and Greeley was chased into a Park Row restaurant, where he hid under a table. He was not found, for the waiter covered him with a cloth. Captain Warlow and a detachment from the First Precinct were returning to their station house in Broad street after a hard campaign against rioters along the water front, when they received telegraphic instructions to rush to the rescue of *The Tribune*. Captain Warlow led his men up Nassau street, and at Printing House Square was met by Captain Thorne and a detail from City Hall. Together, with a force of about one hundred policemen, they attacked the rear of the mob and soon cleared *The Tribune* office of the rioters, extinguishing the fires before they could do much damage. The mob fled in shrieking disorder up Park Row and through City Hall Park, where it was attacked by a large body of policemen under Inspector Carpenter and Inspector Folk of Brooklyn, who had brought a hundred men across the East River and had been doing valiant service uptown. Carpenter formed his men in company front and swept the Park like a storm, soon dispersing the rioters. After this fight Inspector Folk returned with his force to Brooklyn, where great excitement had begun to prevail, although there was no actual rioting in that city until Wednesday night, when several grain elevators in the Atlantic Basin were burned. Two hours later another mob marched against *The Tribune*, but was repulsed by a detachment of fifty policemen who had been left to garrison Printing House Square while Inspector Carpenter led the remainder of his force into other threatened areas. Employees of the newspapers took part in this last fight, for Patrolman Blackwell of the Harbor Police had brought pistols and carbines from the municipal stores on Riker's and Blackwell's Islands, and had distributed them among the men of the mechanical and editorial departments. Lighted lanterns were hung from the windows of *The Tribune* building, illuminating the Square so brightly that there was no possibility of a surprise attack. The next day the police garrison was relieved by a hundred Marines and sailors, and Gatling guns replaced the lanterns, while the black muzzle of a howitzer protruded threateningly from the main entrance of *The Tribune*. The guns were manned by a squad of seamen.

Serious rioting began in the Negro settlements north and east of the Five Points about seven o'clock Monday evening, and for five hours Captain John Jourdan and sixty men of the Sixth precinct patrolled the district, engaging in many battles and leaving scores of disabled rioters in their wake. Returning to City Hall, this detachment joined a force under Inspector Carpenter, and made a tour of the water front district of the Fourth Ward, where mobs had again assembled after the departure of Captain Warlow, and were burning Negro dwellings and looting stores. Several of the notorious water front dives were sacked by the rioters, and a house of prostitution in Water street was burned and the inmates tortured because they refused to surrender a Negro servant. In New Bowery, east of the Five Points, three Negroes sought refuge on a roof, and the mob fired the building beneath them, so that the Negroes were forced to cling with their fingers to the copings of the gable walls, while the rioters screamed madly for them to fall. Finally their hands were burned and they dropped, and were immediately stamped and kicked to death.

Meanwhile the mobs farther uptown had continued their depredations, and throughout the night there was almost constant fighting. Many of the fires which had been set by the rioters were extinguished by a heavy rainstorm, accompanied by great thunder and lightning, which deluged the city about eleven o'clock. Some historians of the riots believe that if the rain had not appeared the lower half of New York would have been destroyed, for several of the fire companies had joined the mobs *en masse,* and others were slow in responding to alarms. And invariably when the engines did roll to a fire the firemen were hindered by the rioters, and in many cases driven away.

6

NOT more than eight hundred policemen were available for duty in Manhattan when the rioting began Monday morning, but by nightfall the men off duty had reported to their station houses, and Commissioner Acton was able to put about 1,500 men in the field, although many were soon disabled by the pistols and clubs of the rioters. The seriousness of the situation had been apparent to both Mayor Opdyke and the Commissioner early in the morning, and the first mob had scarcely begun to mass in Third avenue before they appealed to Major-General Sandford to call out all units of the National Guard which were in the city. Aid was also requested from Major-General John E. Wool, commander of the Eastern Department of the United States Army, which included New York City. General Sandford immediately sent out messengers, and published handbills and advertisements in the afternoon newspapers, calling upon all officers and men of the Guard, as well as other persons who had seen military service, to report at the Arsenal at Seventh avenue and Thirty-fifth street. General Wool sent a gunboat from Governor's Island to the various forts about the city, with orders to the commanding officers to embark every soldier who could be spared from the fortifications, and as much artillery as possible. He also asked Rear Admiral Paulding, commandant of the Navy Yard, to send to Manhattan all available Marines and seamen from the Yard, and from the warships anchored there and in the harbor. All Regular Army troops were placed under the command of Brigadier General Harvey Brown, who made his headquarters in Commissioner Acton's office. Mayor Opdyke remained at City Hall during the day, and at dusk removed to the St. Nicholas Hotel, where he was joined on Tuesday by Governor Seymour, who had hastened down from the state capital at Albany. Late Monday night Mayor Opdyke sent telegrams to the War Department at Washington asking that the New York regiments which had fought at Gettysburg be rushed into the city as quickly as possible. Messages were also dispatched to the Governors of Rhode Island, Connecticut, New Jersey and Massachusetts, requesting them to hold troops in readiness for service if needed.

The first military unit mustered, besides the Invalid Corps which was already under arms, was the Tenth Regiment of the National Guard, which had been ordered to form line on Monday morning in the Arsenal at Elm and Worth streets. Originally it had been intended to embark the troops for the battle front, but instead they remained in the city and did valiant service in suppressing the mobs. On the first day of the rioting two companies remained at the Elm street Arsenal to guard the munitions stored there. They were supported by a battery of three six-pound guns. Fifty men of the Tenth Regiment and fifty of the Invalid Corps relieved the police guard at the Seventh avenue Arsenal, where General Sandford established his headquarters and whence he dispatched details of troops to cooperate with the police. Two more companies of the Tenth marched to the Arsenal in Central Park. By the middle of the afternoon several small detachments of the regular infantry, and some two hundred Marines and sailors, had landed and were marched to Police Headquarters and the Arsenals. Two more companies of regular infantry reached Headquarters at eleven o'clock Monday night, and by midnight about 2,000 regular and state troops were available for service. The enlisting of citizens as Volunteer Special Police had also begun and was proceeding rapidly. Soon after midnight Colonel Henry Moore of the Forty-seventh Regiment of Volunteers reported that the following troops were garrisoned at the Seventh avenue Arsenal:

Several twelve-pounder mountain howitzers from Governor's Island, with artillerists; detachment of Tenth New York State Militia under Major Seeley; detachment of Twelfth Regular U. S. Infantry, from Fort Hamilton, Captain Franklin; ditto, Third Regular U. S. Infantry, from Governor's Island, Captain Wilkins; ditto, Invalid Corps, from Riker's Island; ditto, units of New York State Volunteers, Captain Lockwood.

These troops numbered about one thousand, all well armed and equipped. But only two detachments, Captain Wilkins' infantrymen and a company of Marines, had engaged the rioters. The latter fired into a mob which attempted to stop its march to Headquarters, and the former relieved the citizen guard at Mayor Opdyke's home, repulsing a gang which made a second attack on the building about midnight.

CHAPTER VIII

THE DRAFT RIOTS
(Continued)

1

THE SECOND day of rioting, Tuesday, July 14, 1863, began with two murders. After a night of drinking and carousing in the dives and dance halls of the Bowery and Five Points, more than a thousand frenzied men and women surged into Clarkson street before dawn and hanged William Jones, a Negro, to a tree when he attempted to defend his wife and children and prevent the burning of his home. A fire was lighted beneath him, and the mob danced madly about, shrieking and throwing stones and bricks at his body while it dangled above the flames. Another Negro, named Williams, was attacked at Washington and LeRoy streets. While half a score of rioters held him down, their leader smashed his skull with a huge stone weighing more than twenty pounds, which he dropped time after time on the Negro's head. Women who accompanied the rioters slashed his body with knives and poured oil into the wounds, but before they could ignite it were dispersed by a detachment of police under Drill Officer Copeland and Captain John F. Dickson. This force also defeated the mob in Clarkson street and cut down Jones's body.

Hanging and Burning a Negro in Clarkson Street

It was soon apparent that New York faced a day of even fiercer fighting than on Monday, and that all of the resources of the police and military would be required to save the metropolis from fire and pillage. By six o'clock mobs had begun to assemble throughout the city, sweeping tumultuously through the streets, pursuing and beating Negroes, and looting and setting fire to houses. One of the first crowds to gather appeared suddenly in East Eighty-sixth street and attacked the Twenty-third precinct police station, which was garrisoned only by Doorman Ebling, the patrolmen having been marched downtown to Headquarters soon after midnight. The station house was burned. Another mob made a demonstration before Mayor Opdyke's home, smashing windows and doors with bricks and paving stones before it was driven away by the police and soldiers. A second great mass of shouting men and women surged across Printing House Square to attack the *Times* and *Tribune* buildings, but fled in disorder northward through Park Row and Center street when they saw the Gatling guns and the howitzer which had been moved into position during the night. A third gang burned the home of Colonel Robert Nugent, Assistant Provost Marshal General, in West Eighty-sixth street.

Great throngs of men gathered before daybreak in Ninth and First avenues, and worked furiously, erecting barricades which were to give the police and troops much trouble later in the day. Telegraph poles and lamp-posts were hacked down and laid across the street, and between them the rioters piled carts, barrels, boxes and heavy pieces of furniture stolen from residences and stores in the vicinity. In First avenue the fortifications extended from Eleventh to Fourteenth streets, and in Ninth avenue from Thirty-second to Forty-third streets, with smaller barricades across the intersecting thoroughfares. Throughout the day, when hard pressed by the policemen and soldiers, the rioters sought refuge in these districts, and they were not dispersed and the barricades destroyed until the troops had driven the mob back with heavy volleys of musketry fire.

Inspector Daniel Carpenter mustered a force of two hundred policemen at Headquarters at six o'clock Tuesday morning, and marched them uptown to suppress rioters who had appeared in Second avenue and threatened the plant of the Union Steam Works at Twenty-second street, from which the police had been unable to remove the stores of munitions. The detachment marched into Second avenue a block below the Works, and found a mob which packed the thoroughfare north to Thirty-third street. Hundreds of the rioters possessed muskets, swords and pistols, and boldly confronted the police, while others had invaded the houses on either side of Second avenue between Thirty-second and Thirty-third streets, and lay in wait on the roofs with piles of bricks and stones beside them. As he had done in the Broadway and Amity street battle on Monday, Inspector Carpenter deployed his men as skirmishers, and two lines of policemen marched slowly north-ward, meeting with little resistance except for a few scattering vol-leys which passed harmlessly over their heads, or clipped the pave-ment before them. But at Thirty-second street the rioters on the house-tops suddenly hurled a shower of bricks and stones into the ranks of the police, and many of the patrolmen went down under the shock of the heavy missiles. At the same instant the mob, which had slowly closed in behind the advancing force, attacked front and rear, but Carpenter and his men fought with such fury and disci-pline that within fifteen minutes they had cleared the street, and the rioters huddled in small and sullen groups a hundred feet from the menacing clubs. With the mob thus frightened, fifty patrolmen dashed into the houses and up the stairs to the roofs, where they fell upon the gangsters. The rioters would not stand up before the slashing nightsticks, and many leaped into the street and were killed. Others were clubbed down, and those who escaped into the street were felled by Carpenter and his men. About fifty rioters had taken possession of a saloon at Second avenue and Thirty-first street, and were firing muskets and pistols through the windows, but were driven out without loss to the police, although many patrolmen had narrow escapes. One of the gangsters fired a bullet through a policeman's cap, but the latter seized him about the mid-dle and flung him through a window, dashing out his brains against the pavement.

Word of the fierce battle reached the Seventh avenue Arsenal, and Major-General Sandford dispatched Colonel H. J. O'Brien, of the Eleventh New York Volunteers, with one hundred and fifty infantrymen of various units, to the aid of the police. The troops were accompanied by two six-pound cannon and twenty-five artillerymen, under command of Lieutenant Eagleson. When he saw the troops marching up Second avenue Inspector Carpenter immediately launched another assault against the mob, but the rage of the rioters had increased and they stood their ground, pelt-ing the soldiers and the police with bricks and stones and keeping up a steady fire from their muskets and pistols. Colonel O'Brien wheeled the troops into company front and the infantrymen fired several volleys, but still the rioters pressed forward with great fury. Lieutenant Eagleson was then ordered to fire his guns, and the six-pounders belched a hail of grape and canister into the close packed ranks of the mob, causing frightful havoc. Six rounds were discharged before the rioters fall back, and then they broke and fled in all directions, leaving the sidewalks and pavement strewn with dead and wounded. One of the killed was a woman who carried a baby in her arms. She fell at the first volley, but the baby was underneath and was not injured, although the mother was fearfully trampled as the mob surged back and forth over her body.

With comparative quiet restored in Second avenue, Inspector Carpenter started on a tour of the eastern part of the city, and engaged several mobs which were surging through the streets. Colonel O'Brien marched his soldiers back to the Arsenal, but three hours later returned alone to the scene of the battle, for his home was in the vicinity and he was concerned for the safety of his family, as well as of his property. He reached his house without incident and finding that Mrs. O'Brien and her children had fled to Brooklyn before the fighting began and were with relatives, started to return to his command. But when he rode into Second avenue he was recognized, and several men attempted to pull him from his horse, while others threw bricks at him. He dismounted and entered a saloon at Nineteenth street and Second avenue. When he came out a great crowd of men and women had assembled, and were urging each other to kill him. With his sword in one hand and his revolver in the other, Colonel O'Brien walked deliberately across the street toward his horse. But he had not gone ten feet before the mob surged forward, and he was knocked down with a club. Before he could scramble to his feet the rioters were upon him. He was kicked and beaten, and then a rope was twisted about his ankles and he was dragged back and forth over the cobblestones. A Catholic priest interfered long enough to administer the last rites of the church, and then departed, leaving Colonel O'Brien to the tender mercies of the infuriated rioters. For more than three hours they tortured him, slashing his flesh with knives and daggers, dropping stones upon his head and

Murder of Col. O' Brien

body, and hauling him up and down the street with fierce howls of victory. He was then abandoned, and throughout the long, hot July afternoon lay unconscious on the pavement, none of his friends daring to rescue him or take him water. About sundown a great mob of men and women appeared and proceeded to inflict fresh torments upon his torn and battered body, finally dragging him into his own back yard. There a gang of Five Points harpies squatted about him, and after mutilating him with knives, flung stones at his head until he was dead.

The attention of the rioters had been distracted from the Union Steam Works by the ferocity of the attacks led by Inspector Carpenter and Colonel O'Brien, but when the police and soldiers had marched away the mob reappeared and captured the factory after a brief fight with the small guard of patrolmen. But instead of removing the carbines and distributing them, the rioters did not even break out the cases. They garrisoned the plant with some five hundred thugs, evidently with the intention of using it as a headquarters and a rallying point for the rioters operating along the East Side. Two hundred policemen under command of Inspector George W. Dilks marched into Second avenue when news of the capture of the Steam Works reached Headquarters, and the building was retaken foot by foot after terrific fighting. Many of the rioters were pursued to the roofs and killed, and the dead and dying littered the halls and rooms and the sidewalk in front of the structure. A physician of the neighborhood said afterward that within an hour he dressed twenty-one wounds in the head, all of which were fatal.

During the heavy fighting which preceded the invasion of the Union Steam Works by the police the mob was led by a one-armed giant who wielded a huge bludgeon, employing it as a flail with great effect, and by a young man in dirty overalls who fought valiantly with knife and club. The giant was shot and killed, and the young man was dealt such a terrific blow on the head that he fell heavily against an iron railing, and one of the pickets penetrated his throat beneath the chin. A policeman lifted the body from the paling, and the young man was found to possess aristocratic features, well-cared-for hands, and a fair, white skin. Obviously he was a man unused to physical labor. "Although dressed as a laborer, in dirty overalls and filthy shirt," wrote a chronicler of the riots, "underneath these were fine cassemere pants, a handsome, rich vest, and a fine linen shirt." His identity was never learned, for when the police had gone his body, together with the other dead, was carried away by the rioters. It is believed to have been taken to the Five Points in a cart, and buried beneath one of the tenements at Paradise Square.

All of the carbines and ammunition which remained in the Union Steam Works were loaded into wagons and taken to Police Headquarters under heavy guard. Soon after the recapture of the factory a detachment of soldiers joined the policemen, and the combined forces made a tour of the district, dispersing several large mobs. In Twenty-first street the expedition was met by a galling fire from the windows and roofs, and the policemen fell back, while the troops advanced and silenced the sharpshooters with several well-aimed volleys. One rioter who was shooting from

The Battle for the Union Steam Works

behind a corner of a house was killed when a soldier fired through the building. The Police under Inspector Dilks included, among other units, all of the reserves of the Eighteenth precinct, and while these men were fighting the mobs in First and Second avenues another gang of rioters attacked the station house in East Twenty-second street. Sergeant Burden and three men comprised the garrison, and although they made a determined resistance and kept the mob at bay for half an hour, they were finally driven out and the building burned.

Meanwhile Captain George W. Walling, already noted as one of the fiercest fighters of the Police Department because of his forays against the Honeymoon gang and the thugs of the water front, was having a busy time with a detachment of patrolmen from the Twentieth precinct. Early in the morning they marched into Pitt street, where a mob had surrounded a small body of soldiers, but before they could arrive the troops had fired into the rioters and dispersed them. Captain Walling then marched his men through the Bowery and broke up several large mobs, and an hour later was ordered to the rescue of a company of soldiers who had been attacked in front of Allerton's Hotel, in Eleventh avenue between Fortieth and Forty-first streets, by a gang of rioters who had taken their guns away from them. After defeating this mob and recapturing many of the stolen muskets, Captain Walling marched

Storming the Barricades in Ninth Avenue

across town to Fifth avenue and Forty-seventh street, where rioters had broken into and were looting the homes of Dr. Ward and
other residents of the vicinity. The detachment finally arrived at
the police station in West Thirty-fifth street after several hours of
hard fighting, and joined a force which was being organized to
attack the barricades in Ninth avenue.

So far as the police units were concerned, the formation of this
body had been completed by three o'clock in the afternoon, but it
was almost two hours later before regular army troops under command of Captain Wesson arrived to support them. Meanwhile the
rioters had strengthened their defenses, and had burned the
Weehawken Ferry house at West Forty-second street because a
saloon keeper refused to surrender his stock of liquors. At six
o'clock the combined military and police forces moved out of the
station house and marched into Ninth avenue, where thousands of
rioters, armed with muskets, pistols, bricks and paving stones,
crouched behind the barricades. Captains Slott and Walling led a
large detachment of police as an advance guard, but met with such
a heavy fire from the entrenched mob that they were compelled to
retreat. The soldiers then advanced in line of skirmishers and

routed the mob with several volleys of musketry, killing between twenty and thirty. The police rushed forward, and with their clubs and axes demolished the first line of barricades, while the troops massed in the rear and kept up a steady fire to prevent a counter attack. Similar methods were employed to capture the remaining fortifications, and within two hours the mob had fled, the defenses had been cleared away and the police were in control of Ninth avenue.

While this battle was in progress another great crowd had attacked the home of J. S. Gibbons, a cousin of Horace Greeley, at No. 19 Lamartine Place, near Eighth avenue and Twenty-ninth street. The rioters swarmed into the house, and were looting it when they were attacked from the rear by a police force drawn from the Broadway Squad and the reserves of the Thirty-first precinct, under command of Captain James Z. Bogart. There was fierce fighting for half an hour, and in the midst of the uproar a detachment of soldiers appeared and fired a wild volley which struck policeman and rioter alike. Patrolman Dipple was shot in the thigh, the bullet entering the bone and ranging upward through the marrow. He died soon afterward. Patrolmen Robinson and Hodgson were also seriously wounded. During the pillaging of the Gibbons residence the women caused the police more trouble than the men. Not only did they fight with greater ferocity, but they clung tenaciously to whatever bit of spoil they had been able to lay their hands upon. They were not driven from the house until the police took to spanking them with their clubs.

2

THROUGHOUT the whole of Tuesday the police experienced great difficulty in keeping their lines of communication open, for the leaders of the mob sent out patrols which cut every telegraph wire they could find; and repair crews, escorted by soldiers, were constantly being dispatched from Headquarters to mend breaks. The rioters also tore down the railroad telegraph lines along Eleventh avenue, and ripped up great sections of the Harlem and

New Haven railroad tracks, evidently with the intention of hampering the movement of troop trains. The lines of the Police Telegraph system which remained in operation were congested with important messages, but nevertheless Commissioner Acton suspended all official business for a moment early Tuesday afternoon, and at 1:12 o'clock this telegram was sent to the police of the Fifth Precinct:

> SEND TO DR. PURPLE AT 183
> HUDSON STREET TO GO AS SOON AS
> POSSIBLE TO INSPECTOR
> LEONARD'S HOUSE. BABY VERY
> SICK.

A military escort was provided for the physician, and it is of record that the sick baby recovered.

By noon Tuesday the danger to the armories, arsenals, Navy Yard and other government and state property had been materially lessened. The Seventh Regiment Armory was garrisoned by four hundred men and two howitzers, and detachments almost as large were in the Central Park, Seventh avenue and Worth street arsenals. The sub-treasury in Wall street was guarded by a troop of regular infantry and a battery of field guns, under command of Colonel Bliss of the Volunteers. Rumors of an intended raid upon the Navy Yard in the East River were received at Headquarters, and the war vessels in the harbor and in the Hudson immediately steamed up the East River; and soon all the approaches to the Yard were under the guns of the receiving ship North Carolina, the corvette Savannah, and the gunboats Granite City, Gertrude, Unadilla and Tulip. The ironclad Passaic and the steam gunboat Fuchsia had taken up positions off the Battery to prevent an attempt by the rioters to gain a footing on Governor's Island. Warships also lay at the foot of Wall and other important streets, with their guns trained to sweep the thoroughfares with grape and canister at the first sight of rioting mobs.

About two o'clock in the afternoon the bridge over the Harlem River at Macomb's Dam was destroyed, together with the

Washington Hotel and a large planing mill at Third avenue and 129th street. There was now fierce rioting throughout Manhattan, and from the Battery to the Harlem River detachments of soldiers and policemen were constantly in contact with the mobs, emerging victorious from a great majority of the clashes. By late Tuesday afternoon Special Volunteer Policemen, to the number of almost a thousand, had been equipped with badges, uniforms and clubs, and were doing garrison and guard duty, releasing policemen and soldiers for active work in the field. Little fighting against the mobs was done by the Specials because of their lack of discipline and experience, although good work was done by a few companies composed of men who had seen battle service against the Confederates. They were led against the rioters by the officers who had commanded them in the South.

A large body of rioters attempted to form a troop of cavalry with horses stolen from the stables of the Red Bird Line, but the horsemen could not manage their steeds and accomplished nothing. Another mob launched an attack against a Negro church in Thirtieth street between Seventh and Eighth avenues, and Captain Walling marched to the scene with a large force of patrolmen. The church was already in flames when the police arrived, and the rioters were fighting back the firemen who were endeavoring to put out the blaze. Walling and his men dispersed the mob, killing one man who sat astride the roof hacking at the timbers with an axe. Meanwhile other crowds were looting gun stores in Third avenue near Thirty-seventh street, and had set fire to the buildings after carrying out the arms and ammunition. Later the occupants of the block on Second avenue between Thirty-fourth and Thirty-fifth streets were notified that their homes would be burned that night, but within ten minutes the mob had applied the torch and hanged a Negro who fled from one of the tenements. Ten houses were burned.

There was practically no halt in the fighting on Tuesday night, bloody battles raging at various points throughout the city. For the fourth time a mob made an unsuccessful attack upon *The Tribune* building in Printing House Square; and between eight and nine o'clock Patrolman Bryan of the Fourth Precinct telegraphed to

Headquarters that a huge crowd was threatening to burn Brooks Brothers clothing store in Catherine street.[1] Fifty men were rushed to the building under command of Sergeants Finney and Matthews and Roundsman Farrell, but before they could arrive the attack had begun. Patrolmen Kennedy, Platt and Davis, who had been mingling with the rioters in disguise, checked the mob for a few moments, but they were soon overwhelmed and beaten, and the rioters then smashed the doors and streamed into the store. There they lighted the gas and broke out the windows, and when the police arrived the thugs were hurriedly attiring themselves in new suits and stuffing their pockets with neckties, shirts and other articles of apparel. Great bundles of clothing were also thrown from the windows.

The police quickly dispersed the mob in the street, and then charged inside, clubbing the rioters with their nightsticks and chasing them from floor to floor. Many tried to escape down a rope which led through a trapdoor into the basement, but the police waited for them at the bottom and knocked them senseless as fast as they appeared. During the struggle several policemen were shot and seriously wounded, and it was not until Inspector Carpenter appeared with his roving command that the store was cleared. Throughout the night a heavy guard was maintained, and the next day fifty patrolmen, with a military escort, searched the low rookeries of the vicinity and recovered about $10,000 worth of clothing and other property. In one shanty they found fifty new suits, and in another a huge gunnysack filled with neckties and socks.

3

GOVERNOR Seymour issued a proclamation late Tuesday afternoon declaring the city to be in a state of insurrection, and at midnight Mayor Opdyke received a telegram from Edwin M. Stanton, Secretary of War, that five regiments had been detached

---

[1] Now at Madison avenue and Forty-fourth street

from the victorious Union Armies, and were being rushed to the metropolis. The message was not made public, but encouraged by the prospect of aid and by the success of the previous day's operations, Commissioner Acton announced in Wednesday morning's newspapers that the backbone of the riot had been broken, and that the police were in control of the city. Nevertheless, there was heavy fighting during the next three days, and especially on Wednesday, when five Negroes were hanged and the soldiers again loosed their howitzers and field guns against the raging gangs of rioters. The five thousand liquor stores within the mob-infested areas remained open, but otherwise business had been almost entirely suspended, and the stores and factories sheltered their stocks of goods behind barred doors and shuttered windows. Except for occasional service on Sixth avenue, all of the street cars and omnibuses had ceased to operate, and the drays and carts which ordinarily rumbled through the city bearing loads of merchandise had been hidden to prevent the rioters using them to erect barricades. The roads of Westchester county and northward were crowded with men, women and children fleeing from a city that seemed doomed to destruction; and from Tuesday noon until the end of the rioting the railroad stations and the piers were crowded with great throngs that fought for places on trains and boats.

Wednesday, the 15th of July, was the hottest day of the year, and the stifling heat was made more intolerable by the columns of black smoke which curled upward from the ruins of more than three score houses which had been fired by the rioters. The fighting began before dawn, but the first conflict of importance occurred about nine o'clock, when a detachment of infantrymen of the Eighth Regiment of Volunteers, under command of General Dodge, supported by a troop of cavalry and a battery of howitzers under Colonel Mott of the Regular Army, marched out of Headquarters to disperse a mob which was reported to be hanging Negroes at Thirty-second street and Eighth avenue, within a block of the present Pennsylvania Hotel, and on the site of the Pennsylvania Railroad Station. When the column marched into Eighth avenue the soldiers found three Negroes hanging to lamp-posts, while a gang of ferocious women crowded about the dangling bodies, slashing them with knives as a mob of men estimated at more than five thousand yelled and cheered. The rioters fell back as the troops advanced, and Colonel Mott spurred his horse into their midst and cut down one of the Negroes with his sword, afterward running the weapon through a rioter who tried to drag him from his mount.

Colonel Mott had scarcely returned to his command when the mob surged forward and began the attack with a hail of bricks and stones and a brisk fire from muskets and pistols. Colonel Mott ordered Captain Howell to bring two howitzers into position in Seventh avenue to sweep Thirty-second street, and the guns were loaded with grape and canister. The infantry and cavalry then charged with bayonet and saber, driving the mob back to Eighth avenue. But the rioters came on again when the troops returned to protect the artillery, and Captain Howell shouted that he would fire the guns unless they dispersed. He was answered by jeers and shouts, and the mob rushed forward, the solid mass of humanity packing the street from curb to curb. Captain Howell ordered his gunners to fire, and scores of rioters fell dead or wounded as the shot ripped and tore through their close-packed ranks. But it was not until six rounds had been fired that they scattered and fled into Eighth avenue, and thence northward. The soldiers broke up into small detachments and cleared the side streets, and then cut down the bodies of the Negroes, after which they marched back to Headquarters in Mulberry street. Half an hour later the rioters returned, carried away their dead and wounded, and again strung up the Negroes. They dangled from the lamp-posts until late afternoon, when they were removed by a detachment of police under Captain Brower.

Artillery was again brought into action about an hour after the fighting in Eighth avenue, when the rioters attacked Jackson's Foundry in Twenty-eighth street between First and Second avenues. Driven away in disorder by half a dozen rounds of grape and canister, elements of the mob poured across the city and set fire to several houses at Twenty-seventh street and Seventh avenue, and when the troops had departed mobs again assembled on the East

Side and burned half a dozen dwellings in Second avenue near Twenty-eighth street, although no further move was made against the foundry. During the early afternoon Colonel Nevers led a company of regular infantrymen who frustrated an attempt to destroy the iron clad Dunderberg, which was under construction in Webb's Shipyard. Another military detachment, comprising thirty-three men of Hawkins' Zouaves and a company of regular infantry, captured a house at Broadway and Thirty-third street in which the rioters had secreted several thousand muskets. This expedition was supported by a battery of rifled cannon which had arrived in the city about noon.

Several times on Wednesday afternoon large bodies of troops were routed by the mobs, and two howitzers were captured by the rioters after the artillerymen had been clubbed down. However, the guns were of no value to the mobs, for they had no ammunition. The most serious of the day's defeats occurred about six o'clock, when Colonel Cleveland Winslow marched against a great mob in First avenue between Eighteenth and Nineteenth streets, with a force of two hundred volunteers commanded by Major Robinson, about fifty soldiers of the Duryea Zouaves, and two howitzers commanded by Colonel E. E. Jardine of Hawkins' Zouaves. While the infantrymen were engaging the rioters, Colonel Jardine unlimbered his guns and trained them to sweep the avenue, but before he could fire the mob had scattered into the houses on either side of the street. Within a few minutes a heavy fire was being directed upon the troops from the roofs and windows. More than a score of soldiers were killed and wounded. The howitzers poured a rain of shot through the street with little effect, and the soldiers attempted unsuccessfully to pick off the sharpshooters, but the latter fired with such deadly accuracy that within half an hour half of the military force was dead or wounded. Among the latter was Colonel Jardine, who was shot in the thigh by a rioter who stepped into the middle of the street while the howitzers were being loaded, rested his musket on the shoulder of a comrade, and took deliberate aim. Realizing that his command would be overwhelmed if the rioters made an attack in force, Colonel Winslow ordered the troops to fall back until the police could arrive with clubs and clear the houses, and drive the thugs into the street where the artillery would be effective. But at the first sign of a retreat the mob swarmed from the buildings and launched such a savage attack that the soldiers abandoned their dead and wounded, and their artillery, and fled in disorder, only a few escaping. Colonel Jardine, with two officers of the Duryea Zouaves who had also been hurt, crawled into the basement of a dwelling in Second avenue near Nineteenth street. There two women hid them beneath a great pile of kindling wood, but they were soon found by rioters who broke into the house. Colonel Jardine's companions were immediately clubbed to death, and he would have suffered a similar fate had not one of the leaders of the mob recognized him as an old acquaintance, and prevailed upon the rioters to spare his life. Several hours later, when the district had become quiet, the women carried Colonel Jardine to the home of a surgeon. Eventually he recovered from his wounds.

4

THE victory in First avenue was the last important success won by the mob. The regiments which had been ordered into New York began to arrive early Wednesday evening, and on Thursday morning Commissioner Acton and General Brown were able to supplement their tired forces with several thousand fresh troops who had been hardened by the campaign against the Confederates. The Seventy-Fourth Regiment of the National Guard reached the city about ten o'clock Wednesday night, and was immediately marched through the riot areas, as was the Sixty-Fifth, a Buffalo regiment, which had arrived half an hour later. At four o'clock Thursday morning the Seventh Regiment of the National Guard landed at Canal street, and soon after daybreak marched through the streets of the East Side, to the dismay of its old enemies among the gang leaders. The Sixty-Ninth Regiment detrained Thursday morning, and a few hours later the streets also resounded to the tramp of the Twenty-Sixth Michigan and the Fifty-Second and

152nd New York Volunteers. From then until Friday night troops arrived in the city in ever increasing numbers, and with the additional forces at their command General Brown and Commissioner Acton were able to effect an organization which had hitherto been impossible. Manhattan Island was divided into four districts, and headquarters were established in Harlem, in West Twenty-second and East Twenty-ninth streets, and at City Hall. In each area large bodies of soldiers and policemen were kept on reserve, while smaller detachments kept up a continuous patrol of the streets, preventing the formation of mobs. Much of this work was performed by the troops, for the police had engaged in such hard fighting since Monday that scarcely a man was unwounded, and the remainder were so weary from constant marching and battling that they could no longer cope effectively with the rioters.

Mayor Opdyke published an encouraging proclamation in the Thursday morning newspapers, urging the citizens to return to their usual occupations, and some of the street car and omnibus lines resumed operations. An official announcement, later discovered to be erroneous, was issued that the draft had been suspended in New York, and would not thereafter be enforced, and the Board of Aldermen held a special meeting and appropriated $2,500,000 with which to pay the exemption fees of all poor men who were chosen but did not want to go to war. But despite these measures fighting continued throughout the day. The most serious encounter was in Second avenue between Twenty-ninth and Thirty-first streets, where a mob defeated several small detachments of policemen and soldiers, and pursued about twenty-five of the latter into Jackson's Foundry, which was besieged. General Brown dispatched Captain Putnam to the rescue with a battery of field guns, fifty policemen and a full company of regular infantry. When the mob attacked, Captain Putnam swept the street with his artillery, killing eleven men and wounding many more. The rioters then scattered into the buildings on either side of Second avenue, but both policemen and soldiers pursued them, and with clubbed muskets and nightsticks drove them into the street, where they were again raked by the guns. They soon fled, and the troops marched to the rescue of their beleaguered comrades in the foundry.

This was the last fight of any consequence, although there were frequent minor clashes throughout Thursday night, and a few on Friday. Another proclamation by the Mayor on Friday declared that the riotous assemblages had been dispersed, and that a sufficient military force was now on hand to suppress any illegal movement, however formidable. At eleven o'clock Friday morning a crowd of some three thousand men and women assembled before the residence of Archbishop Hughes, at Madison avenue and Thirty-sixth street, and the prelate addressed them from a chair on his balcony, as he was so afflicted with rheumatism that he could not stand. He appealed to their religious pride and urged them to cease rioting:

"Every man has a right to defend his home or his shanty at the risk of life. The cause, however, must be just. It must not be aggressive or offensive. Do you want my advice? Well, I have been hurt by the report that you were rioters. You cannot imagine that I could hear these things without being grievously pained. Is there not some way by which you can stop these proceedings and support the laws, none of which have been enacted against you as Irishmen and Catholics? You have suffered already. No government can save itself unless it protects its citizens. Military force will be let loose on you. The innocent will be shot down, and the guilty will be likely to escape. Would it not be better to retire quietly?"

A strong force of soldiers and policemen attended the meeting, but did not molest the Archbishop's audience, which dispersed quietly as soon as the prelate had finished speaking. "They were on the whole a peaceable crowd," wrote Headley in *Sketches of the Great Riots of New York*, "and it was evidently composed chiefly if not wholly of those who had taken no part in the riot. None of the bloody heads and gashed faces, of which there were so many at that moment in the city, appeared. The address was well enough, but it came too late to be of any service. It might have saved lives and much destruction had it been delivered two days before, but now it was like the bombardment of a fortress after it had surrendered—a mere waste of ammunition. The fight was over, and to use his own not very refined illustration, he 'spak' too late.' "

General Brown was relieved by General E. R. S. Canby on the morning of Friday, and on Saturday General John A. Dix took over the command of the Department of the East from General Wool. On orders from General Dix the troops assumed the duty of guarding the city, while the police devoted several days to the recovery of stolen property. Large detachments, some with military escorts, visited the rookeries and dives of the Five Points, the Bowery and the slum districts along the Hudson and East Rivers, and in cellars and garrets found loot of every description, from barrels of sugar and luxurious rugs to tobacco and bird-seed. "Mahogany and rosewood chairs with brocade upholstering, marble top tables and stands, costly paintings and hundreds of delicate and valuable mantel ornaments are daily found in low hovels," said a newspaper. "Every person in whose possession these articles are found disclaims all knowledge of the same, except that they found them in the street, and took them in to prevent them being burned. The entire city will be searched, and it is expected that the greatest portion of the property taken from the buildings sacked by the mob will be recovered."

The casualties of the four days' fighting were never exactly computed, but were as high as those of some of the important battles of the Revolution and the Civil War, including such famous engagements as Shiloh and Bull Run. Conservative estimates placed the total at two thousand killed and about eight thousand wounded, a vast majority of whom were rioters. Practically every man on the police force was injured, although only three died. The losses of the various military units were not disclosed by the War Department, but were at least fifty men killed and some three hundred wounded. Eighteen Negroes were hanged by the rioters, and about seventy others were reported missing. Five were known to have been drowned when mobs pursued them into the East and Hudson Rivers. The police and troops captured eleven thousand stand of arms, including muskets and pistols, together with several thousand bludgeons and other weapons. The property loss was estimated at about $5,000,000, and the loss to business was incalculable, due to the stoppage of trade and the exodus of thousands of citizens, many of whom did not return to the city for several months. More than a hundred buildings were burned, including a Protestant Mission, the Colored Orphan Asylum, three police stations, an Armory, three Provost Marshals' offices, and a great number of dwellings, factories and stores. About two hundred other structures were looted and damaged.

Throughout the rioting the police and military authorities were hampered, and their plans often frustrated, by the politicians, especially the Democratic members of the Board of Aldermen and the State Legislature, who seized the opportunity to embarrass the administrations of the Republican President and the Republican Mayor. These worthy statesmen frequently appeared at Police Headquarters, and at a time when houses were being looted and burned and Negroes tortured and hanged, when business was at a standstill and the streets were filled with surging mobs, demanded that the police and soldiers be withdrawn from their districts, complaining that they were murdering the people. A Democratic Police Magistrate held a special session of his court, brought forward a test case, and solemnly pronounced the draft law to be unconstitutional, and urged the people to resist its enforcement. Most of the prisoners taken by the police during the last two days of the rioting, and during the search for stolen goods, were immediately freed through political influence, and were never brought to trial. Many of the gang leaders of the Five Points, the water front and other criminal infested areas were caught leading their thugs on looting expeditions, but politicians rushed to their aid and saved them from punishment. When the rioting had ceased only twenty men, out of the thousands who had formed the mobs, were in jail. Of these nineteen were tried and convicted, and were sentenced to an average of five years each in prison.

5

ALTHOUGH the gangsters and other criminals had been defeated and hammered from pillar to post by the police and soldiers during the desperate fighting of that strenuous week in July, they continued to give the police much trouble during the remaining years of the Civil War. In May, 1864, mobs began to assemble when the *World* and the *Journal of Commerce* published what purported to be a proclamation by President Lincoln, recommending a Fast Day and calling upon the city to provide 400,000 men for the Northern armies. A huge crowd swarmed for more than an hour about the office of the *Journal of Commerce* in Wall street, demanding that the proclamation be rescinded, while every available policeman was rushed into the district and the garrison at Governor's Island stood to arms. The mob was only quieted when extra editions of other newspapers appeared with information from Washington that the proclamation was a hoax. Both the *World* and the *Journal of Commerce* were temporarily suppressed by the government, and the *Associated Press* offered a reward of $1,000 for the conviction of the author of the bogus document. Detectives learned that it had been written by Joe Howard, Jr., who was immediately arrested and sent under strong military guard to Fort Lafayette.

Burning of Barnum's Museum

A few months later the city was again thrown into terror by the famous Black Bag conspiracy. Fire was discovered at 8:43 o'clock on the evening of November 25, 1864, in a bedroom of the St. James Hotel in Broadway, and a few minutes later Barnum's

Museum was found to be in flames. Then in rapid succession fires were started in the St. Nicholas, United States, New England and Metropolitan Hotels, and in the La Farge House and Lovejoy's, among the most prominent hostelries in the metropolis. At midnight several gangs appeared along the Hudson River water front and attempted to set fire to the shipping tied up at the docks, and between that hour and dawn fires were discovered in the Belmont, Fifth avenue, Howard and Hanford Hotels, and in the Astor House and Tammany Hall, as well as in several lumber yards and more than a score of factories and important stores in various parts of the city. Fortunately the Fire Department, assisted by the police and great numbers of citizens, was able to extinguish all of the fires in time to prevent a general conflagration. Bags of black canvas were discovered in the hotel rooms, and when examined at Police Headquarters were found to contain a quantity of paper, a pound and a half of rosin, a bottle of turpentine and bottles containing phosphorous in water. The incendiaries started the fires by piling the bedding in the center of the room, saturating it with turpentine, and applying a match, after which they locked the door. The hotel keepers offered a reward of $20,000 for the apprehension of the criminals, but none was caught.

Another attempt to burn Barnum's Museum was made early in 1865, but it was not until July of that year that it was finally destroyed, together with almost the entire block bounded by Fulton, Ann and Nassau streets and Broadway, with a total loss of about $2,000,000. The fire started in the upper stories of the Museum and spread downward, gradually igniting the neighboring buildings. During the conflagration the entire police force was kept busy fighting the crowds of gangsters and other thieves who flocked to the scene and attempted to loot nearby business houses as they had done during the great fire of 1835. Several stores were broken into and robbed despite the vigilance of the police, among them Knox's Hat Store, the hats being offered for sale by the thieves within sight of the shop from which they had been stolen.

WHEN NEW YORK WAS REALLY WICKED

I

AT THE close of the Civil War, while the statesmen of Tammany Hall dipped greedy fingers into the city's money chests, New York entered upon an unparalleled era of wickedness; so demoralized were the police by political chicanery and by widespread corruption within their own ranks that they were unable to enforce even a semblance of respect for the law. For more than twenty-five years the criminal classes revelled in an orgy of vice and crime; and the metropolis, then comprising only Manhattan Island, richly deserved the title of "the modern Gomorrah," which is said to have been first applied by the Rev. T. DeWitt Talmage in a sermon in the Brooklyn Tabernacle during the middle seventies. Both the Rev. Talmage and the Rev. Henry Ward Beecher, pastor of Plymouth

CULVER PICTURES

"STOP THIEF!"—A SKETCH OF LIFE IN NEW YORK CITY.

"Stop Thief"—A Sketch of Life in New York City. October 31, 1868

Church in Brooklyn, made frequent pilgrimages to Manhattan and visited the shrines of wickedness under escort of Central Office detectives, acquiring sermon material which they employed in the point-with-horror manner still used so effectively by modern clergymen.

Before the War the dives, dance halls, and houses of ill-fame were largely confined to the Five Points, the Bowery and Water, Cherry and other streets along the East River water front in the old Fourth Ward. But scarcely had the South laid down its arms at Appomattox than hundreds of bagnios, with red lanterns gleaming from the windows or dangling from beams on the porches, appeared throughout the city. They operated without molestation so long as the owners paid the assessments imposed by their political overlords, and even advertised with great boldness in the newspapers and by printed circular. The most celebrated single group of these places was the Sisters' Row in West Twenty-fifth street, near Seventh avenue, where seven adjoining houses were opened in the sixties by seven sisters who had come to New York from a small New England village to seek their fortunes, and had

The Rev. T. DeWitt Talmage in Satan's Circus

fallen into ways of sin. These were the most expensive bordellos in the city, and were conducted with great style and ceremony. On certain days of the month no gentleman was admitted unless he wore evening dress and carried a bouquet of flowers, and the inmates were advertised as cultured and pleasing companions, accomplished on the piano and guitar and familiar with the charms and graces of correct social intercourse. The proceeds of Christmas Eve were always given to charity. Another noted resort was Josephine Woods', in Eighth street near Broadway, where a grand blind man's buff party was held every New Year's Eve, and open house was kept throughout New Year's Day in imitation of the prevailing custom in more refined society.

In a speech at Cooper Union in January, 1866, Bishop Simpson of the Methodist Episcopal Church made the startling and discouraging announcement that prostitutes were as numerous in New York as Methodists, and later, in a sermon in St. Paul's M. E. Church, fixed the number at twenty thousand, approximately one-fortieth of the population. John A. Kennedy, Superintendent of Police, vigorously denied the truth of the Bishop's statements, and said that although he had no figures on the Methodists, who had not come under his jurisdiction, the records of the police force showed that there were but 3,300 public prostitutes in the city, distributed among 621 houses and ninety-nine assignation hotels, and including 747 waiter girls employed in concert saloons and dance halls. However, Bishop Simpson and other reformers produced considerable proof, and it is quite likely that his figures more nearly approached the truth than those of the Superintendent, for the latter dealt only with the professional aspects of the problem, and, moreover, did not include the thousands of street women who swarmed the thoroughfares of the city. Originally women of this class were known as night-walkers, for they were seldom seen on the streets before dusk, but as they became bolder they were called street-walkers.

Many of the worst of the dives with which New York was infested during these days of iniquity, and which were utilized as rendezvous by the gangs of criminals and the hordes of fallen women, were in the area between Twenty-fourth and Fortieth streets and Fifth and Seventh avenues, a region of such utter depravity that horrified reformers referred to it as Satan's Circus. As late as 1885 it was estimated that at least half of the buildings in the district were devoted to some form of wickedness, while Sixth avenue, then the wildest and gayest thoroughfare in the city, was lined with brothels, saloons and all-night dance halls, and was constantly thronged by a motley crowd seeking diversion and dissipation. This area was a part of the old Twenty-ninth police precinct, which ran from Fourteenth to Forty-second streets and from Fourth to Seventh avenues, and was the original Tenderloin, so named by Captain, later Inspector, Alexander S. Williams. After long and unrewarded toil in outlying districts, Captain Williams was transferred to the command of the Twenty-ninth in 1876. A few days later a friend, meeting him on Broadway and noting his expansive smile, asked the cause of his merriment.

"Well," said Williams, "I've been transferred. I've had nothing but chuck steak for a long time, and now I'm going to get a little of the tenderloin."

CULVER PICTURES

A Street Arrest.—[Drawn by C. Kendrick.] May 18, 1878

Perhaps the most famous of the dives which came under Williams' jurisdiction was the old Haymarket, in Sixth avenue just south of Thirtieth street. Because of its long life—it survived several closings and was in active operation until late in 1913—the Haymarket became widely known throughout the United States, and was a favorite place for the plucking of yokels who ventured into the metropolis to see the sights of the great city. The house was opened as a variety theater soon after the Civil War, and was named after a similar playhouse in London. But it was unable to compete with such celebrated theaters as the Tivoli in Eighth street and Tony Pastor's in Fourteenth street, and was closed about the first of December, 1878. However, within a few weeks it was remodeled and reopened as a dance hall, which it remained to the end of its days.

The Haymarket was housed in a three-story brick and frame building, which by day was dismal and repulsive, for it was painted a dull and sulphurous yellow and showed no signs of life. But with the coming of dusk, as the performers in Satan's Circus assembled for their nightly promenade of Sixth avenue, the shutters were removed and lights blazed from every window, while from huge iron hooks before the main entrance hung a sign, "Haymarket—Grand Soiree Dansant." Women were admitted free, but men paid twenty-five cents each for the privilege of dancing, drinking and otherwise disporting themselves within the resort. The galleries and boxes which had extended around three sides of the main floor when the house was a theater were retained, and off them were built small cubicles in which, at the height of the Haymarket's glory, women habitues danced the cancan and gave exhibitions similar to the French peep shows. The descriptive title of "circus," which is now generally applied to such displays in this country, is said to have originated in the Haymarket. The dictionary defines the cancan as "a rollicking French dance, accompanied by indecorous or extravagant gestures," but it appears to have been much more than rollicking as performed in the old Haymarket, especially during the early morning hours when the place was hazy with smoke and the tables and floors filled with drunken revellers, among whom lush workers and pickpockets plied nimble fingers. In more recent years the cancan has given way to the hoochy-coochy and other forms of muscle dancing, which first became popular with the appearance of the original Little Egypt at the Chicago World's Fair.

The French Madame's, in Thirty-first street near Sixth avenue, took its name from the nationality of its proprietor, an obese, bewhiskered female who sat throughout the night on a high stool near the cashier's cage. She acted as her own bouncer, and acquired great renown for the manner in which she wielded a bludgeon, and for the quickness with which she seized obstreperous women customers by the hair and flung them into the street. While the resort was ostensibly a restaurant, practically no food except black coffee was sold, although a big business was done in wines and liquors. The place was much frequented by the street women, who readily accepted offers to dance the cancan, which was performed in small chambers above the dining-room. For a dollar they danced nude, and for an additional small fee gave exhibitions similar to those provided in the booths of the Haymarket. Resorts similar to the French Madame's, except that they had small dance floors, were the Idlewile in Sixth avenue near Thirty-first street, and the Strand, a few doors south, which was operated by Dan Kerrigan, a member of the Tammany Hall General Committee during the late seventies. The Rev. T. DeWitt Talmage spent an evening in each of these places in 1878, and raised such a furore with his sermons that the police, upon orders from Mayor Cooper, closed them to women for a period of several months.

Other famous dives of the Satan's Circus district were the Cremorne, in Thirty-second street west of Sixth avenue; Egyptian Hall in Thirty-fourth street, east of Sixth avenue; Sailors' Hall in Thirtieth street, which was frequented principally by Negroes; Buckingham Palace in Twenty-seventh street, noted for its masked balls; Tom Gould's in Thirty-first street, a drinking dive with rooms for rent upstairs, and the Star and Garter, an establishment of a slightly higher class which was opened at Sixth avenue and Thirtieth street in 1878 by Ed Coffee, a famous sportsman of the period. The Star and Garter enjoyed an immediate success, largely because of the popularity of the head bartender, Billy Patterson, a rotund and jovial genius who was one of the really great drink mixers of the age. It was his boast that he did not have an enemy in the world, and that he could concoct a drink which would make any man his abject admirer; it was considered a great honor to have Billy Patterson, in person, prepare a beverage. When he was finally struck down by a mysterious assailant who attacked him with a slung-shot one night as he left the side door of the Star and Garter, the circumstance caused so much comment throughout Satan's Circus that it gave rise to the famous query, "Who struck Billy Patterson?"

The Haymarket in 1879

The Cremorne occupied the basement of a building in Thirty-second street just west of Sixth avenue, and was regarded by the police as one of the most abandoned dives of the period. The origin of its name is unknown, but it is likely that, in common with many other resorts of the district, it was named for a London dance-hall or bar-room. The street entrance led directly to the bar, at the end of which, behind a large and handsomely carved desk, sat the manager, a huge, pompous, unapproachable personage whose great walrus mustaches and luxuriant beard gave him the sobriquet of Don Whiskerandos. Beyond the manager swinging doors opened into a large room, garishly decorated with paintings and statues noted more for nudity than artistic merit, where men and women sat together at tables and drank to the accompaniment of music from a squeaky violin, a booming bull fiddle and a rattling piano. The women here, as in most of the other resorts, received a commission on all drinks; small brass checks were given them for mixed beverages and straight liquors, and when wine was bought by their friends they saved the corks. Drinks for ladies were twenty cents, but gentlemen paid the standard price of fifteen cents or two for a quarter. Next door to the Cremorne was another establishment which bore the same name, but it was a mission conducted by Jerry McAuley, a reformed gambler and drunkard whose name has been immortalized by the present McAuley Mission in Water street, where religion and sandwiches are now available nightly for the bums of the water front. Befuddled customers of the dive frequently wandered into McAuley's Cremorne by mistake, whereupon he promptly locked the doors and preached to the roisterers before he would permit them to resume their round of dissipation.

2

A new type of resort, the concert saloon, appeared in New York in 1860, when a Philadelphian opened the Melodeon in the old Chinese Assembly Rooms in lower Broadway. These places soon became very popular, and within a few years there were at least two hundred of them scattered throughout the lower part of the city. They provided dancing and liquor, but the principal attractions were the waiter girls and the low, and frequently lewd, theatrical performances, although some of the cheaper establishments, especially those along the Bowery, offered as entertainment only a piano virtuoso, who was always drunk and was called Professor.

The most celebrated of these resorts was that operated by Harry Hill in West Houston street east of Broadway. For many years Hill's place was rightly considered one of the sights of the metropolis, to which visiting clergymen repaired to gather material for sermons on the iniquities of Gotham. It occupied the whole of a sprawling, dingy, two-story frame house, which had two front entrances, a small door for ladies, who were admitted free, and a larger one for gentlemen, who paid twenty cents. Before the main doorway a huge red and blue lantern shed its rays against a gigantic sign-board which leaned against the side of the house, and upon which were lettered half a dozen lines of doggerel, composed by Hill and inviting the wayfarer to partake of

Punches and juleps, cobblers and smashes,
To make the tongue waggle with wit's merry flashes.

Harry Hill prided himself on his religious habits, and went to
church regularly every Sunday, and to prayer meeting on Wednesday
night; and frequently donated large sums to charity, as evidence
of his willingness to co-operate in good works. He was an inveter-
ate poet, and once a week mounted the stage and gave a recital of
his output, while the other activities of the resort ceased, not even
drinks being served until the master had finished. It is distressing
to note that on this night the attendance was generally very slim.
The rules of the house were written in rhyme, and were prominently displayed upon the walls. "The pith of these rules is," says
a contemporary writer, "no loud talking; no profanity; no obscene
or indecent expressions will be allowed; no one drunken, no one
violating decency, will be permitted to remain in the room; no
man can sit and allow a woman to stand; all men must call for
refreshments as soon as they arrive, and the call must be repeated after each dance; if a man does not dance he must leave. Mr.
Hill himself is a man about fifty years of age, small, stocky and
muscular, a complete type of the pugilist. He keeps the peace of
his own concern, and does not hesitate to knock any man down,
or throw him out of the door, if he breaks the rules of the establishment. He attends closely to all departments of the trade. He
is at the bar; in the hall, where the dancers must be kept on the
floor; at the stage, where the low comedies and broad farces are
played. He keeps the roughs and bullies in order; he keeps jealous
women from tearing out each other's eyes. With burly face and
stocky form, he can be seen in all parts of the hall, shouting out,
'Order! Order! Less noise there! Attention! Girls, be quiet!' And
these he shouts all evening."

The dance hall proper had originally been a series of small
rooms, which had been made into one by the removal of parti-
tions. There was no regular bar on the main floor, but on one side
of the long hall was a counter over which drinks were served, and
from which they were distributed by the waiter girls after they had
been brought up from the basement, where the more disreputable

of Hill's customers spent their evenings in sorry debauch. On the other side of the room was the stage, with a tall box for the Punch and Judy show which was then a popular form of entertainment. Hill's place was a favorite resort of pugilists, and he frequently varied his theatrical entertainment with a prize fight. It was there that John L. Sullivan made his first New York appearance on March 31, 1881, when he defeated Steve Taylor in two and one-half minutes.

Harry Hill competed, on more or less even terms, with such celebrated downtown hells as the American Mabille at Bleecker street and Broadway, the Black and Tan in the basement of No. 153 Bleecker street, and Billy McGlory's Armory Hall at No. 158 Hester street. The American Mabille, which was named for the Jardin de Mabille in Paris, was owned by Theodore Allen, better known as The Allen, member of a family which was originally devoutly Methodist but later notoriously criminal. Three of his brothers, Wesley, Martin, and William, were professional burglars, while a fourth, John, ran a gambling house. The Allen is said to have owned more than half a dozen resorts, and financed gambling houses and places of ill-fame. He was also a friend and patron of the gang leaders, and planned and participated in a large number of bank and store burglaries. He finally killed a gambler and disappeared from the scene. His resort occupied the basement and first floor of the Bleecker street house, with a dance hall in the basement and the concert saloon upstairs, where dissolute women in gaudy tights danced and sang ribald songs.

The Black and Tan was operated by Frank Stephenson, a tall, slim man with a curiously bloodless face. Contemporary writers marked his resemblance to a corpse; his face was almost as white as snow and his cheeks were sunken, while his eyebrows and hair were black as ink. His eyes were deep set, and very keen and piercing. It was his custom to sit bolt upright in a high chair in the center of his resort, and remain there for hours without displaying any other sign of life than the baleful glitter of his eyes. His establishment was largely frequented by Negroes, but the women were all white and appear to have been quite abandoned. Four bartenders served drinks over a long counter, and behind each was a

A Night-Scene at Harry Hill's Concert Saloon

long dirk and a bludgeon which were frequently used to silence fractious customers. The closing hours of the Black and Tan, as of the other principal resorts, were enlivened by the cancan and licentious displays. For many years one of the regular frequenters of the Black and Tan was an old woman known as Crazy Lou, who was said to have been a daughter of a wealthy Boston merchant. At the age of seventeen she was seduced, and coming to New York to seek the author of her shame, fell into the hands of procurers, who sold her to one of the Seven Sisters in West Twenty-fifth street. When her beauty faded she was dismissed, and thereafter became a frequenter of the Haymarket, the Cremorne, Harry Hill's, Billy McGlory's and finally the Black and Tan. In her old age she lived on scrapings from garbage pails, and the few pennies she could beg or earn by selling flowers. But each evening she went regularly to the Black and Tan, arriving promptly at midnight and remaining for exactly two hours. She wore a faded, ragged shawl, and always sat at a certain table in a corner, where Stephenson in person served her with a huge tumbler of whiskey which cost her nothing. This she sipped until the time came for her to leave. But one night she failed to appear, and the next morning her body was found floating in the East River. Stephenson expressed his sorrow by setting a glass of whiskey on her accustomed table each night at midnight for a month, permitting no one to sit there until two o'clock in the morning.

All of these dives were havens of grace compared to Billy McGlory's Armory Hall at No. 158 Hester street, for McGlory's was probably the most vicious resort New York has ever seen. McGlory was born in a Five Points tenement before that district had been regenerated by the Five Points Mission and the House of Industry, and was reared in an atmosphere of vice and crime. In his youth he fought with and captained such famous gangs as the Forty Thieves and the Chichesters, but in the late seventies removed to Hester street, where he opened his dance hall and drinking den in the midst of a squalid tenement district which fairly swarmed with criminals and harlots. Armory Hall became the favorite haunt of the gangsters of the Fourth and Sixth Wards and the Bowery, and of the thieves, pickpockets, procurers and knockout drop artists who flourished throughout the city. Scarcely a night passed that the resort was not the scene of half a dozen gory fights; and it was not unusual to see a drugged and drunken reveller, his pockets turned inside out by the harpies who had fawned upon him but a few minutes before, dragged from a table by one of McGlory's capable bouncers and lugged into the street, where his pockets were searched anew by the lush workers. Frequently the latter stripped the victim of his clothing and left him naked in the gutter. The thugs who kept the peace of McGlory's were all graduates of the Five Points and water front gangs, and included some of the most expert rough-and-tumble fighters of the period; throughout the night they strode menacingly about the dive, armed with pistols, knives, brass knuckles, and bludgeons which they delighted to use.

McGlory's place was entered from the street through a dingy double doorway, which led into a long, narrow passageway with walls painted a dead black, unrelieved by a gas light or splash of color. Fifty feet down the passage was the bar-room, and beyond that the dance hall with chairs and tables for some seven hundred persons. A balcony ran around two sides of the hall, with small boxes partitioned off by heavy curtains and reserved for the best customers, generally parties of out-of-town men who appeared to be willing to spend considerable money. In these boxes were given exhibitions even more degraded than at the Haymarket. Drinks were served by waiter girls, but as an added attraction McGlory also employed half a dozen male degenerates who wore feminine clothing and circulated through the crowd, singing and dancing. Music was provided by a piano, a cornet and a violin. A night in McGlory's was thus described by a writer for the *Cincinnati Enquirer*, who went slumming, or as it was then called, elephant hunting, among the dives of New York in the early eighties:

> There are five hundred men in the immense hall. There are a hundred females—it would be mockery to call them women. The first we hear of them is when half a dozen invade our box, plump themselves on our laps and begin to beg that we put quarters in their stockings for luck. There are some shapely limbs generously and immodestly

shown in connection with this invitation. One young woman startles the crowd by announcing that she will dance the cancan for half a dollar. The music starts up just then, and she determines to do the cancan and risk the collection afterward. She seizes her skirts between her limbs with one hand, kicks away a chair or two, and is soon throwing her feet in the air in a way that endangers every hat in the box. The men about the hall are all craning their necks to get a sight of what is going on in the box, as they hear the cries of 'Hoop-la!' from the girls there.

Some of my companions have been drawn into one of the little boxes adjoining ours. They come back now to tell of what depravity was exhibited to them for a fee. . . . It is getting late. Across the balcony a girl is hugging her fellow in a maudlin and hysterical manner. Another girl is hanging with her arms around the neck of one of the creatures I described some time ago. His companion joins him—a moon-faced fellow—and they come around to our box and ogle us. They talk in simpering, dudish tones, and bestow the most lackadaisical glances on different members of our party. . . . Billy McGlory himself is at the bar, to the left of the entrance, and we go and take a look at him. He is a typical New York saloon keeper—nothing more, nothing less. A medium sized man, he is neither fleshy nor spare; he has black hair and mustache, and a piercing black eye. He shakes hands around as if we were obedient subjects come to pay homage to a king. . . . I have not told the half, no, nor the tenth, of what we saw at his place. It cannot be told. . . . There is beastliness and depravity under his roof compared with which no chapter in the world's history is equal.

Many of the most depraved of the downtown dives were in the vicinity of Police Headquarters at No. 300 Mulberry street. Half a block from Headquarters was a gambling house which catered only to policemen, and at No. 100 Mott street, a short distance away, was a saloon kept by Mike Kerrigan, better known as Johnny Dobbs, who served an apprenticeship with the river pirates of the Fourth Ward and then became a celebrated bank robber and fence. Dobbs is said to have handled more than $2,000,000 in stolen money, of which probably one-third went to him as his

Satan's Circus—Sixth Avenue at 3 A.M.

share of various adventures. But he ran through it, and eventually, in the middle nineties, was found unconscious in the gutter, and died in the alcoholic ward of Bellevue Hospital a few days later. It was Johnny Dobbs who, when asked why the crooks flocked to the neighborhood of Police Headquarters, replied, "The nearer the church the closer to God."

Tom Bray operated a similar resort at No. 22 Thompson street, but he was a more intelligent man than Dobbs, and banked his money, so that when he died he left an estate of more than $200,000. The House of Lords and the Bunch of Grapes, neighboring dives at Houston and Crosby streets, were much frequented by English thieves and confidence men. Among them were such famous crooks as Chelsea George, Gentleman Joe, Cockney Ward and London Izzy Lazarus, who was killed by Barney Friery in a dispute over the division of a plug hat full of jewelry, which London Izzy had stolen from a jewelry store after smashing the show window with a brick. The St. Bernard Hotel at Prince and Mercer streets was one of The Allen's resorts, and along Broadway from Chambers to Houston streets were at least fifty basement drinking dens, of which the Dew Drop Inn was the most famous. At Broadway and Houston street, near Harry Hill's concert saloon, was Patsy Egan's dive, where Reddy the Blacksmith, a celebrated Bowery Boy, killed Wild Jimmy Hagerty, a Philadelphia gangster who had tried to make Reddy the Blacksmith stand on his head. Reddy was a brother to Mary Varley, a notorious shoplifter, confidence woman and fence, who kept a house in James street.

Peter Mitchell amassed more than $350,000 in two years, from the profits of a saloon and assignation house at Wooster and Prince streets, but hanged himself to a whiskey tap before he could spend his fortune. He is said to have become religious in his middle age, and thereafter was afflicted with remorse over the way he had acquired his fortune. Johnny Camphine kept one of the most notorious dives in the city at Mercer and Houston streets, and in lieu of whiskey commonly sold colored camphine, or rectified oil of turpentine, which had its legitimate uses as a solvent for varnishes and as a fuel for lamps. It has been said that at least a hundred men were driven insane by drinking Johnny Camphine's beverage, and over a long period an average of two men a night were taken out of the place, howling with delirium tremens. Within a few doors of Johnny Camphine's place was a resort owned by a thief and gang leader called Big Nose Bunker, who was accounted one of the great brawlers and rough-and-tumble fighters of his time. But at last he became embroiled in a fight with a water front gangster who chopped off four of his fingers and stabbed him six times in the stomach. Big Nose carried his fingers to the police station in a paper bag and asked that a surgeon be sent for to sew them on, but before an ambulance could arrive he collapsed and died. There was great sorrow throughout the underworld.

The reputation of the Bowery and the Five Points did not suffer from the fame of the resorts around Headquarters and in Satan's Circus along Sixth avenue. Owney Geogheghan operated his celebrated dive at No. 105 Bowery, and next door at No. 103 was the Windsor Palace, owned by an Englishman and named in honor of the residence of Their Britannic Majesties. Both of these places were hells of exceptional fragrance, wherein raw whiskey was sold for ten cents a drink and crowds of lush workers, pickpockets and blackjack artists waited for a visitor to fall unconscious so they could rob him. Murders were frequent in both Geogheghan's and the Palace. Gunther's Pavillion was another celebrated Bowery dive, and Bismarck Hall, at Pearl and Chatham streets, was noted for its annex, a series of cave-like rooms under the sidewalk, which were used for immoral purposes. The Hall acquired further renown when the Grand Duke Alexis of Russia visited it in the seventies and recognized one of the waiter girls as a Russian countess who had fallen into misfortune. The legend goes that he bought her freedom from the owner of the dive, to whom she had bound herself for a term of years, and took her back to Russia. Accounts of the incident do not divulge her name. Bismarck Hall and the House of Commons, nearby, were also the haunts of a Bowery character called Ludwig the Bloodsucker, who quaffed human blood as if it were wine. Ludwig was a very squat, swarthy German, with an enormous head crowned with a shock of bristly black hair. Huge bunches of hair grew out of his ears, and his unusual appearance was accentuated by another tuft which sprouted from the end of his nose.

Milligan's Hell was at No. 115 Broome street, and on Center street, near the Tombs, Boiled Oysters Malloy ran a basement resort called the Ruins, where three drinks of terrible whiskey were sold for a dime. Mush Riley added to the fame of the district with a dive only a few doors away. Riley acquired his nickname because of a fondness for corn meal mush dipped in hot brandy. He once gave an elaborate dinner to Dan Noble, Mike Byrnes, Dutch Heinrichs and other famous criminals, and served a Newfoundland dog as the *pièce de résistance*, a fact unknown to his guests until they had eaten heartily and praised the unusual flavor of the roast. Noble was chief of a gang of bank robbers and burglars, and to insure the success of his operations cannily obtained places for twenty of his men on the police force. They stood guard for their fellow criminals, and received shares out of the common funds. Noble finally reformed and invested his money in apartment houses.

3

THE dives which flourished around Police Headquarters and along the Bowery were favorite resorts of the pickpockets, sneaks, panel thieves, badger game experts, lush workers, and knock-out-drop artists who operated in great numbers throughout the city. They also offered excellent business opportunities to the gangs of banco, confidence, and green goods men, for this was the period when countrymen actually bought gold bricks and counterfeit money, and were easy prey for the accomplished city slickers. The gold brick game, perhaps the most celebrated of all swindles, is supposed to have been invented by Reed Waddell, who was born in Springfield, Illinois, a few years before the Civil War. Waddell was a member of a prosperous and highly respectable family, but the gambling fever was in his veins, and even in his boyhood he acquired considerable local fame because of his willingness to

Owney Geoghegan's and the Windsor Palace

take chances and the recklessness with which he played for high stakes. His family soon cast him off, and in 1880, when he was but twenty-one, he appeared in New York with the first gold brick ever offered for sale. Waddell's brick was of lead, but he had it triple gold-plated wth a rough finish, and in the center sunk a slug of solid gold. It was marked in the manner of a regulation brick from the United States Assayer's office, with the letters "U.S." at one end and below them the name of the assayer. Underneath the name appeared the weight and fineness of the supposed chunk of bullion. When Waddell caught a sucker he was taken to an accomplice who posed as an assayer, with an office and all necessary equipment to delude the victim. This man tested the brick, and if the prospect was still dubious Waddell impulsively dug out the slug of real gold and suggested that the dupe himself take it to a jeweller. The latter's test, of course, showed the slug to be actually of precious metal, and in ninety-nine cases out of a hundred the sale was completed. Waddell sold his first brick for four thousand dollars, and thereafter never sold one for less than three thousand five hundred dollars. Sometimes he obtained twice that amount. In ten years he is said to have made more than $250,000 by the sale of gold bricks and green goods, for he branched out into the latter scheme after a few years of concentrated effort on the bricks. The green goods swindle, which was also called the sawdust game, first made its appearance in New York in 1869. It required two operators, who simply sold the victim a package of genuine money and then exchanged it for a bundle of worthless sheets of green or brown paper, or, if the currency was packed in a satchel, for another bag filled with sawdust. The green goods man first obtained the names of people who were regular subscribers to lotteries and various gift book concerns, and agents were sent over the country to look up the most promising. In due time those chosen for the sacrifice received one of several circular letters which were in general use, of which the following was the most popular:

Dear Sir: I will confide to you through this circular a secret by which you can make a speedy fortune. I have on hand a large amount of counterfeit notes of the following denominations: $1, $2, $5, $10 and $20. I guarantee every note to be perfect, as it is examined carefully by me as soon as finished, and if not strictly perfect is immediately destroyed. Of course it would be perfectly foolish to send out poor work, and it would not only get my customers into trouble, but would break up my business and ruin me. So, for personal safety, I am compelled to issue nothing that will not compare with the genuine. I furnish you with my goods at the following low price, which will be found as reasonable as the nature of my business will allow:

> For $1,200 in my goods (assorted) I charge $100
> For $2,500 in my goods (assorted) I charge 200
> For $5,000 in my goods (assorted) I charge 350
> For $10,000 in my goods (assorted) I charge 600

These circulars, as well as follow-up letters and other literature, were sent boldly through the mails. Some of the green goods swindlers prepared elaborate booklets, illustrated with photographs of bank notes, which the prospective victim was told were counterfeit.

In time Reed Waddell extended his operations to Europe, and was killed in Paris in March, 1895, during a dispute over the division of earnings with Tom O'Brien, a banco man whose only peers were Joseph Lewis, better known as Hungry Joe, and Charles P. Miller, who was called King of the Banco Men. Miller began his career as capper for a New Orleans gambling house, but came to New York when he had saved thirty-five thousand dollars, and opened a small house of chance which was notorious as a skinning dive. Within a few years he was chief of a gang of banco and green goods men who worked principally in the Astor House and the Fifth Avenue Hotel. Miller's headquarters were a lamp-post on the southwest corner of Broadway and Twenty-eighth street, against which he could generally be found leaning. In later years the term banco was confused by hurried writers with Buncombe or bunkum, and so degenerated into bunco, and was applied indiscriminately to every type of swindler; but originally it referred only to the operator of banco, an adaptation of the old English gambling pastime of eight dice cloth. Banco was introduced into the United States by a noted sharper who played it with great success in the western gold fields, and brought it into New York about 1860, after he had been driven out of San Francisco by the Vigilantes. Sometimes it was also called lottery. A variation of it was recently introduced in Chicago, but it has been unheard of in New York for many years.

The game was played either with dice or cards. If the former, a layout of fourteen spaces was used, but if the latter the layout contained forty-three spaces. Of these forty-two were numbered, thirteen contained stars also, and one was blank. Twenty-nine of the numbers represented prizes ranging from two dollars, to five thousand dollars, depending upon the size of the bank. The cards were numbered from one to six, and eight were dealt to each player. The numbers were then counted, the total representing the number of the prize drawn on the layout. If the victim drew a star number, which had no prize, he was allowed to draw again on putting up a specified sum of money. He was usually permitted to win at first, and eventually the bank owed him from one hundred dollars to five thousand dollars. He was then dealt a hand which totaled twenty-seven, the number of the conditional prize, the condition being that he stake a sum equal to the amount owed him and draw again. Then, of course, he drew a blank or star number and lost all he had put up. The banco steerer, who performed an office similar to that of capper for a gambling house, lost also, and it was his duty to cause such an uproar that the woes of the victim were overwhelmed. The swindle sounds a bit silly to our modern ears, but it was much in vogue for years throughout the United States and many of the banco men amassed fortunes. Hungry Joe, Tom O'Brien and Miller specialized in bankers, wealthy merchants, and other people of prominence, for not only did they have more money to lose, but were less apt to complain to the police. Hungry Joe scraped acquaintance with Oscar Wilde when the English author visited the United States on a lecture tour, and after dining with him several times at the Hotel Brunswick, inveigled him into a banco game. Wilde lost five thousand dollars, and gave Hungry Joe a check on the Park National

Bank, but stopped payment when he learned that he had been swindled. Hungry Joe's own boastful account of the affair, however, was that he took one thousand five hundred dollars in cash from the writer.

The late sixties also saw the beginning of the reprehensible practice of using knock-out drops to deaden the senses of a victim while the thieves picked his pockets or appropriated his jewelry. Laudanum had occasionally been employed by the crimps of the old Fourth Ward water front to drug a sailor so he could be shanghaied without too much protest, but no effective use of drugs for the sole purpose of robbery was made in New York until a California crook, Peter Sawyer, appeared in 1866, and aroused such a furore in police and criminal circles that the former honored him by calling the practitioners of his art peter players. At first Sawyer used nothing more deleterious than snuff, which he dropped into his victim's beer or whiskey, but later he and other peter players came to depend principally on hydrate of chloral. Occasionally they used morphine. Since Prohibition bootleg liquor has generally been found to be sufficiently efficacious.

The medicinal dose of hydrate of chloral is from fifteen to twenty grains, but from thirty to forty grains were used for knock-out purposes. The drug was compounded in the proportion of one grain to a drop, and a teaspoonful was commonly employed to dose a glass of beer. The action of the drug is to decrease the action of the heart, and an overdose is apt to cause paralysis of the heart and lungs. Few men can stand a larger dose than thirty grains, but occasionally the old time peter players were compelled to give up to sixty grains to a victim who had been drinking heavily.

The practice of using knock-out drops became so popular that large gangs of both men and women thieves were formed, and employed no other method to prepare a victim for robbery. They generally worked in pairs, and while one distracted the attention of the dupe the other dropped the poison into his beverage. For many years the police seldom arrested a street walker who did not have chloral or morphine in her purse or secreted in the lining of her muff. The largest and most successful of the knock-out gangs maintained a headquarters in a dive in Worth street near Chatham Square, at the southern end of the Bowery, employing street boys to trail well-dressed men who ventured into the territory and notify members of the gang when the visitors appeared to be ready for the final touches. More than a score of men amassed fortunes from the sale of small vials of chloral at two dollars each, but eventually the bulk of the business fell into the hands of Diamond Charley, a notorious Bowery character whose shirt front blazed with precious stones in the manner of the later but respectable Diamond Jim Brady. Each evening at dusk Diamond Charley sent out a dozen salesmen carrying small satchels packed with vials of chloral, which they sold openly in the dives and on the street corners. They also offered a small morphine pill which could be hidden under a finger ring, but it would not dissolve readily and was never in great demand. Soon after he had obtained a monopoly Diamond Charley increased the price of chloral to five dollars and then to ten dollars a vial, to the great indignation of the users of the drops, for the cost of manufacturing a dose was not more than six cents. Thereafter many of the thieves compounded their own mixtures, and in their eagerness for quick action added other poisons to the chloral, frequently with fatal consequences which worried no one except the police and the victim's relatives.

Knock-out drops were also used with great success by the cadets and procurers, who conducted their business with the utmost brazenness. Many of the former were organized into associations, and maintained club rooms, where they met for discussion of business problems; while the latter frequently operated from elaborate offices. Red Light Lizzie, perhaps the most famous procurer of her time, employed half a dozen men and women to travel through the small villages of New York and adjacent states, and lure young women into the metropolis with promises of employment; and several young men received salaries from her for enticing girls into dives and plying them with drugged liquor. Red Light Lizzie herself owned half a dozen houses of ill-fame, but she supplied other places as well, and each month sent a circular letter to her clients. Her principal rival was Hester Jane

Haskins, also called Jane the Grabber, who became notorious as an abductor of young girls for immoral purposes. She came at length to specialize in young women of good families, and the disappearance of so many aroused such a commotion that in the middle seventies Jane the Grabber was arrested by Captain Charles McDonnell and sent to prison.

The procurers also obtained many recruits from the flower and news girls who were about the streets in great numbers. Many of these, some no more than children, were prostitutes on their own account, and there were half a dozen places of assignation which catered solely to them. The owner of one such establishment advertised that her place was frequented by flower girls under sixteen years of age; another kept nine small girls, ranging in age from nine to fifteen, in the back room of an oyster saloon near the corner of Chatham street, now Park Row, and William street. It was the custom of these girls to approach a man in the street, and instead of asking him to purchase flowers or newspapers, hail him with "Give me a penny, mister?" For several years this was the common salutation of the street girls, and the manner in which the more dissolute of the flower and news vendors made known their calling.

Many of the girls were also members of the panel and badger game gangs which abounded throughout the vice area. These methods of thievery were brought to great perfection by the gang captained by Shang Draper, who kept a saloon in Sixth avenue between Twenty-ninth and Thirteenth streets. Draper is said to have employed thirty women on salary to entice drunken men into a house in the vicinity of Prince and Wooster streets, where they were victimized by the badger game or robbed by thieves who crept into the room through hidden panels cut into the wall, and stole the victim's valuables while his attention was distracted. Draper's gang was finally broken up by Captain John H. McCullagh, although he continued to operate his saloon until late in 1883, when Johnny Irving was killed in a pistol duel with Johnny Walsh, better known as Johnny the Mick, who was immediately shot to death by Irving's friend, Billy Porter. Irving and

Walsh were captains of rival gangs of sneak thieves and pick-pockets, and there had been bad blood between them for many years. Draper himself was also a famous bank robber, and was implicated in the celebrated robbery of the Manhattan Savings Institution, as well as many other crimes.

The Panel Game

CHAPTER X

THE KING OF THE BANK ROBBERS

1

PRACTICALLY EVERY burglar and bank robber of note in the United States made New York his principal headquarters during the twenty years which followed the Civil War, but the only one to whom the police were willing to award the palm of genius was George Leonidas Leslie, also known as George Howard and Western George. Leslie was the son of an Ohio brewer and a graduate of the University of Cincinnati, where he had specialized in architecture and won high honors. He could probably have amassed a fortune by the practice of his profession, but upon the death of his mother, soon after he had completed his work at college, he came to New York and fell in with bad company, and so became a criminal.

Within a few years after the close of the Civil War Leslie had become the head of the most successful gang of professional bank robbers that ever infested the continent. In the opinion of George W. Walling, who was Superintendent of Police from 1874 to 1885, Leslie and his followers were responsible for eighty per cent. of the bank thefts in America from the time of Leslie's first appearance in the East, about 1865, until he was murdered in 1884. Walling estimated the total stealings of the gang at from $7,000,000 to $12,000,000, with the former as a conservative minimum. Probably one-third of their loot was taken from financial institutions in the metropolis, including $786,879 from the Ocean National Bank at Greenwich and Fulton streets on June 27, 1869, and $2,747,000 from the Manhattan Savings Institution in Bleecker street at Broadway, on October 27, 1878. In the Ocean Bank robbery the thieves left almost $2,000,000 in cash and securities scattered upon the floor beside the vault. The gang also carried out the famous raids against the South Kensington National Bank of Philadelphia, the Third National Bank of Baltimore, the Saratoga County Bank of Waterford, N. Y., and the Wellsbro Bank of Philadelphia. It was largely the activity of Leslie and his associates, together with the frequent forays of sneak thieves, burglars and confidence men, that caused Inspector Thomas Byrnes to establish his famous Dead Line on March 12, 1880, when he opened a branch office of the Detective Bureau at No. 17 Wall street and ordered the arrest of every known criminal found in the area bounded by Fulton street on the north, Greenwich street on the west, the Battery on the south, and the East River.

But it was only to the police and the underworld that Leslie was known as a criminal genius. He posed as a man of independent means, and because of his education and family connections was accepted in good society in New York; he belonged to several excellent clubs and was known as a *bon vivant* and a man about town. He was a familiar figure at theater openings and art exhibitions, and acquired a considerable reputation as an amateur bibliophile; he possessed a fine group of first editions, and was frequently consulted by other collectors. He patronized the most exclusive tailors and haberdashers, and seldom associated with his fellow criminals, except in a business way, until the early eighties, when he became enamoured of Babe Irving, a sister to the Johnny Irving who was killed in Shang Draper's saloon by Johnny the Mick. He was also smitten by the charms of Shang Draper's mistress, and spent much time and money on both women.

The police found ample indications of Leslie's skill and leadership in more than a hundred robberies, but only once were they able to obtain evidence sufficient to warrant his arrest. That was in 1870, at the outset of his career, when he and Gilbert Yost undertook to rob a jewelry store in Norristown, near Philadelphia. They were captured while trying to enter the establishment, but Leslie had already made connections with Philadelphia politicians, and was promptly released on bail, which he forfeited. Yost was convicted and served two years in prison. The Norristown job was one of the few occasions when Leslie found it necessary to take an active part in the actual commission of a robbery. Ordinarily his work consisted in making the plans, making the preliminary surveys, handling the bribe and graft money and arranging with the fences for the disposal of the plunder.

It was Leslie's custom, whenever a bank had been selected as a pudding, to obtain, if possible, architects' plans of the building; if none were available he visited the institution in the guise of a depositor and drew plans of his own from observation. He then prepared a large scale drawing of the ground floor and the basement, carefully plotting all entrances and exits, the exact location of the safe or vault, and all pieces of furniture which might be stumbled over in the darkness, or which blocked the way to a door or window. Sometimes he was able to insinuate one of his gang into the bank as a watchman or porter, and valuable information was then obtained in great and exact detail. The type of strong box was noted, together with the name of the manufacturer, and from a clerk or other employee of convivial habit something could usually be learned of the routine of the institution.

Leslie possessed great mechanical skill, and was thoroughly familiar with every type of safe and bank vault manufactured in the United States, many of which he could open by manipulating the dial. Of the majority he owned stock models or small replicas in wood or metal, which were stored in a loft in the lower part of the city. There he sometimes spent a week experimenting on the model which corresponded to the safe or vault in the prospective pudding, until he had learned to throw the combination out of gear and bring the tumblers into line. This was generally accomplished by boring small holes above or below the dial, and worrying the tumblers with a thin piece of steel. When this knowledge has been acquired respecting a certain type of safe, Leslie summoned the men chosen for the enterprise, and in his work room carefully explained his drawings and allotted each man a definite task. Sometimes a room was fitted up to resemble the interior of the bank, and the robbers felt their way to the safe through the darkness and opened it while Leslie watched and criticised the performance.

Preparations of this character were made for the robbery of the Manhattan Savings Institution, but they miscarried through sheer carelessness, and the vault was finally forced with a remarkably fine kit of burglar tools which had been constructed especially for Leslie at a cost of more than three thousand dollars. Leslie began planning the Manhattan job late in 1875, three years before the crime was actually committed, when he selected as his principal assistants Jimmy Hope, Jimmy Brady, Abe Coakley, Red Leary, Shang Draper, Johnny Dobbs, Worcester Sam Perris, and Banjo Pete Emerson. After a careful survey of the vault Leslie decided against the use of dynamite or powder, for the shock of the explosion would shatter the plate glass windows of the bank, and the noise would certainly be heard by the janitor, Louis Werckle, who lived with his family in the basement, as well as by guests and employees of the St. Charles Hotel, next door.

Having learned the style of the combination lock to the Manhattan vault, Leslie procured another of the same make from the manufacturers, Valentine & Butler, and proceeded to experiment with it. He found that the combination could be thrown out of gear and the notches of the tumblers brought into line by boring a hole underneath the indicator, and then working the tumblers around with his thin piece of steel. In the course of the next few months Leslie obtained a job in the bank for Patrick Shevlin, an obscure member of the gang, and some six months later

Shevlin was able to admit him into the bank at night. Leslie bored a small hole in the safe and threw two of the tumblers in line, working behind a black screen which had been placed in front of the vault to hide it from the view of persons passing in the street. But it was very nerve-wracking work, and although Leslie puttied up the hole he had bored, he forgot to replace the tumblers in their original positions, so that next morning the bank employees could not open the vault. The manufacturers installed a new lock plate, and when Leslie returned to the bank to complete his experiments he found that he could no longer move the tumblers, although he learned later that he could have done so had he bored a new hole an eighth of an inch below his previous opening.

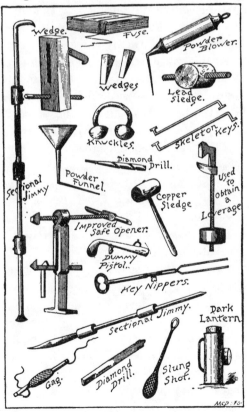

A Bank Burglar's Outfit

Leslie then decided to commit the robbery by force, but this was not attempted until the policeman on post, John Nugent, had been bribed to remain away from the bank until he should be needed to guard the retreat of the robbers and, if possible, delay pursuit. At six o'clock Sunday morning, October 27, 1878, Jimmy Hope, Abe Coakley, Banjo Pete Emerson, and Bill Kelly, a strong arm man who was taken along in case fighting became necessary, slipped into the bank, all wearing masks. They went directly to the apartment occupied by Werckle, and there bound and gagged the janitor, his wife, and his mother-in-law. Kelly remained to guard them, while the others repaired to the main offices of the bank and began operations on the vault, which they opened after three hours of hard work. The interior compartments, constructed of the finest steel, resisted their most persistent efforts, although they finally forced an entrance into one which contained a large sum in cash, belonging to a depositor.

While Hope and Emerson were at work behind the screen which hid the safe, Abe Coakley removed his hat and coat and puttered about the bank as though he belonged there, dusting and rearranging the furniture and performing other tasks. While he was thus engaged Patrolman Van Orden of the Fifteenth precinct passed on his way home, and casually looked into the window. He was surprised to see the vault hidden by a screen, but his suspicions were allayed when Coakley waved to him in friendly greeting. A few minutes later the thieves slipped out of the back door of the bank with the loot packed in small satchels, one of which was carried by Patrolman Nugent.

The fact of the robbery was discovered within an hour, when Werckle burst his bonds and rushed into the hotel barbershop. But it was not until late in May, 1879, that the police were able to make any arrests. Coakley and Banjo Pete Emerson were acquitted, but Hope and Kelly were convicted and sentenced to long prison terms. Patrolman Nugent is said to have escaped by bribing a juror, but a few months later he was arrested in Hoboken and sent to jail for highway robbery. The police could not obtain enough evidence against Leslie to bring him to trial. While the total sum stolen was enormous, only $300,000 worth of the bonds were negotiable, and the cash amounted to but $11,000. The bank afterward recovered $257,000 worth of the bonds, so that the actual loss was $11,000 in cash and $43,000 in securities.

The success of Leslie's various operations soon brought him nationwide renown, and in the last years of his life he became a consulting bank robber, and was frequently called upon for advice by other gangs. For a stiff fee or a percentage of the gains, with a guarantee, he planned bank and store burglaries all over the United States. He is said to have received twenty thousand dollars to make a trip to the Pacific Coast to look over plans for a bank robbery contemplated by a syndicate of San Francisco thieves. But this period of his career was short, for the liaisons with Babe Irving and Shang Draper's mistress consumed more and more of his time and thought, and he lost much of his sagacity and prudence. He also became extremely apprehensive over the murder of J. W. Barron, cashier of the Dexter Savings Bank of Dexter, Maine, during an ill-starred attempt to rob that institution. Several other enterprises failed through faulty planning and direction, and his gang began to lose confidence in him. Draper, angry at Leslie's attentions to his mistress, attributed to the King of the Bank Robbers the talk which led to police knowledge of the Dexter crime, and to the arrest of Hope, Coakley, Banjo Pete and others for the Manhattan robbery.

It soon became common knowledge throughout the underworld that Leslie was destined for a violent end, and no one was surprised when, on the morning of June 4, 1884, Mounted Patrolman Johnstone found his decomposed body lying at the base of Tramps' Rock, near the dividing line between Westchester and New York counties beyond the Bronx River. He had been shot in the head, and a pearl-handled revolver lay beside him. Leslie's corpse was identified by Herman Steid, an agent for Marm Mandelbaum, the notorious fence, who gave the dead robber decent burial. But the police were never able to find the murderers, although they suspected Shang Draper, Johnny Dobbs, and Worcester Sam Perris. Only two weeks before his body was found Leslie had returned to New York from a brief visit to Philadelphia, and had gone to a house at No. 101 Lynch street,

Brooklyn, where Shang Draper was in seclusion with Jemmy Mooney and Gilbert Yost, and to which Worcester Sam and other members of the gang made frequent trips from Manhattan. The police always believed that Leslie was murdered in the Brooklyn house, and his body hauled away in a cart by Dobbs, Worcester Sam and Ed Goodie, a sneak thief who sometimes worked with the Leslie combination. These three were seen near Yonkers about the time that Leslie's body must have been placed at Tramps' Rock. But little evidence could be obtained, and the killing remains on the long list of unsolved crimes.

2

THE extraordinary success of the many well organized bands of thieves which flourished in New York during the city's great era of wickedness would scarcely have been possible had they not possessed an equally efficient outlet for the distribution of their plunder. This was accomplished through the fences, or receivers of stolen property, who operated in the recognized criminal districts within easy reach of the resorts frequented by crooks, and masked their real business with small stores, generally carrying an imperishable stock which was never changed and was seldom removed from the shelves, for legitimate customers were few and were not encouraged.

Nothing was so large or so small that the fences would not undertake to convert it into cash; in the middle seventies one even handled successfully fifty thousand dollars worth of needles and thread which had been stolen from the warehouse of H. B. Claflin & Company. While such receivers were probably no more numerous than they are today, they had better political and police connections than their modern prototypes, and were consequently bolder and more powerful. Many scornfully refused to resort to any subterfuge whatever; one of the notorious places of the city was the Thieves' Exchange in the Eighth Ward, near Broadway and Houston street, where fences and criminals met each night and dickered openly over their beer and whiskey for jewelry and other loot. Annual retainers were paid to criminal lawyers, and politicians and policemen received stated fees, and occasionally commissions on gross business. Some of the more successful of the fences not only disposed of the goods brought to them, but tided thieves over periods of adversity, and provided funds for the preliminary surveys which were necessary before a bank vault or the strong box of a store could be successfully attacked.

The first of the great fences of whom there is extensive record was Joe Erich, who kept a place in Maiden Lane before the Civil War. Erich's principal rival was Ephraim Snow, better known as Old Snow, who owned a small dry goods store at Grand and Allen streets and dealt in stolen property of every description. It is related of Old Snow that he once disposed of a score of sheep which a gang of Bowery thugs, on a vacation in the country, had stolen from a Westchester county farmer and driven through the streets of the city to the shop of the fence. Old Unger's house in Eldridge street was also a favorite bargaining place for the thieves, especially sneaks and pickpockets. Equally popular were Little Alexander, whose real name was never known to the police, and Bill Johnson, who operated a dry goods store in the Bowery.

All of these fences were still in operation at the close of the Civil War, but they were soon eclipsed by the brilliant successes of Marm Mandelbaum and John D. Grady, better known as Travelling Mike, a thin, stooped, shabby, dour-visaged little man who padded about the streets wearing a heavy overcoat summer and winter and bearing a peddler's box on his shoulder. Ostensibly Travelling Mike sold needles and other small articles for the use of the housewife, but his box was more apt to contain pearls and diamonds, or stolen bonds, than legitimate objects of barter. Travelling Mike seldom went abroad with less than ten thousand dollars worth of goods in his box or on his person. He maintained no regular establishment, but he was a frequent visitor to the Thieves' Exchange, and from time to time called upon his clients to suggest robberies and dicker for anything they might have stolen since his last visit. He had an especial fondness for jewelry and bonds, and rarely bought anything which he could not carry away in his box. His occasional exception was silk, which was always in great demand. One of his most brilliant sneak thieves was the original Billy the Kid, otherwise William Burke, who was arrested one hundred times before his twenty-sixth birthday.

Travelling Mike was believed by the police to have suggested the raid upon Rufus L. Lord's treasure in 1866 by Greedy Jake Rand, Hod Ennis, Boston Pet Anderson, and Eddie Pettengill, which resulted in the greatest single haul ever made by sneak thieves in the United States. Lord was an important financial figure of the time, and is said to have been worth, in bonds, stocks, and real estate, more than four million dollars. His business acumen was remarkable, but he was so grasping and penurious that he had the reputation of being a miser, and had no friends and few acquaintances. He maintained a dingy, shabby office in the rear of No. 38 Exchange Place, where he spent much of his time clipping coupons and sorting them into bundles, or listening eagerly to the clink of the double eagles which he kept in great canvas bags. He wore disreputable clothing which was constantly in need of patches, and in summer his footgear was a pair of worn felt slippers. He had a burglar and fire proof safe built in the rear wall of his office, but during his latter years became so feeble and absent-minded that he frequently went home and left it unlocked, with several millions of dollars in cash and securities at the mercy of thieves. His office was always in semi-darkness, for he would not burn more than one candle at a time, and there was but one small window through which sunlight could penetrate.

Greedy Jake and his accomplices made several calls upon the capitalist, ostensibly to discuss a proposed loan or investment; and on the afternoon of March 7, 1866, a dark, foggy day, Greedy Jake entered the office in Exchange Place and proceeded to distract Lord's attention with much glib talk about the high rate of interest he was willing to pay. When he offered twenty per cent., and high-class collateral, Lord became frantic with eagerness, and clutching Greedy Jake's coat lapels implored him to consummate the deal immediately. While he was so engaged Boston Pet and Eddie Pettengill sneaked into the darkened office, and a few moments later sneaked out again bearing two tin boxes containing $1,900,000 in cash and securities, most of which were negotiable. The boxes were planted in a saloon at Spring and Wooster streets for a few weeks, and after the hue and cry had slackened, about two hundred thousand dollars of the negotiable bonds found their way into the hands of Travelling Mike Grady, who speedily converted them into cash. The remainder of the stolen property was recovered by the police within two years, but the shock was so great that Lord became more misanthropic than ever, and thereafter would not permit a stranger to enter his office, which he barricaded with a steel door.

Fredericka Mandelbaum, better known as Marm or Mother, was probably the greatest and most successful fence in the criminal annals of New York. She was a huge woman, weighing more than two hundred and fifty pounds, and had a sharply curved mouth and extraordinarily fat cheeks, above which were small black eyes, heavy black brows and a high sloping forehead, and a mass of tightly rolled black hair which was generally surmounted by a tiny black bonnet with drooping feathers. She owned a three-story building at No. 79 Clinton street, on the corner of Rivington, and lived with her husband, Wolfe, and their son and two daughters, on the second and third floors, which were furnished with an elegance unsurpassed anywhere in the city; indeed, many of her finest pieces of furniture and some of her most costly draperies had once adorned the homes of the aristocrats, from which they had been stolen for her by grateful and kind-hearted burglars. In these apartments Marm Mandelbaum entertained lavishly with dances and dinners which were attended by some of the most celebrated criminals in America, and frequently by police officials and politicians who had come under the Mandelbaum influence.

On the ground floor, at the Rivington street corner, Marm Mandelbaum operated a small haberdashery, but her real business was carried on in a clapboarded wing which sprawled down Clinton street, where she handled the loot and financed the operations of a majority of the great gangs of bank and store burglars. In the early days of her career she peddled the plunder from house to house. Among the famous criminals who dealt with her were Shang Draper, George Leonidas Leslie, Banjo Pete Emerson, Mark Shinburn, Bill Mosher, and Joe Douglas. Shinburn was a bank burglar of distinction who complained that he was at heart an aristocrat, and that he detested the crooks with whom he was compelled to associate. He lived frugally and invested all his gains in foreign money orders payable to relatives in Prussia. Eventually he retired and sailed to Europe, where, by the judicious expenditure of a part of his fortune, he became Baron Shindell of Monaco, and lived happily and aristocratically ever after. Mosher and Douglas were the men who stole four-year-old Charley Ross from his home in Germantown, Pa., on July 1, 1874, this precipitating the greatest kidnapping mystery this country has ever known. They were soon suspected, and were trailed all over the East by New York detectives; but they were not found until the morning of December 14, 1874, when they were killed while trying to rob the home of Judge Van Brunt in Bay Ridge, Brooklyn. Mosher was shot by Judge Van Brunt's son, Albert, and the Judge himself fired a bullet into Douglas's back as the burglar ran from the house. Mosher was killed outright, but Douglas lingered for several moments, and as Judge Van Brunt approached Douglas raised himself on one elbow and said, "It's no use lying now. Mosher and I stole Charley Ross from Germantown!" But he died before he could divulge the whereabouts of the boy, and Charley Ross has never been found, although about once every two years someone appears and lays claim to being the missing child.

Marm Mandelbaum also had an especial soft spot in her heart for female crooks, and was the friend and patron of such famous women criminals as Black Lena Kleinschmidt, Big Mary, Ellen Clegg, Queen Liz, Little Annie, Old Mother Hubbard and Kid Glove Rosey, all sneaks, pickpockets and blackmailers; and Sophie Lyons, perhaps the most notorious confidence woman America has ever produced. Her husband was Ned Lyons, a bank burglar. Black Lena obtained enormous sums of money through thievery and blackmail, but in her middle age she became ambitious for social conquest and removed to Hackensack, N. J., where she posed as the wealthy widow of a South American mining

Old Mother Hubbard

Black Lena

Marm Mandelbaum

Kid Glove Rosie

Queen Liz

Sophie Lyons

MARM MANDELBAUM AND SOME OF HER CLIENTS

Marm Mandelbaum's Dinner-Party

engineer. She gave elaborate functions, and aroused such a furore in New Jersey society that she became known as the Queen of Hackensack. But she remained a practical pickpocket and shoplifter, and spent two days of each week in New York replenishing her coffers. She was finally dethroned when she wore an emerald ring which one of her dinner guests, whose husband Black Lena had appropriated for her own uses, recognized as having been stolen from her handbag during a shopping trip to the metropolis.

The New York Police first listed Marm Mandelbaum as a suspected fence in 1862; and during the next twenty years she is estimated to have handled between $5,000,000 and $10,000,000 worth of stolen property. Several times during her long career she made the experiment of putting a few of her clients on salaries, binding them to deliver to her everything they stole, and to exercise reasonable industry and sagacity. However, she soon became convinced of the truth of Inspector Thomas Byrnes' dictum that there is no honor among thieves, and abandoned the practice after she had caught several of her hirelings disposing of loot to Travelling Mike Grady. She is said also to have been a Fagin and to have maintained a school in Grand street, not far from Police Headquarters, where small boys and girls were taught by expert pickpockets and sneak thieves. She also offered advanced courses in burglary and safe-blowing, and to a few of the most intimate of her associates gave post graduate work in blackmailing and confidence schemes. The fame of this institution became wide-spread, but Marm Mandelbaum became alarmed and dismissed her teaching staff when the young son of a prominent police official applied for instruction.

In all of her operations Marm Mandelbaum had the benefit of the expert legal counsel of Big Bill Howe and Little Abe Hummell, comprising the celebrated law firm of Howe & Hummell, to whom she paid an annual retainer of five thousand dollars. They not only appeared in her behalf on those rare occasions when the law made an impudent gesture in her direction, but also represented her clients whenever any of them were caught *flagrante delicto*. But they were unable to save her in 1884, when the reform element came into power and the District Attorney procured several indictments charging her with grand larceny and receiving stolen goods. The case was called for trial in December of that year, but Marm Mandelbaum had forfeited her bail and fled to Canada, where she spent the remainder of her days, although she is said to have made several visits to New York in disguise. But the state received nothing for its trouble, as Marm's bondsmen had transferred the property which they had pledged for her appearance by means of back-dated instruments, and Marm herself had shifted her holdings to her daughter. Of her noted lawyers, Howe died in 1903, and two years later District Attorney William Travers Jerome sent Little Abe to prison for various malpractices.

3

SEVERAL well-organized gangs of ghouls operated in New York during the post-bellum period, but for the most part they confined their activities to the tombs of Negroes and paupers, selling the bodies to doctors and medical students. They were seldom molested by the police and attracted little attention until the death of Alexander T. Stewart, a pioneer merchant prince around whom, after his death, was enacted one of the most extraordinary crimes ever perpetrated in the metropolis. Stewart began his business career in a very humble way, acting as his own bookkeeper, salesman, porter, and errand boy, but by the exercise of vast industry and excessive shrewdness he died the foremost store-keeper of his age. He became the owner of a fine store at Broadway and Chambers street, in a building now occupied by *The Sun*, and later of a great emporium which covered the block between Fourth avenue and Broadway and between Ninth and Tenth streets. It is now a part of the Wanamaker store. He did business for cash only and defied competition; at the height of his commercial power many of his clerks were merchants whom he had driven out of business. He had several children, but all died in infancy: and he had few if any friends, although because of his wealth and position he possessed great influence. His attitude toward everyone was suspicious and forbidding, and he is said to have made it his rule never to trust either man or woman. He was undersized and thin, with coarse, reddish hair and sharp features, and slate-grey eyes of almost unbelievable coldness. He died in 1876, worth thirty million dollars, and was buried in the church-yard of St. Mark's-in-the-Bouwerie, at Second avenue and Tenth street.

Stewart's body had scarcely been lowered into the grave before rumors were afloat that ghouls planned to steal the corpse and hold it for ransom. Several well known criminals were found loi-tering near the churchyard during the succeeding few weeks, and the police investigated reports that George Leonidas Leslie and his gang of bank robbers were planning a raid upon the burial ground, but no actual attempt was made to enter the vault until the night of October 8, 1878, when Sexton Hamill discovered that the name slab had been clumsily lifted from the grass. It was feared that the intruders had descended into the vault, where four other bodies were interred beside that of the great merchant, but nothing had been disturbed beneath the surface of the ground. By direction of Henry Hilton, attorney for Mrs. Stewart and the estate, new locks were put on the churchyard gates, and the name plate was removed to a point some ten feet southwest of the grave, where it was sunk into the grass to mislead the ghouls. The old location of the slab was carefully sodded over, and as an addition-al precaution, the watchman of a livery stable in Second avenue was employed to visit the churchyard every hour during the night and warn trespassers from the enclosure. But nothing further occurred and on November 3, 1878, the guard was dismissed, Attorney Hilton believing that all danger had passed.

Four days later, on the morning of November 7, the assistant sexton, Frank Parker, entered the churchyard an hour after dawn and was horrified to find a great mound of earth upturned at the mouth of the Stewart vault. Without investigating he hurried to the home of Sexton Hamill in Tenth street, and the latter went immediately to the church, where he entered the vault and found that the body of the merchant had been stolen. He hastened to the Stewart store, and learning that Hilton had not yet arrived, hired a cab and drove at top speed to the lawyer's home in Thirty-fourth street, adjoining the marble mansion occupied by Mrs. Stewart. Hilton immediately notified the police, and Superintendent George W. Walling took personal charge of the investigation.

The Stewart vault was of brick, ten by fifteen feet and twelve feet deep, and had been covered over by three feet of earth. It had been dug in almost the exact center of the yard, east of the church, and was flanked on either side by the graves of Benjamin Winthrop and Thomas Bixby, members of old New York families. The ghouls had ignored the decoy name slab, and had gone straight to the grave, into which they had descended after removing the protecting layer of earth. They had unscrewed the cover of a great cedar chest and cut through a lead coffin, and had then forced the casket containing the body. They also carried away with them the expensive knobs and the name plate of the casket, and a piece of the velvet lining, which they had cut out in the shape of an irregular triangle. As further evidence of their visit they had left a new coal shovel and a tin bull's-eye lantern. The body of the merchant weighed about one hundred pounds, and had not been embalmed. It had apparently been hauled away in a cart, the tracks of which were found near the eastern gate.

In the morning newspapers of November 8, Attorney Hilton announced that a reward of twenty-five thousand dollars would be paid for the return of the corpse and the arrest and conviction of the ghouls. The crime aroused a tremendous sensation throughout the East, and for months amateur sleuths busily searched barns and out-houses, and pried into the interiors of suspicious-looking carts and wagons. A score of new graves were opened in the belief that they might contain the missing body, and the newspapers printed many pages of comment and speculation. A double guard was placed over the grave of Commodore Vanderbilt at New Dorp, Staten Island, while armed men patrolled cemeteries throughout the city. The police soon learned where the shovel and lantern had been purchased, but there all clues ended, although more than a hundred professional criminals were summoned to Headquarters and compelled to furnish accounts of their movements on the night the body was stolen. For the theft of the corpse of a great and powerful merchant was quite different from the ordinary crime, and it was generally understood in the underworld that the ghouls need not expect the usual protection from police and politicians.

But nothing developed until the following January, when General Patrick H. Jones, of No. 150 Nassau street, a lawyer who had formerly been postmaster, called upon Superintendent Walling and displayed the knobs and two of the silver handles from the Stewart casket, together with a small strip of velvet and a triangular piece of paper, all of which he said he had received by express from Canada. He also showed several letters signed by Henry G. Romaine, asking him to act as intermediary in arranging for the return of the corpse, which Romaine said would be promptly done upon the payment of two hundred and fifty thousand dollars in cash. General Jones was further requested to conduct the negotiations by personals in the *New York Herald*. In one of the letters Romaine said:

> The remains were taken before twelve o'clock on the night of the 6th and not at three o'clock on the morning of the 7th. They were not taken away in a carriage but in a grocer's wagon. They were not taken to any house near the graveyard, but to one near 160th street. They were then enclosed in a zinc-lined trunk and left on an early morning train. They went to Plattsburg and from there to the Dominion. There they were buried. Except that the eyes have disappeared, the flesh is as firm and the features as natural as on the day of interment, and can therefore be instantly identified. The enclosed piece of paper is exactly the size of the piece of velvet taken from the coffin, while the small strip sent you will prove to be of the same piece as that of the coffin.

After a conference with Hilton and Superintendent Walling, General Jones was instructed to publish a personal in the *New York Herald* on February 5, offering to open negotiations. On the 11th a reply, postmarked Boston, was received, in which Romaine offered to deliver the corpse on the following conditions:

1. The amount to be paid shall be $200,000.
2. The body will be delivered to yourself and Judge Hilton within twenty-five miles of the city of Montreal, and no other person shall be present.
3. The money is to be placed in your hands or under your control until Judge Hilton is fully satisfied, when you will deliver it to my representative.
4. Both parties to maintain forever an unbroken silence in regard to the transaction.

Hilton would not agree, and refused to continue the negotiations. Romaine then instructed General Jones to communicate with Mrs. Stewart, but the General refused to do so. About the middle of March Hilton offered twenty-five thousand dollars for the body or bones of Stewart, but Romaine "respectfully but firmly" declined. There the matter rested for more than a year. But late in the winter of 1880, Mrs. Stewart, who had been fearfully upset by the theft of her husband's body, approached the ghouls on her own account through General Jones, and Romaine wrote that he would return the corpse for one hundred thousand dollars. Mrs. Stewart favored the immediate payment of this sum, but General Jones countered with an offer of twenty thousand dollars, which Romaine accepted, but again laid down stringent conditions for the payment of the money and the delivery of the body. He directed that the funds, in currency, be placed in a canvas bag, and that a messenger leave New York alone at ten o'clock of a designated evening in a one-horse wagon, and drive into Westchester County along a lonely road which was indicated on a map of the district. Romaine wrote that some time before morning the messenger would be met and given further directions.

A relative of Mrs. Stewart volunteered to act as messenger, and at the appointed hour drove into the country. Several times during the night he thought he was being watched, but it was not until three o'clock in the morning that a masked horseman appeared and directed him to turn his cart into a lane. At the end of a mile the messenger came upon a buggy drawn across the road, from which two men clambered and approached him. Both were masked, and one carried a heavy gunny sack. A triangular strip of velvet was offered to the messenger as proof of identity, and the money was promptly paid over, whereupon the ghouls dumped the gunny sack into the wagon and drove northward in their own vehicle. The messenger hurried back to the city with the bones of the merchant rattling in the sack beneath his feet. An undertaker packed them into a trunk, and the next night they were taken in a special freight car to Garden City, L. I., where an empty coffin had been prepared in the burial vault of the Garden City Cathedral. In it the sexton and the messenger deposited the bones, and the coffin was then hidden in an inaccessible place beneath the dome of the Cathedral. There they remain to this day, and for many years were protected by a hidden spring which, if touched, would have shaken a cluster of bells in the church tower and sent an alarm throughout the village.

The Return of A. T. Stewart's Bones

CHAPTER XI

THE WHYOS AND THEIR TIMES

1

THE GREATEST of the gangs which came into existence in New York after the Civil War was the Whyos, as vicious a collection of thugs, murderers, and thieves as ever operated in the metropolis; they were at least the peers of the fierce river pirates of the old Fourth Ward. The origin of the name is unknown, but is believed to have arisen from a peculiar call sometimes employed by the gangsters; the gang itself appears to have been an outgrowth of the Chichesters of the old Five Points, who thus outlived the Dead Rabbits, Plug Uglies, Shirt Tails, and other combinations of the Paradise Square district. The Whyos maintained their principal rendezvous in Mulberry Bend, slightly north and east of the Five Points proper, although during the summer many

"Hell's Kitchen," New York.—[Drawn by Charles Graham]

of them could always be found lounging in a churchyard at Park and Mott streets. The principal thoroughfare of the Whyo domain was Baxter, the Orange street of the old Five Points, which later became famous for its secondhand clothing shops and the pullers-in who dragged customers in from the sidewalks by main strength. Baxter street was the home of the original Harris Cohen, who opened a store and achieved such a tremendous and immediate success that at least a dozen other enterprising Jewish merchants quickly flung out signs bearing his name, so that all the shops for more than a block were apparently operated by the original Harris Cohen. One of the Cohens kept a cage filled with English sparrows in his window, because to his delighted ears their song was "cheap! cheap! cheap!" The money spent for bird seed was his advertising appropriation.

Although they were at home in Baxter street and the other thoroughfares of Mulberry Bend, the Whyos extended their operations throughout the city, and made some of their most celebrated raids along the lower West Side and in the Greenwich Village district. They fought many desperate battles with other gangs and with the police, and were not finally exterminated until the middle nineties. The last haunts of these eminent thugs were an Italian dive at Worth and Mulberry streets, and a Bowery drinking place called the Morgue, the owner of which boasted that his product was equally efficient as a beverage or an embalming fluid. It was in

Big Frank Mccoy

Johnny Dobbs

Eddie Goodi

Sheeny Mike Kurtz

Billy the Kid

Banjo Pete Emerson

Worcester Sam Perris

Max Shinburn

SOME FAMOUS BANK ROBBERS

Red Rocks Farrell

Googy Corcoran

Clops Connolly

Piker Ryan

Bull Hurley

Dorsey Doyle

Mike Lloyd

Big Josh Hines

Baboon Connolly

SOME FAMOUS MEMBERS OF THE WHYO GANG

the Morgue that the Whyos had their last great fight, which began when English Charley and Denver Hop quarrelled over the division of loot and started shooting at each other. Soon a score of men were blazing away with revolvers, but all were drunk and no one was injured. The proprietor of the Morgue said they were very silly to expect to hit anyone after drinking his liquor.

The Whyos were at the height of their power during the eighties and early nineties, when the membership of the gang included many celebrated criminals, among them Hoggy Walsh, Fig McGerald, Bull Hurley, Googy Corcoran, Baboon Connolly and Red Rocks Farrell. These heroes were not only thugs and brawlers of the first water, but a majority were also expert sneak thieves, burglars and pickpockets, and many owned dives, panel houses and places of prostitution. Big Josh Hines became famous as the first man to hold up a stuss game, a gambling pastime which in later years became an important source of revenue for the Jewish and Italian gangs. Stuss made its appearance in New York about the middle eighties, and games soon dotted the area east of the Bowery from Chatham Square to Fourteenth street, and westward to Broadway.[1] Night after night Big Josh went from place to place, armed with two revolvers, exacting as tribute a percentage of the gains. When the stuss owners complained, Big Josh indignantly pointed out that he had been very generous; that no man could say the whole of his earnings had been taken.

"Them guys must be nuts," he peevishly told a detective. "Don't I always leave 'em somethin'? All I wants is me share!"

---

[1]Stuss was an adaptation of faro, and there were several variations, but the most popular was played with a layout of thirteen spaces, numbered from ace to king. The dealer shuffled the deck and placed it face downward upon the table. The players made their bets on whatever cards they hoped would appear, and the entire deck was then turned over. The card now on top was the dealer's, and all money which had been bet on it went to the house. The next card was the players', and the house paid off on it. Every other card was the dealer's, so that the players could not possibly win on more than six of the thirteen. The percentage in favor of the house was enormous. The game was widely known in the underworld as Jewish Faro.

It has been said that during their period of greatest renown the captains of the Whyos would accept no man as a member until he had committed a murder, or at least had made an honest effort to thus enroll himself among the aristocracy of the underworld. This legend probably grew out of a remark made by Mike McGloin, an early Whyo who was hanged in the Tombs on March 8, 1883, for the murder of Louis Hanier, a saloon keeper of West Twenty-sixth street. Hanier protested when he came upon McGloin robbing his till, and the indignant gangster promptly killed him with a slung-shot. Said McGloin the day after the murder: "A guy ain't tough until he has knocked his man out!" The later Whyos were devout believers in McGloin's dogma; many of them eagerly accepted blackjacking, murder and mayhem commissions, and advertised by means of printed and written price lists their willingness to maim and kill. The pioneer in this method of procuring clients was Piker Ryan, who appears to have been a thug of exceptional enterprise. When he was at length brought to book for one of his many crimes, the police found this list in his pocket:

Punching	$2
Both eyes blacked	4
Nose and jaw broke	10
Jacked out (knocked out with a blackjack)	15
Ear chawed off	15
Leg or arm broke	19
Shot in leg	25
Stab	25
Doing the big job	100 and up

Ryan made good use of his opportunities, as was apparent from a notebook which was also in his possession. One page was headed "Jobs," and below the heading were half a dozen names. Some had check marks after them, which Ryan explained meant that the tasks had been completed to the satisfaction of his clients.

The greatest leaders of the Whyos were Danny Lyons and Danny Driscoll, who exercised joint dominion over the gang.

Appropriately enough, they were hanged in the Tombs within eight months of each other. In 1887 Driscoll and John McCarthy became involved in a quarrel over a Five Points girl named Beezy Garrity, and in the furious gunfight which followed a bullet struck and killed her. Driscoll was convicted of the crime, and was hanged on January 23, 1888. Lyons was probably the most ferocious gangster of his period, a worthy rival of the earlier Mose the Bowery Boy and the later and equally eminent Monk Eastman. He was also one of the first of the great gang leaders to avail himself of feminine counsel. He frequently consulted his girls, Lizzie the Dove, Gentle Maggie, and Bunty Kate, all of whom proudly walked the streets for him and faithfully gave him their earnings. But Lyons was not satisfied with the manner in which they maintained him, and added a fourth girl, Pretty Kitty McGown, to his entourage. He expelled her lover, Joseph Quinn, who vowed eternal enmity, and for several months he and Lyons went gunning for each other. Both celebrated the Fourth of July, 1887, by drinking heavily, and when they met next morning at the Five Points their dispositions were even more murderous than usual. They blazed away at each other across Paradise Square, and Quinn fell dead with a bullet in his heart. Lyons went in hiding for a few months, but was finally captured, and was put to death on August 21, 1888. Bunty Kate and Pretty Kitty shrugged their shoulders and obtained other lovers immediately, but Gentle Maggie and Lizzie the Dove aroused much comment in the underworld by donning widow's weeds and refusing to accept any business engagements until they had observed a decent period of mourning. However, they occasionally went out for refreshments, and met one night in a Bowery dive, where they undertook to decide whose sorrow was greatest, and to whom Lyons had been more affectionate. Gentle Maggie finally settled the argument by stabbing Lizzie the Dove in the throat with a cheese knife, and Lizzie died. Her last words were that she would meet Gentle Maggie in hell and there scratch her eyes out.

Another shining light of the old Whyos, before the time of Driscoll and Lyons, was Dandy Johnny Dolan, who was not only a street brawler of distinction, but a loft burglar and sneak thief of rare talent as well; nothing was too great or too trivial for him to steal. His fellow gangsters regarded him as something of a master mind because he had improved the technique of gouging out eyes; he is said to have invented an apparatus, made of copper and worn on the thumb, which performed this important office with neatness and dispatch. His invention was used by the Whyos with great success in their fights with other gangs. He was also credited with having imbedded sections of sharp axe blade in the soles of his fighting boots, so that when he overthrew an adversary and stamped him, results both gory and final were obtained. But ordinarily Dandy Johnny did not wear his fighting boots. He encased his feet in the finest examples of the shoemaker's art, for he was the Beau Brummel of the gangland of his time, and was extraordinarily fastidious in his choice of raiment and in the care of his person. Under no circumstances, not even to take part in a brawl or raid that promised to be rich in loot, would he appear in public until his hair had been properly oiled and plastered against his skull, and his forelock tastefully curled and anointed. He had a weakness for handkerchiefs with violent red or blue borders, and for carved canes, especially if the handle of the stick bore the representation of an animal. Of these he owned a great store, to which he added as opportunity offered; he frequently promenaded the Five Points and Mulberry Bend with a vivid kerchief knotted about his throat and others peeping from his pockets, while he jauntily swung a handsome cane.

It was his passion for these adornments that cost him his life. James H. Noe, a brush manufacturer, decided to enlarge his business during the summer of 1875, and began the erection of a new factory at No. 275 Greenwich street. It was his custom to walk to the property each Sunday morning and observe the progress of the work. On Sunday, August 22, 1875, he entered the structure as usual, and climbed the ladders and temporary stairways to the roof. There he came upon Dandy Johnny Dolan, his eye gouger upon his thumb and a blue bordered handkerchief knotted about his throat, ripping away the lead of the gutters. Mr. Noe marched him downstairs, but when they reached the ground floor Dandy Johnny struck the manufacturer on the head with an iron bar,

Dandy Johnny Dolan Surprised by Mr. Noe

inflicting injuries from which Mr. Noe died in a week. With his victim unconscious, Dandy Johnny proceeded to rob him, taking a small sum of money and a gold watch and chain, and also carrying away Mr. Noe's cane, which had a metal handle carved in the likeness of a monkey. Then Dandy Johnny very foolishly tied his own handkerchief about the manufacturer's face. The story goes that the thug appeared in the haunt of the Whyos in Mulberry Bend with one of Mr. Noe's eyes in his pocket, but the tale is probably apocryphal.

Detective Joseph M. Dorcy was put to work upon the case, and within a few days learned that the watch and chain had been pawned at a small shop in Chatham street, the present Park Row. Some time later two women who had walked the streets for Dandy Johnny, but had been dismissed in favor of younger and handsomer girls, recognized the handkerchief as his, and reports were received by the detective that Dandy Johnny had been seen about the resorts of the Bend and Five Points proudly displaying a cane with a monkey's head in metal for a handle. He was immediately arrested, and at his trial was identified as the man who had pawned the watch and chain. On April 21, 1876, he was hanged in the courtyard of the Tombs. His captor, the astute Detective Dorcy, became one of the most celebrated sleuths of his time. Another of his famous exploits was the capture of Canon Leon L. J. Bernard, who had embezzled $1,400,000 of the funds of the See of Tournai, Belgium. Dorcy pursued the reverend scoundrel to Vera Cruz, and not only arrested him but recovered $1,200,000 of the stolen money.

2

ABOUT the time the Whyos were coming into prominence the gangsters of the Hartley Mob, who made their rendezvous in the dives around Broadway and Houston street, were attracting much attention by using a hearse and carriages to transport their plunder through the streets. The vehicles proceeded like a funeral, with the stolen goods concealed behind the black drapings of the hearse and on the floors of the carriages, in which rode the gangsters heavily armed and dressed in funereal garments. The Hartley Mob chieftains also employed the hearse to haul their battlers. Once some twenty members of the gang set out to avenge an insult which had been offered to them by one of the Five Points gangs, and the latter gathered in force in Mulberry street to repel them. But the Five Pointers divided their ranks to permit a hearse and funeral carriages to pass, and were surprised and overwhelmed when the Hartley Mob thugs suddenly swarmed out of the vehicles and attacked them. The Hartley Mob numbered among its members some expert burglars and thieves, but was broken up by the police within a few years, for its leaders were never able to make proper political connections and so received scant protection.

The Molasses Gang, captained by Jimmy Dunnigan, Billy Morgan, and Blind Mahoney, was also a contemporary of the Whyos. The members of this outfit were for the most part till-tappers and cheap sneak thieves, although Dunnigan and Blind Mahoney were expert pickpockets as well. It was Dunnigan's custom, with other members of the gang, to enter a store and ask the owner to draw his soft hat full of molasses, preferably sorghum, explaining that he had a bet with a friend as to how much the head-gear would hold. When the hat was full Dunnigan promptly clapped it on the storekeeper's head and pulled it down over his eyes, so that he was almost blinded by the molasses. While he struggled to free himself the gangsters robbed the till, picked up everything else they could carry, and departed.

Under the leadership of Sheeney Mike, Little Freddie, and Johnny Irving, the Dutch Mob operated with great success from Houston to Fifth streets east of the Bowery until 1877, when Captain Anthony J. Allaire took command of the police of the Eighteenth precinct and clubbed them out of the district. The area bounded by Eleventh and Thirteenth streets and by First avenue and Avenue A was kept in a continual uproar by the Mackerelville Crowd, while farther north the Battle Row Gang appeared and ranged through the sixties from the East to the Hudson rivers. The original Battle Row was in Sixty-third street between First and Second avenues, but in later years the name was also used to designate a block in West Thirty-ninth street, between Tenth and Eleventh avenues. The Rag Gang was one of the most notorious of the many newly formed combinations along the Bowery, while on the West Side the original Hell's Kitchen Gang came into being about 1868 and soon became a collection of the most desperate ruffians in the city.

The name Hell's Kitchen was first applied to a dive near Corlear's Hook on the East Side north of Grand street, but soon after the Civil War it became the popular designation of a considerable area north and south of West Thirty-fourth street west of Eighth avenue. Under the leadership of Dutch Heinrichs this gang roamed through Hell's Kitchen, levying tribute on the merchants and factory owners, breaking into houses in broad daylight, beating and robbing strangers, and keeping the entire district in a chronic state of terror. Much of their stealing was done at the old Thirtieth street yards and depot of the Hudson River railroad. Heinrichs was sent to prison for five years after he and two of his gangsters had attacked Captain John H. McCullagh, then a patrolman, who had ventured alone into Hell's Kitchen to investigate the theft of two hogsheads of hams from a freight car. McCullagh battled with the three thugs for more than half an hour, and finally knocked them unconscious with his nightstick. He then tied their arms behind their backs with their own belts, loaded them into a cart and hauled them to the police station in West Thirty-fifth street. The Hell's Kitchen Gang eventually absorbed the Tenth Avenue Gang, whose most noted exploit was the robbery of an express train of the Hudson River Railroad. Led by Ike Marsh, the gangsters boarded the train at Spuyten Duyvil, at the northern end of Manhattan Island, and clambered into the express car, where they bound and gagged the messenger and then threw off an iron box containing a large sum of greenbacks and government bonds.

The district around Broadway and Houston street, besides being the resort of bank burglars, panel thieves, and other criminals, was also infested by many small gangs. None were of any permanent importance, but their membership comprised some of the most ferocious street brawlers of the period. Several policemen who attempted to subdue them and stop their depredations were killed or badly beaten, and little progress was made against them until the appearance of Patrolman Alexander S. Williams, who was destined to become an Inspector and one of the most famous of New York policemen. Williams was a huge and powerful man with a great bull voice which had been strengthened by many years at sea as a ship's carpenter. Two days after he had been assigned to the Houston street area he selected the two toughest characters of the neighborhood, picked fights with them and knocked them unconscious with his club. He then hurled them one after the other through the plate glass window of the Florence Saloon, from which they had issued to attack him. Half a score of their comrades came to their rescue, but Williams stood his ground and mowed them down with his nightstick. Thereafter he averaged a fight a day for almost four years. His skill with the nightstick was extraordinary, and the fame of his powerful blows became so widespread that he was hailed as Clubber Williams, a sobriquet which he retained to the end of his career.

Williams was appointed a captain in September, 1871, and assigned to the command of the Twenty-first precinct, which had a station house in East Thirty-fifth street, between Second and Third avenues. This was the original Gas House district, and was one of the most turbulent sections of the city, for the celebrated Gas House Gang was just coming into power, and was terrorizing a large area. Scarcely a night passed in which the gangsters did not loot houses and stores and fight among themselves in the streets and dives, and the police were powerless to stop them. But Williams invoked the gospel of the nightstick, and organized a strong arm squad which patrolled the precinct and clubbed the thugs with or without provocation. The district was soon comparatively quiet, and remained so throughout Williams' administration. Indeed, so thoroughly had the gangsters been cowed that three months after he took command Williams made a demonstration for the benefit of police reporters, and citizens who had

Inspector Alexander S. Williams

protested against his wholesale use of the nightstick. While a small group watched, Williams hung his watch and chain on a lamp-post at Third avenue and Thirty-fifth street. The party then walked around the block, and when it returned to the post the jewelry had not been disturbed. After a few years in this precinct, and in the Eighth and Fourth, Williams was transferred in 1876 to the command of the Twenty-ninth, or Tenderloin district. He resigned in 1879 to become Superintendent of the Bureau of Street Cleaning, but after two years in that office returned to the Police Department and was again assigned to the Tenderloin, where he remained for six turbulent but prosperous years. Charges were brought against him eighteen times, but he was invariably acquitted when tried by the Board of Police Commissioners. Throughout his career he continued to pin his faith to the nightstick, and when complaints were made of his furious clubbing he justified his course with the famous observation, "There is more law in the end of a policeman's nightstick than in a decision of the Supreme Court."

Along the lower West Side, in the area now inhabited principally by Turks, Syrians, and Armenians, several notable gangs were organized and soon became the rulers of the district, protected, as usual, by the politicians. The Stable Gang, which had some fifty members, made its headquarters in an old barn in Washington street, and devoted its talents entirely to robbing immigrants. The Silver Gang also had a rendezvous in Washington street; but pursued the more refined occupation of burglary. The most ferocious of the gangs in this section was the Potashes, who roamed the neighborhood of the Babbitt Soap Factory in Washington street near Rector. They were very fierce fighters, and with Red Shay Meehan as captain dominated the other gangs and kept for themselves the choicest morsels of thievery and brawling. A nest of double tenements in the block bounded by Greenwich, Washington, Spring, and Canal streets was the home of half a dozen gangs. Among them was the Boodle Gang, which raided the stores in Centre Market and attacked the provision wagons which passed through their territory. The operations of this crowd were similar to those of the butcher cart gangs, which had made their appearance in the late fifties. At first the butcher cart thieves confined their activities to meat wagons and butcher shops; a dozen thugs rode up to a store, rushed inside and seized a carcass of beef or as many hams and cuts of small meat as they could carry, which they flung into their cart. Then they went pelting down the street at top speed. In the middle sixties these gangs turned their attention to the financial district and began robbing messengers who carried money and securities from one bank to another. The first important theft of this character occurred on January 19, 1866, when Samuel Terry was robbed of a satchel containing fourteen thousand dollars in checks and money, which he was carrying from the Farmers & Citizens Bank of Williamsburg to the Park National Bank of New York. As Terry crossed Beekman street near Park Row two men jumped from a butcher's cart and approached him. One knocked him down with a slung-shot, while the other snatched the satchel. Both then sprang into their vehicle and whipped up the horses, easily making their escape. In recent years this method of robbery has been used extensively by automobile bandits, and by the hi-jackers, who specialize in liquor.

3

THE period in which the Whyos and their contemporary gangs began shooting, stabbing, and stealing their way toward the natural destiny of children born and reared in such frightful habitations as the Old Brewery, Cow Bay, and Gotham Court, also saw an enormous increase in the number of juvenile gangsters, who were to provide material for the great gangs of the nineties and the early part of the present century. Before the Civil War the juvenile as well as the adult gangs were largely confined to the Five Points, the lower Bowery district, and the Fourth Ward, simply because these were the congested and poverty stricken areas of the city; as the slums increased in extent, gangsters of all types and ages multiplied in numbers and power. By 1870 the streets throughout the greater part of New York fairly swarmed with prowling bands of homeless boys and girls actively developing the criminal instinct which is inherent in every human being. While all of these gangs chose their titular leaders from their own ranks, a majority were at the same time under the domination of adult gangsters or professional thieves, who taught the children to pick pockets, snatch purses and muffs, and steal everything they could lay their hands upon, while they masked their real business by carrying bootblack outfits, baskets of flowers, or bundles of newspapers. They lived on the docks, in the cellars and basements of dives and tenements, and in alleys and area ways; and when their masters could not feed them, which was often, they ate from swill barrels and garbage pails.

When the Rev. L. M. Pease went to the Five Points in 1850 to open a mission he found that all of the great brawling, thieving gangs of Paradise Square had their sycophantic gangs of youngsters. There were the Forty Little Thieves, the Little Dead Rabbits, and the Little Plug Uglies, the members of which emulated their elders in speech and deed, and as far as possible in appearance. And in the Fourth Ward, along the water front, were the Little Daybreak Boys, composed of lads from eight to twelve years of age, who were almost as ferocious as the older gangsters whose name they adopted and whose crimes they strove mightily to imitate. Some accompanied the Daybreak Boys on various enterprises, acting as lookouts and decoys, and crawling through the portholes of ships and lowering ropes up which the adult thugs clambered to the decks. But they also planned and executed many adventures on their own account, and were believed by the police to have committed several murders. One of their famous exploits was performed in the Harbor just off the Battery, when half a dozen in rowboats attacked three boys who where out for a pleasure sail in a small sloop. The lads were robbed and beaten and then thrown into the river, while the young pirates triumphantly sailed the sloop up the East River and sold it to a junkman for a few dollars. Luckily their victims could swim, and reached the Battery in safety. Many of the most noted leaders of the Daybreak Boys, including Saul and Howlett, graduated from the ranks of these young miscreants.

Some of the early juvenile gangs were led by girls, notably the Forty Little Thieves, who swore undying loyalty to Wild Maggie Carson, a fierce little vixen who had her first bath at the age of nine and was not tamed until the end of her twelfth year, when the Rev. Mr. Pease taught her the joy of sewing buttons on shirts. She became as enthusiastic a seamstress as she had been a brawler and roughneck, and when she was about fifteen was adopted into a good family. She finally married well. But not many of the juvenile gangsters were reclaimed. Jack Mahaney, a contemporary of Wild Maggie, who led a gang of his own, became in later life one of the most celebrated criminals in America, and because of the frequency of his escapes from prison and from the custody of policemen, was known as the American Jack Sheppard. He twice escaped from Sing Sing, as well as from the Tombs and almost every other important prison in the East, and several times leaped from fast trains to what appeared to be certain death. But he was never injured.

Jack Mahaney Escaping from a Train

Mahaney was born in New York City in 1844, and was the son
of a well-to-do family. His father died when he was about ten
years old, and his mother sent him to boarding school, where a
naturally reckless and mischievous disposition soon got him into
trouble. He ran away after he had been repeatedly flogged, and
when the police found him in company with a gang of notorious
little dock rats he was sent to the House of Refuge. He not only
escaped from this institution, but took a dozen other boys with
him and fled into the Five Points, where he fell into the hands of
Italian Dave, a famous Fagin and sneak thief. Italian Dave had
under his wing some thirty or forty boys between the ages of nine
and fifteen, whom he housed in a rickety tenement on Paradise
Square and taught to steal, conducting daily classes with the aid
of fully dressed dummies of men and women, which were placed
in various postures while the boys practiced picking pockets and
snatching muffs and purses. They were also instructed in the fine
points of begging and stealing articles from store windows and
counters, and whenever they were clumsy Italian Dave ceremoniously clad himself in a policeman's uniform and beat them with
a nightstick.

When the boys had completed their laboratory work Italian
Dave sent them into the streets to practice their art, or hired them
out to sneak thieves and burglars to act as lookouts. Sometimes a
thief would pay the Fagin a stated sum and engage the services of
a certain number of boys for a definite period, during which time
everything they stole belonged to him. However, he was obliged to
provide them with food and shelter, and it was always very much
of a gamble. Mahaney became such an accomplished pickpocket
and sneak that he was retained by Italian Dave as his own personal boy and allowed privileges none of the others received. He frequently accompanied the Master on marauding expeditions.
Sometimes he picked the pockets of a drunken man pointed out
to him by Italian Dave, or snatched the purse of a careless
woman; again he engaged a well dressed man in conversation and
so distracted his attention while Italian Dave knocked him senseless with a slung-shot, after which Dave retired and the boy went
through the victim's pockets. When he grew older Mahaney sev-

ered his connection with Italian Dave and joined one of the Five Points gangs. Later, having served his apprenticeship, he organized his own gang of butcher cart thieves, and in time became a burglar, a confidence man, and an all-around crook.

Within ten years after the close of the Civil War conditions even worse than those of the Five Points and the Fourth Ward prevailed in many of the lower and middle sections of the city. With the connivance of crooked officials and politicians, contractors had hurriedly flung together cheap and flimsy tenements in the congested districts to house the hordes of immigrants, and these structures soon degenerated into slums of the utmost depravity. The Tenth Ward, north of Chatham Square and Division street and comprising much of the territory which is now known as the lower East Side, was particularly squalid. Conditions in this district were especially bad in Hester street and in the block bounded by Pitt, Stanton, Willett, and Houston streets, which contained a double row of tenements called the Rag Pickers' Den.

But these slums were equalled if not surpassed by such places as Rotten Row in Laurens street, Poverty Lane and Misery Row in Ninth and Tenth avenues, and Dutch Hill, a group of shanties in East Fortieth street near the East River. An avalanche of juvenile gangs poured out of these slums. The Nineteenth Street Gang, a particularly vicious collection of young thugs with whom even the police did not care to battle, was composed of boys living in Poverty Lane and Misery Row; and the tenements around Second avenue and East Thirty-fourth street, populated principally by Irish Catholics, gave to juvenile gangland a youthful leader called Little Mike, who led his gang on many forays against the Protestant missions and schools which were opened from time to time. It was Little Mike's delight to break up the classes and religious services by hurling stones through the windows, after which he poked his red head into the room and yelled, "Go to hell, you old Protestants!" Half a dozen gangs of small beggars and sneak thieves made life miserable for the merchants and householders on the lower West Side, around Greenwich and Washington street and within the shadow of old Trinity Church.

In Worth, Mott, Mulberry, Baxter and other streets of the Bowery and Five Points areas saloons and dives were opened which catered solely to the street boys, selling them frightful whiskey at three cents a glass and providing small girls for their amusement. For the favor of one of these children two boys of a Mackerelville gang once fought a duel with knives in City Hall Park, surrounded by a mob of howling youngsters armed with dirks, clubs and stones. One of the boys was killed, and the affair ended in a free-for-all battle in which more than fifty juvenile gangsters were engaged. In various parts of the city were half a dozen gambling houses wherein the boys frittered away their meager earnings at faro and policy; and keepers of assignation houses and places of prostitution employed them as cappers, while independent harlots engaged them to distribute printed cards and act as guides for men in quest of amorous adventure. Hundreds of boys and girls roamed the streets producing squeaky noises from violins, harps, and other musical instruments, begging pennies which they turned over to their masters. A majority of the child minstrels lived in the slums of Mulberry Bend, where a strong colony of Italians had been established soon after the Civil War and was gradually ousting the Irish. In many instances the children had been indentured to thieves by their parents in Italy.

One of the notorious early groups of juvenile terrorists was the Fourth Avenue Tunnel Gang, which had a rendezvous in the street car tunnels along Fourth avenue, now lower Park avenue, from Thirty-fourth to Forty-second streets. Richard Croker, of Tammany Hall fame, is said to have been a leader of this gang. In later years, before he gravitated through the natural course of events into politics, Croker was a pugilist of parts, and engaged in several formal bouts from which he emerged victorious. Another famous juvenile gang was the Baxter Street Dudes. These lads made their appearance in the seventies under the leadership of an angelic appearing but in reality tough little boy known as Baby-Face Willie. The Dudes operated their own playhouse, which they called the Grand Duke's Theater, in the basement of a stale beer dive at No. 21 Baxter street. There they wrote and performed plays and musical shows, and produced them at slight expense, for whenever they required scenery or properties they simply stole what they needed from the larger theaters along the Bowery or from the merchants. The theater became a favorite resort of street boys from all parts of the city, and of elephant hunters, or slummers, and the Dudes did a handsome business, dividing the profits on a *pro rata* basis. The admission charge was ten cents. But other juvenile gangs of Five Points and Mulberry Bend became jealous of their success, and began to bombard the theater with stones every time a performance was attempted, and scarcely a night passed without a fight. The police finally closed the play-house, partly on this account and partly because the boys persist-ently refused to pay the regular city amusement tax.

During the reign of Monk Eastman as king of the gangsters, in the late nineties and the early part of the present century, the most efficient gang of youngsters in the city was a group of pick-pockets dominated by Crazy Butch, one of Eastman's henchmen who was finally slain by Harry the Soldier in a fight over a woman, an expert shoplifter known as the Darby Kid. Crazy Butch him-self was thrown onto the world at the tender age of eight, and within two years had abandoned the arduous labor of shining shoes and selling newspapers for the larger profits of picking pockets. When he was thirteen he stole a dog, named him Rabbi, and in the course of time trained the animal to snatch a handbag from a careless woman's hand and race with it through the streets until he had shaken off pursuit. Then he met Crazy Butch at Willett and Stanton streets, and with proudly wagging tail turned over the spoil. In his late teens Crazy Butch assumed the leader-ship of an East Side gang of small boys, and within a few months had a fleet of between twenty and thirty youngsters prowling the streets snatching purses and muffs. They went abroad on daily expeditions, Crazy Butch riding a bicycle slowly down the street while his young thieves flanked him on either sidewalk. Presently Crazy Butch bumped into a pedestrian, preferably an old woman, whereupon he alighted from his machine and launched into a tirade of abuse which quickly drew an indignant throng. And while the crowd pressed closer to see and hear what was transpir-ing, the boys flitted into the street, and in a moment their gifted fingers were prying into pockets and handbags. When the crowd had been thoroughly plundered, or if a policeman appeared, the boys scattered, and Crazy Butch suddenly apologized to the victim of his rough riding and pedalled away to the appointed rendezvous, where he collected the stealings of the boys and rewarded each of them with a few cents.

The character of the juvenile gangs changed in proportion to the increased activity of welfare agencies, better housing conditions, greater efficiency of the police and, especially, to reforms in the educational system which permitted effective supervision and regulation of the children of the tenement districts. It is quite likely that there are as many juvenile gangs in New York today as there have ever been, for forming in groups and fighting each other is part of the traditional spirit of play, but in general they have become much less criminal. Until recent years, when the custom has fallen somewhat into disuse, the election-night bonfires were a prolific source of fights between the juvenile gangs, for when one group ran short of material it raided the blazing heaps of wood around which another gang capered. These fights always resulted in a more or less permanent enmity, and election nights were followed for several weeks by frequent battles as the despoiled gang sought revenge. In many parts of the city, particularly the Harlem and upper East Side districts, the boys fought with wooden swords and used wash-boiler covers for shields. But invariably the excitement of battle overcame them and they resorted to bricks and stones, with the result that a few heads and many windows were broken.

CHAPTER XII

KINGDOMS OF
THE GANGS

1

THERE WERE two important Democratic factions in New York when the mayoralty campaign opened in 1886—Tammany Hall, and the New York County Democracy, which had been organized in 1880 by Abram S. Hewitt and other prominent Democrats who had become disgusted with the rapacity of the Tammany dictators. Hewitt was nominated for Mayor by the County Democracy, the Republicans took the field under the banner of Theodore Roosevelt, and the Union Labor Party, which had recently been formed and had shown considerable strength, named Henry George. At the behest of Richard Croker, that remarkably astute politician who ruled the metropolis for so many years, Tammany Hall endorsed the candidacy of Hewitt, who was elected by a majority of about twenty-two thousand over George and more than thirty thousand over Roosevelt. But the new Mayor, although he owed his election largely to Tammany, soon displayed an astonishing honesty, and had scarcely been inaugurated before he began to rid the city of some of its wickedness. He closed Billy McGlory's, the Black and Tan, Harry Hill's, the American Mabille and other resorts in the lower part of the city, as well as the Haymarket, the French Madame's and the dives which had made the Satan's Circus district around Sixth avenue such a noted area of vice and dissipation. He also raided many of the luxurious gambling houses which had hitherto operated under the special protection of the police and the politicians, and launched vigorous campaigns against the gangsters and other criminals.

Mayor Hewitt naturally incurred the enmity of his erstwhile political supporters, and in 1888, when he ran for re-election as the candidate of the County Democracy, Tammany Hall overwhelmingly defeated him with Hugh J. Grant. The Haymarket and other uptown resorts promptly reopened their doors, but only a few were ever restored to their former splendour, for business and residential encroachments caused Sixth avenue to become less and less vicious, and the center of vice and crime soon shifted to the old Tenth Ward. By the early nineties this district had acquired great renown as the most depraved area in the United States, with street after street lined with brothels and dives and infested by prowling thugs. The white slave industry during this period was carried on almost entirely in the Tenth Ward, and the pimps and procurers organized into gangs and boldly held meetings at which they exchanged and sold women as the traders at the old Bull's Head Tavern used to sell cattle. One of these groups maintained elaborate club rooms in Allen street, where its members met formally twice a week to discuss market conditions and make various business arrangements. For many years the Ward was under the domination of Charles R. Solomon, who called himself Silver Dollar Smith and owned the famous Silver Dollar Saloon in Essex street, across from the Essex Market Court. His handy man and fixer was a lawyer named Max Hochstim, hero of a story which is still related with relish along the East Side. Said Hochstim to a judge with whom he wished to curry favor: "Your Honor, you sure look swell in the judicial vermin."

Alexander S. Williams was appointed Police Inspector in 1887, and because of the many scandals which had arisen during his administration of the Tenderloin precinct, was transferred to the East Side. Four years later William S. Devery, better known as Big Bill, was appointed to a captaincy and assigned to Williams' district. He assumed command of the Eleventh precinct, which comprised the nine blocks bounded by Chatham Square, the Bowery, and Division, Clinton, and Houston streets. The Rev. Charles H. Parkhurst, as head of the New York Society for the Prevention of Crime, began a crusade against Inspector Williams and Captain Devery during the early nineties, and provided much of the evidence upon which the Lexow and Mazet committees based their respective investigations in 1894 and 1899, through which the extent of the police and political graft was revealed. It was shown by testimony that the influence of Tammany Hall had so permeated the Police Department that the district leaders dictated appointments and assignments, and that practically every member of the force had joined Tammany organizations, and paid without protest the contributions which were levied upon them for the maintenance of the Tammany chieftains. Captain Creedon confessed that he had paid fifteen thousand dollars to political henchmen to obtain his promotion to a captaincy, and Captain Max Schmittberger, later Chief Inspector, who had been a Sergeant in the Tenderloin precinct, admitted that he had collected money from gamblers and keepers of disorderly resorts, and had paid it over to Inspector Williams. Testimony was also produced that Williams was interested in a brand of whiskey, and had foisted it upon the saloon keepers, raiding their places if they failed to push it. One woman who owned a chain of houses of prostitution testified that she paid thirty thousand dollars annually for protection, and others said that when they opened their establishments they were called upon for an initiation fee of five hundred dollars, and that thereafter a monthly charge ranging from twenty-five dollars to fifty dollars was placed upon each house according to the number of inmates. Street walkers told the investigators that they paid patrolmen for the privilege of soliciting, and gangsters, sneak thieves, burglars, pickpockets, footpads, and lush workers, all testified that they gave the police or politicians a percentage of their stealings. More than six hundred policy shops paid an average of fifteen dollars a month each, while three hundred dollars was collected from pool rooms, and even larger sums from the luxurious gambling houses.

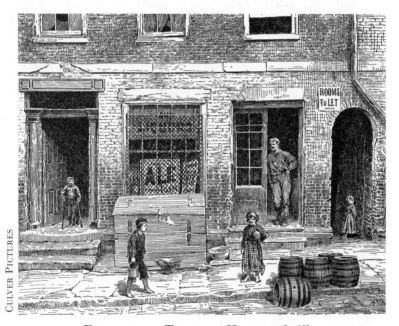

Entrance to a Tenement-House and Alley
The door at the left leads directly into a tenement. The archway at the right is a dark passageway leading to filthy yards and tenements in the rear

Inspector Williams denied any wrong-doing, but admitted that although his salary had been small throughout his career, he had been thrifty enough to purchase a valuable estate at Cos Cob, Connecticut, the dock alone costing thirty-nine thousand dollars, and that he owned a yacht, a house in the city and other property, and had several large bank accounts. He told the committee that he had amassed his fortune by speculating in building lots in Japan. No action was begun against him as a result of the revelations before the Lexow Committee, but within a year he voluntarily resigned from the police force and entered the insurance business, where he soon ran his fortune into the millions. He died in 1910. But the evidence against Big Bill Devery was so strong that the Board of Police Commissioners dismissed him from the force in 1894. He was indicted for extortion a few months later, but was acquitted when tried before a jury in 1896. Meanwhile he had been restored to duty as captain by a ruling of the Supreme Court, and within a few months the Police Commissioners exhumed the old charges and again endeavored to rid the department of him. But Devery promptly obtained another order from the Supreme Court, and the Commissioners were forbidden to bring him to trial. So great was the Tammany influence, and so high did Devery stand in the councils of the Wigwam, that early in 1898 he was appointed Inspector, and within six months became Chief of Police. Devery was a huge man, seldom without a big black cigar tilted in a corner of his mouth, and he possessed a likable personality and various tricks of expression which made him very picturesque and popular.

Robert A. Van Wyck, the last Mayor of New York before the Bronx, Brooklyn, Queens, and Richmond were merged with Manhattan to form the present Greater City, was a staunch admirer of Devery, and called him the best chief of police New York ever had. Dr. Parkhurst, however, continued to produce evidence of graft and corruption, and the newspapers conducted extensive campaigns to clean up the city, attributing to Devery's demoralizing administration practically every crime committed in the metropolis. The *New York Herald* was especially antagonistic during the race riots of August, 1900, when mobs of black and white men fought for two days through the streets and on the housetops of Hell's Kitchen. The trouble began when Negro gangsters murdered a patrolman who was searching for a criminal among the tenements along Thirty-seventh street between Eighth and Ninth avenues. He was killed in the afternoon, and that night members of the white gangs assembled on the corner of Thirty-seventh street and Ninth avenue, where they assailed passing Negroes with stones and brickbats, seriously wounding several. The Negroes soon attacked in large numbers, reinforced by the gangs of San Juan Hill, as the district north of Fiftieth street west of Eighth avenue had been called in honor of the exploits of the Negro troops during the Spanish-American War. The *Herald* charged that the trouble soon degenerated into a police riot, with patrolmen actively aiding the white gangsters. "In each case," said the *Herald*, "the white youths were the aggressors. After they had started the game several policemen would rush in and complete their work by battering the unfortunate colored men with nightsticks, frequently arresting them. This attitude of Devery's men was not calculated to stop the turmoil between the races. When the chief ordered his men to clear Eighth avenue many persons attracted by curiosity were hurt. The police made a magnificent charge down Eighth avenue, past Devery's 'four corners' at Twenty-eighth street, injuring many women and children who were gathered there."

Despite the attacks upon him, Big Bill Devery remained in power until early in 1901, when the Legislature passed a law abolishing the office of Chief of Police and reorganizing the Department. The head of the force was thereafter called Commissioner. Devery became a Deputy Commissioner, but his turbulent spirit was restless under the quiet of a desk job, and he soon resigned and went into the real estate business. He died in 1919 and was highly eulogized by the press.

2

WHILE Inspector Williams and Big Bill Devery waxed fat and prosperous by their despotic rule of the lower East Side, and other police officials emulated them throughout the city, the Whyos and their contemporaries were vanishing and many new gangs were appearing which equalled the earlier thugs in fighting qualities and excelled them in criminal achievement. Their names even yet cause great fear and trembling, and are frequently taken in vain by crowds of upstart young hoodlums. For almost fifteen years Manhattan Island south of Times Square was divided by the gangs into clearly defined kingdoms, and the boundaries were garrisoned and as carefully guarded as are the frontiers of civilized nations. The Five Pointers, successors to the Dead Rabbits, the Plug Uglies, and the Whyos, mustered fifteen hundred members and were lords of the area between Broadway and the Bowery, and Fourteenth street and City Hall Park. Their principal rendezvous was the New Brighton Dance Hall in Great Jones street, owned by Paul Kelly, chieftain of the gang. There they held their social functions and planned raids upon enemy territory. The gang led by that prince of thugs, the great Monk Eastman, could call more than twelve hundred warriors to the colors, and ruled the territory from Monroe to Fourteenth streets and from the Bowery to the East River; including the treasure-laden Red Light district. This gang scorned to adopt an euphonious pseudonym, but called itself, with simple pride, the Eastmans. Its headquarters were in an unsavory dive in Chrystie street near the Bowery, from which the police in an indignant moment once removed two wagon loads of slung-shots, revolvers, blackjacks, brass knuckles, and other implements of gang warfare. For more than two years a bitter feud raged between the Eastmans and the Five Pointers over a delicate question of territorial rights, and the dispute was never settled, although a score of pitched battles were fought and the lives of perhaps thirty gangsters were sacrificed. Monk Eastman contended that the domain of the Five Pointers ended at Nigger Mike Salter's dive, the Pelham, in Pell street, but Paul Kelly held that the frontier of his kingdom was the Bowery, and that he was entitled to whatever spoil might be found on the eastern side of that thoroughfare.

The Gas House Gang, with about two hundred thugs under its banner, had moved southward from the old Gas House district around East Thirty-fifth street, and ranged Third avenue from Eleventh to Eighteenth street. In this comparatively restricted area the Gas Housers found much to amuse and enrich them, and when suitable opportunities failed to present themselves, invaded the territory of other gangs. They were especially adroit footpads, and in their heyday averaged about thirty holdups a night.

The Gophers were lords of Hell's Kitchen, their domain running from Seventh to Eleventh avenues and from Fourteenth street to Forty-second street. They were fond of hiding in basements and cellars, hence their name. The Gophers could put no more than five hundred men into the field, but every man was a thug of the first water, and not even Monk Eastman cared to lead his gangsters into Hell's Kitchen unless he outnumbered them at least two to one; and on those rare occasions when the Gophers made an excursion in force into the East Side, there was great scurrying among the gangs of the latter area. A favorite resort of the Gophers was a saloon in Battle Row (Thirty-ninth street between Tenth and Eleventh avenues) kept by Mallet Murphy, who was so called because in lieu of a bludgeon or common bung starter, he employed a huge wooden mallet to repel intruders and silence obstreperous customers. The Gophers were so turbulent and so fickle in their allegiance that their leaders seldom retained the crown more than a few months at a time, so that the gang produced no outstanding figure of the stature of Monk Eastman or Paul Kelly. However, many are recorded in police history as desperate criminals and fierce fighters. Newburg Gallagher, Marty Brennan, and Stumpy Malarkey were noted Gophers of their time, and Goo Goo Knox also acquired considerable fame, both as a Gopher and as one of the founding fathers of the Hudson Dusters. Another great hero of the Gophers was One Lung Curran, who, when his girl bewailed the lack of a suitable fall coat, strode into the street and blackjacked the first policeman he encountered. Removing the uniform blouse from the prostrate officer, One Lung Curran presented it to his sweetheart, who stitched it into a smart jacket of military cut which created a fashion, so that every Gopher in Hell's Kitchen felt impelled to follow One Lung Curran's example. For some time a constant procession of policemen staggered into the West Forty-seventh street station house in their shirt sleeves. The fad was not checked until the police began to patrol the district in parties of four and five, and the Strong Arm Squad made frequent excursions into the Kitchen and left bruised and battered Gophers in its wake. Still another Gopher of distinction was Happy Jack Mulraney, so called because he always appeared to be laughing. However, the smile was caused by a partial paralysis of the muscles of the face. In reality Happy Jack was a verjuiced person and very sensitive about his deformity; when his chieftains wished to enrage him against an enemy they told him that slighting remarks had been made about his permanent grin. Happy Jack was finally sent to prison for the murder of Paddy the Priest, who owned a saloon in Tenth avenue and was a staunch friend of Happy Jack's until he asked the gangster why he did not laugh on the other side of his face. Happy Jack then shot him and for good measure robbed the till.

A score of smaller gangs in Hell's Kitchen were proud to owe allegiance to the Gophers and fight under the leadership of One Lung Curran and other captains, who had made the name of their gang a synonym for ferocity and Hell's Kitchen one of the most dangerous areas on the American continent. Chief among these lesser bands were the Gorillas, the Rhodes Gang, and the Parlor Mob. The Gophers also had the support of the Battle Row Ladies' Social and Athletic Club, better known as the Lady Gophers, which was composed entirely of women whose mettle as fighters had been tested in frequent combats with the police. This organization was led by Battle Annie, the sweetheart of practically the entire Gopher gang, and one of the most popular figures in the history of Hell's Kitchen. Like her illustrious predecessors, Gallus Mag, Sadie the Goat, and Hell Cat Maggie, she was partial to mayhem, and is said to have held classes in the art, giving her followers the benefit of her experience and researches. Over a period of more than a half dozen years Battle Annie was the Queen of Hell's Kitchen, and acquired widespread renown as the most formidable female of her time. When the practice of hiring gangsters was begun by the labor unions and employers, Battle Annie earned a handsome income by supplying female warriors to both sides in industrial disputes. For many years there was scarcely a strike in which women were engaged that did not find Battle Annie and her gangsters enthusiastically biting and scratching both pickets and strike-breakers.

The Hudson Dusters controlled the West Side of Manhattan below Thirteenth street and eastward to Broadway, the western frontier of Paul Kelly's kingdom, although their right to the latter thoroughfare was bitterly contested by a small gang called the Fashion Plates. They also ranged as far south as the Battery, but their principal theater of operations was the Greenwich Village district, where a maze of crooked, winding streets offered excellent hiding places. There they had displaced the Potashes, the Boodle Gang, and other combinations of the early nineties. The Dusters were friends and allies of the Gophers, many of their leaders having formerly been members of the Hell's Kitchen gang who had moved southward when the Kitchen became too hot to hold them, but they held aloof from the feuds of the Eastmans, the Five Pointers, and other gangs of the East Side. Their principal enemies were the Marginals and the Pearl Buttons, who disputed with them for the privilege of plundering the docks and shipping along the Hudson River water front. In later years, after the Hudson Dusters had been smashed by the police and their captains had succumbed to the drug habit or had been sent to Sing Sing for various crimes, the Marginals, under the leadership of Tanner Smith, became the dominant gang of the district, subduing the Pearl Buttons and reducing them to the status of vassals.

The Hudson Dusters were organized in the late nineties by Kid Yorke, Circular Jack, and Goo Goo Knox, who had fled the Gopher domain after leading an abortive insurrection against the reigning prince. Later leaders of unusual notoriety and prowess were Red Farrell, Rickey Harrison, Mike Costello, Rubber Shaw, and Honey Stewart, while Ding Dong became known as the most accomplished thief of the gang. Ding Dong prowled the streets attended by half a dozen young ragamuffins, who clambered onto express wagons and threw off packages to their master. Ding Dong clutched them to his bosom and fled into the crooked streets of Greenwich Village, while the driver of the wagon and the police bent themselves to the hopeless task of catching the boys. When the gang was founded headquarters were established in a building at Hudson and Thirteenth streets, the owner of which, under compulsion, donated two rooms for a club house. As the gang increased in numbers and power these quarters became too small, and the Dusters came into possession of an old house in Hudson street below Horatio, later the site of the Open Door Mission. There they installed a piano, and at all hours of the night danced and caroused with the prostitutes of the water front, becoming a nuisance and an affliction unto the honest house-holders and merchants of the neighborhood, upon whom they levied for supplies. But few complaints were made, for the Dusters were quick to revenge slights or betrayals, whether fancied or real. Once when a saloon keeper scornfully refused to provide half a dozen kegs of beer for a party, the Dusters invaded his establishment, wrecked the fixtures, and carried away his entire stock of liquors. But the police eventually took cognizance of the situation and made several raids upon the Hudson street house, at length smashing the piano and throwing the furnishings into the street. The Dusters moved into Bethune street, and thence to various points as the Strong Arm Squad searched them out.

The journalists were very fond of the Hudson Dusters, and their activities were much described, so that they became one of the best known gangs of the period. And while they were never such fighters as the Eastmans, the Five Pointers, and the Gophers, they were a rare collection of thugs and much of their reputation was deserved. Perhaps ninety per cent. of the Dusters were cocaine addicts, and when under the influence of the drug were very dangerous, for they were insensible to ordinary punishment, and were possessed of great, if artificial, bravery and ferocity. They seldom attacked the police in force, but whenever they had a grievance against an individual officer it was well for him to request a transfer, for sooner or later he was assaulted and maimed. Such a catastrophe happened to Patrolman Dennis Sullivan of the Charles street station, who announced during the last years of the Dusters' power that he intended, single-handed, to smash the gang. He succeeded in arresting ten of the gangsters, including Red Farrell, the leader, and his ambitions were discussed at great length at various meetings of the Dusters in Hudson and Bethune streets. It was finally decided that Sullivan must be taught a lesson, and the decision was approved by a Greenwich Village politician who utilized the Dusters at election time as repeaters and sluggers, and who felt that an attack upon the policeman would prove to the political higher-ups that the Hudson Dusters really controlled their territory. So one night in Greenwich street, as Patrolman Sullivan was about to arrest a member of the gang against whom a tradesman had complained, the Dusters pounced upon him when his back was turned, and he went down fighting valiantly against a score of slugging, kicking thugs. His coat was stripped from his back, his nightstick, shield and revolver taken away, and he was badly beaten with stones and blackjacks. When he had been knocked unconscious the Dusters withdrew, but determined to give him a permanent injury. He was therefore rolled over on his back, and four of the gangsters stepped forward and ground their heels in his face, inflicting frightful wounds. Police reserves took him to a hospital, where he remained for many weeks.

The successful attack upon Patrolman Sullivan aroused a sensation throughout gang circles, and the Gophers formally congratulated the Hudson Dusters upon the thoroughness of the job, and especially upon the added touch of stamping. One Lung Curran, who finally succumbed to the affliction which had given him his sobriquet, was in the tuberculosis ward of Bellevue Hospital when he heard the news, and celebrated the exploit in poetry, for he had long been the acknowledged bard of the West Side gangsters:

Says Dinny, "Here's me only chance
    To gain meself a name;
I'll clean up the Hudson Dusters,
    And reach the hall of fame."
He lost his stick and cannon,
    And his shield they took away,
It was then that he remembered
    Every dog has got his day.

There were half a dozen other verses, describing the assault in great detail. The Hudson Dusters had the poem printed on sheets of coarse paper, and copies were left at every barber shop and drinking place in the Duster kingdom. Especial care was taken to get them into the hands of the police of the Charles street station, and a dozen were sent to Police Headquarters and to the hospital where Patrolman Sullivan was a patient. For months the ditty was sung in the streets by Ding Dong's juvenile thieves, and by the other gamins who admired the mighty deeds of the Dusters and, as they grew older, joined the gang.

3

THESE were the principal gangs of the period, but by no means all of them; they were numbered by the score. Perhaps fifty small groups which operated south of Forty-second street owed allegiance to the Gophers, Eastmans, Five Pointers, Gas Housers, and Hudson Dusters, and in the event of a general gang war rallied under the banners of the great captains. Each of these small gangs was supreme in its own territory, which other gangs under the same sovereignty might not invade, but its leader was always responsible to the chieftain of the larger gang, just as a prince is responsible to his king. The McCarthys, the Batavia Street Gang, the Squab Wheelman, and the Cherry Street Gang, which strove mightily to revive the glories of the old Fourth Ward river pirates, were among Eastman's free companies. Crazy Butch organized the Squab Wheelman at a time when Eastman rented bicycles and ran a bird and animal store in Broome street, thus paying a compliment to a branch of his chief's business as well as to his passion for pigeons. Those who would win the favor of the great gang leader were sedulous in their devotion to bicycling, and the Squab Wheelmen were expected to rent a wheel at least once a week, whether they could ride one or not. Crazy Butch maintained his headquarters in a hall in Forsyth street, and one summer night, having received information that the Five Pointers proposed paying him a call in force, he resolved to test the courage of his warriors. Accompanied by three of his closest advisers, Crazy Butch rushed up the stairs and into the hall, blazing away with two revolvers. Some sixty of the

Wheelmen were playing cards and drinking, and all but two or three promptly went out the windows or down the back stairs. Little Kishky, sitting on a window sill, became so excited that he fell backwards into the street and was killed.

Another of Eastman's beloved lieutenants was a beetle-browed thug who had been born Charles Livin, but whose great strength and ferocity gave him the sobriquet of Ike the Blood, although so far as the police ever learned he had no notches on his gun. Ike the Blood followed Eastman on many desperate forays, and was always much in demand whenever a stabbing or blackjacking commission came to the chieftain. He was finally killed by the Gophers in a dive at Seventh avenue and Twenty-eighth street, whither he had gone to the rescue of a friend who had been cornered by the terrors of Hell's Kitchen and was trying to shoot his way to freedom. One of the Gophers was also killed, but it was never known whether the bullet that dropped him was fired by Ike the Blood.

Such noted Five Pointers as Johnny Spanish, Biff Ellison, Eat 'Em Up Jack McManus and Nathan Kaplan, otherwise Kid Dropper,[1] who was destined to become the last of the great gangsters, led their own groups and at the same time were loyal to Paul Kelly. McManus began his career as a prize fighter, but was unsuccessful and abandoned the prize ring to become bouncer in McGuirk's Suicide Hall on the Bowery. Later he became Sheriff of the New Brighton, and was high in the confidence of Paul Kelly. He earned his title of Eat 'Em Up Jack because of his fondness for mayhem; he would have been much at home during the early days of the Fourth Ward. McManus was finally killed as a result of a quarrel with Chick Tricker, who kept a saloon of singular depravity in Park Row. Tricker criticized the manner in which several of the ladies of the New Brighton flung their feet in the dance, and Eat 'Em Up Jack took it upon himself

---

[1]A dropper was a thief who dropped a wallet filled with bad money at the heels of a victim and then pretended to find it. Pleading that he was in a great hurry, the thief induced the sucker to purchase the wallet with the avowed intention of finding the rightful owner. Kid Dropper was especially adroit at this swindle in his youth, hence his nickname.

to avenge the insult. After the dive had closed for the night the pair met at Third avenue and Great Jones street, and in the pistol battle which followed Tricker was shot in the leg. Twenty-four hours later, while Tricker was in a hospital and so had a perfect alibi, a gangster crept up behind Eat 'Em Up Jack in a darkened block of the Bowery and cracked his skull with a piece of lead pipe wrapped in a newspaper. It was common knowledge in the underworld that Sardinia Frank had wielded the bludgeon, but he was never arrested. In later years Sardinia Frank became bouncer at the Normandie Grill at Broadway and Thirty-eighth street, and when he was asked what he was doing so far away from his usual haunts, he replied, simply:

"I'm here to keep out everybody I know!"

Johnny Spanish, whose real name was John Weyler—he was a Spanish Jew and claimed kinship with Butcher Weyler of Cuban fame—was a slim, undersized youth of seventeen when he first began to make a stir in the underworld. Spanish was very taciturn and morose, and was inclined to brood over his troubles, real and imaginary. For several years he kept strictly to himself, operating as an independent thug and accepting commissions from all who would pay his price, but later he attached himself to the Five Pointers and led a small gang during the final years of the Paul Kelly dynasty. Spanish never stirred abroad without two revolvers stuck in his belt, and when he was on important errands carried two more stuffed into his coat pockets, besides the regulation equipment of blackjack and brass knuckles. One of his chief exploits, which won him favorable mention among the gangsters, was the robbery of a saloon in Norfolk street, owned by Mersher the Strong Arm. Spanish served notice that he would call at a certain hour to empty the till, and promptly on the minute appeared in the doorway with his hat drawn down over his eyes, and with two revolvers in his hands. Another man was behind him, but apparently was serving only as gun-bearer, for although he also carried two guns, he did not offer to use them. Spanish, however, sent a bullet crashing through the mirror over the bar, and then strode into the saloon, where he not only emptied the till but the pockets of some ten customers as well, lining them up against the bar while his assistant searched them.

Louie the Lump

Biff Ellison

Kid Twist

Humpty Jackson

Monk Eastman

It was soon after the adventure in Norfolk street that Johnny Spanish fell in love, and was seized with a burning desire to ornament his adored one with silks and precious stones. But he had not sufficient money, and naturally thought of stuss, and principally of the game operated by Kid Jigger in Forsyth street between Hester and Grand, one of the most prosperous on the East Side. Kid Jigger bore a wide reputation as a gun fighter, and the gangsters respected his prowess and left him in peace, but Spanish was blinded by love and avarice, and so was undeterred by Jigger's renown. He visited the stuss game and calmly notified Kid Jigger that thereafter the profits were to be equally divided, although Kid Jigger could continue to do the hard work of running the game.

"An' why," demanded Kid Jigger, "do I give youse half my stuss graft?"

"Because," said Spanish, "if youse don't I'll bump youse off an' take it all."

Kid Jigger laughed loud and long, and Spanish glared at him balefully from his brooding black eyes.

"All right," he said. "I'll bump youse off tomorrow night."

And on the appointed evening, as Kid Jigger stepped from his stuss house into Forsyth street, he found Johnny Spanish waiting for him on the corner. Spanish immediately opened fire with both guns. Jigger scurried back into his castle and escaped injury, but one of Spanish's bullets struck and killed an eight-year-old girl, who was playing in the street. Spanish fled the city, and when he returned a few months later found that the woman for whom he had gone to so much trouble had abandoned him for the more imposing figure of Kid Dropper. He made no threats against her, but one night bundled her into a taxicab and drove into a marsh near Maspeth, Long Island. There he backed her against a tree and fired several shots into her abdomen. She was found unconscious several hours later, but meanwhile had given birth to a baby, three of whose fingers had been shot away. The police caught Spanish after awhile, and early in 1911 sent him to prison for seven years. Kid Dropper was imprisoned a few months later, receiving a sentence of seven years for robbery, complicated by general cussedness.

4

IN addition to the great gangs and their vassal combinations, there were also a large number of independent groups which controlled small areas within the domains of the larger gangs, and vigorously opposed any attempt to absorb or suppress them. As we have recorded, the Marginals, Pearl Buttons, and Fashion Plates laid claim to small portions of the Hudson Duster kingdom; and in the Eastman territory the Fourteenth Street Gang, under the leadership of Al Rooney, successfully maintained its hegemony for several years, as did the Yakey Yakes, the Lollie Meyers and the Red Onions. The Yakey Yakes operated around Brooklyn Bridge under the leadership of Yakey Yake Brady. They finally left the field when Yakey Yake died of tuberculosis.

The most famous of the independent gangs was that captained by Humpty Jackson, whose activities centered around an ancient graveyard in the block bounded by First and Second avenues and Twelfth and Thirteenth streets. Jackson was a unique figure in the underworld of his time. He was fairly well educated, and was seldom to be seen without a book in his pocket. His favorite authors were Voltaire, Herbert Spencer, Darwin, and Huxley. He owned a good library, comprising principally works on philosophy, and is said to have had more than a casual knowledge of Greek and Latin. His disposition, however, was anything but philosophical; he was morose and quick-tempered, and would shoot at the slightest provocation. He carried no less than three revolvers, one in his pocket, another slung under his hump, and a third in a special rack built into his derby hat. His gang numbered some fifty thugs, including such celebrated heroes as Spanish Louie, Nigger Ruhl, the Lobster Kid, and the Grabber.

These worthies met in the cemetery at regular intervals, with Jackson sitting on a tombstone like a crooked little gnome, while his followers disposed themselves upon the graves. They were so at ease one summer evening when Crazy Butch and a score of Eastman gangsters pounced upon them, trussed them up and plundered them of their money and weapons. The police never made a charge of homicide against Humpty Jackson, but they arrested him more than a hundred times and sent him to prison for twenty different offenses. At one of his trials it was shown that he had accepted one hundred dollars from a stranger to blackjack a man he had never seen before. But Humpty himself, of course, did not do the slugging. A gang leader seldom demeaned himself so, any more than a boss contractor shovels dirt or a civilized ruler goes to war. He pocketed his fee, pointed out the prospective victim to a blackjack or slung-shot artist if the affair was to be a mere matter of bruising, or to a gunman if permanent results were desired, and then retired to his favorite dive to await the report of his henchman. Some of the gangsters insisted upon making written reports; one of Monk Eastman's most efficient blackjackers always turned in a formal, type-written document, designating the victim as the subject and himself as the operative. Oddly enough, this man's ambition was to get on the police force.

Next to Jackson himself, the most celebrated of the gangsters who haunted the old graveyard was Spanish Louie, also known as Indian Louie. There was much uncertainty about Louie's ancestry; he talked vaguely, on occasion, about his noble Spanish and Portuguese forefathers, and also let it be known that the hot blood of Indian chieftains flowed in his veins, and that he had inherited all of the vices and none of the virtue of the red man. He was also said to have been in the army and navy, although rumor failed to name the regiment or the ship. Tall tales of his prowess drifted into the dives of Chinatown and the Bowery, where he was most often to be seen, and Spanish Louie neither denied nor affirmed them, for he had a genius for mystery, and so contrived that everything he did played upon that note. He carried a brace of heavy Colt's revolvers, the most massive artillery in gangland, and supplemented this armament with a pair of eight-inch dirks, which he thrust into special scabbards built into his trousers. His clothing was solid black, and was topped by a great sombrero of funereal hue, while instead of a shirt he wore a black sweater drawn close up to his chin. As he strode the streets, with his piercing black eyes glaring from beneath his black-brimmed sombrero, he was a figure calculated to inspire awe and respect; but his fellows could never make up their minds whether he was all that he pretended to be.

He always had money, for no fewer than three girls walked the streets for him, and when he was finally killed he had one hundred and seventy dollars in his pocket, seven hundred dollars in his shoe and three thousand dollars in the Bowery Savings Bank. But he performed no exploits of great moment and acquired no police record; and after he had been about the lower East Side less than a year his bullet-ridden body was found in Twelfth street near Second avenue. His murderer was never found, but the underworld suspected the Grabber, for it was known that the latter had accused Spanish Louie of withholding his share of the proceeds of a social function which the pair had sponsored in Tammany Hall. But at any rate the death of Spanish Louie dispelled the mystery about his ancestry, for a man from Brooklyn claimed the body and gave it orthodox Jewish burial.

Northward along the East Side to the Harlem River a large number of independent gangs ruled their kingdoms with a ferocity equal to that of the downtown groups. The Red Peppers and the Duffy Hills engaged in constant and bitter warfare for the privilege of plundering East 102nd street and adjacent territory, while the Pansies, under the inspired leadership of Rags Riley, maintained a rendezvous at Avenue A and Eighty-first street and looted the East River water front, as well as a considerable area inland. Still further north, the Italian gangs of Harlem's Little Italy held forth, most of their murders being committed in the vicinity of the famous Murder Stable in East 125th street, which became noted as the scene of more killings than any other spot in America, with the exception of the Bloody Angle of Doyers street, in Chinatown. But a majority of these homicides were the result of feuds transplanted from Sicily, and had little to do with ordinary gang operations. The most celebrated of the Italian gangs was that captained by Ignazio Lupo, better known as Lupo the Wolf, who was one of the most desperate and blood-thirsty criminals this country has ever seen. And his followers were just as ferocious. They were greatly feared by their simple countrymen, for not only were they amazingly proficient in the use of the bomb, revolver and stiletto, but were reputed to be able to cast the evil eye, and to possess other magical powers. Whenever an honest

Italian so much as heard the name of Lupo the Wolf he felt impelled to cross himself, and to extend his crossed fingers to ward off the spells which the evil man might throw about him. Frantic men who had been marked for slaughter or robbery frequently appealed to their priests to protect them against Lupo's magic, but the holy men had scant success. Besides participating in the vendettas of the Mafia and the Black Hand, Lupo the Wolf hired his killers and thugs out to other Italian secret orders, and was also an expert counterfeiter. His principal lieutenant was Giuseppi Morello, whose eighteen-year-old stepson was tortured and murdered because he was suspected of betraying gang secrets. William J. Flynn, Chief of the United States Secret Service, traced sixty murders to Lupo's gang, including the killing of Detective Lieutenant Joseph Petrosino in Palermo, Italy, whither he had gone to collect information about the records of Italian criminals in this country. Practically every victim of the Italian gangs was found with his tongue slit in approved Sicilian fashion, and the gangsters also showed a fondness for cramming bodies into barrels, trunks and baskets, and shipping them to other cities. Most of the barrel murders which were so common during the first ten years of the present century were the result of this custom.

5

AS rapidly as the ranks of the gangs were depleted, either by death or by the occasional activity of the police, they were filled by the street boys and by recruits from the young men's social clubs which abounded throughout the East and West Sides, bearing such names as the Twin Oaks, the Yankee Doodle Boys, the Go-Aheads, the Liberty Athletic Club, the Round Back Rangers, the Bowery Indians, the East Side Crashers, the East Side Dramatic and Pleasure Club, the Jolly Forty-eight, the Soup Greens and the Limburger Roarers. These organizations were patterned after, and in many instances controlled and supported by, the political associations which had been formed in large numbers by the Tammany district leaders, who thereby strengthened their

hold upon the voting masses. Such societies had been an important source of Tammany's power since the early days of New York
politics, but it was not until the nineties that they approached the
full flower of perfection. They generally bore the names of the
district leaders or local bosses, who dominated them and provided funds for their frequent social functions, for the outings upon
which the poor women and children were taken during the summer months, and for the gifts of coal, shoes and other necessities
which were showered upon the tenement population in the winter.
It was usually through these organizations, also, that arrangements were made with the gang leaders for thugs to black-jack
voters at the polls, act as repeaters and, on occasion, remove opponents who had made themselves obnoxious and dangerous.

Under the patronage of the political associations, the young
men's clubs appeared during the early nineties in greater numbers than ever before, although they had for many years been a
feature of life in the congested tenement districts, where there
was little opportunity for legitimate pleasure. Some remained
respectable, but a majority were composed of young hoodlums
and petty sneak thieves, all of whom were potential if not actual
gangsters. They greatly admired such redoubtable heroes as
Monk Eastman, Paul Kelly and Humpty Jackson, and hundreds
had no higher ambition than to win commendation from the
reigning monarchs of the underworld. Sometimes their women
friends were admitted to full membership privileges, and names
were chosen which complimented the ladies. Hence the Lady
Locusts, the Lady Barkers' Association, the Lady Flashers, the
Lady Liberties of the Fourth Ward, and the Lady Truck Drivers'
Association.

Many of the clubs made their rendezvous in tumbledown
barns, in the basements of tenement houses, or in halls and audi-
toriums, but others met at regular intervals in the back rooms of
saloons or dives, where certain corners were set apart for their
business and carousing sessions. All gave frequent social affairs,
which they called rackets, resorting to intimidation to compel
merchants and other business men to buy tickets. These methods
were generally adopted by the gangsters, for they were typical

gang practices, and it became customary for a gangster who was widely known as a desperado and a killer to organize an association of which he was the only member, and then give as many rackets in the course of the year as the traffic would bear. One of the most successful of these was the Biff Ellison Association, composed solely of Biff Ellison himself, which sponsored three rackets a year at Tammany Hall. From these affairs Ellison received an annual income of some three thousand dollars, no mean sum in those days, which enabled him to live a life of leisure. But eventually he became weary of such easy graft and opened a sink of sin in the Bowery near Cooper Union, which he aptly named Paresis Hall. It was closed after a few months.

Many of the rackets given by the gangsters, the social clubs and the political associations were held in Tammany Hall, but even more popular were Walhalla Hall, better known as Walla Walla, in Orchard street near Grand, and New Irving Hall in Broome street, successor to the old Green Dragon resort which was wrecked by the Dead Rabbits during their fight with the Bowery Boys in 1857. For a few hours the functions were always conducted with great decorum, and the utmost care was taken to observe the niceties of correct social intercourse. But the bar was always well patronized, the ladies were beautiful and amiable, and the gentlemen hot-blooded, and it was seldom that an East Side ball did not end in a free-for-all fight. Sometimes a battle started because members of one club attended the affair of another wearing dress suits; and their rivals were frequently so demoralized by the spectacle that they forthwith, in order to obtain money, embarked upon a clumsy robbery of which the police were compelled to take notice. Such an incident marred the ball of the William J. Sullivan Association at New Irving Hall in the middle nineties, and prevented several members of that organization from attending the festivities. The Cherry Hill Gang announced that its members would attend *en masse* wearing dress suits, and five members of the Sullivan Association, who were also shining lights of the Batavia Street Gang, felt that it was incumbent upon them to equal if not excel the display. Led by Duck Reardon and Mike Walsh, they cast about for ways and means, and after much cogitation two of them sneaked a watch out of Herman Segal's jewelry store in New Chambers street. They raffled the time-piece at Coyne's saloon in James street, and so manipulated the drawing that one of their own number won it. But their work was crude, and when they again attempted to dispose of the watch they could sell no raffle tickets. So they returned to Segal's, where they smashed a show window with a brick and carried away forty-four gold rings, valued at from four to forty-five dollars each. These were sold, but the thieves were captured by the police while trying on dress suits in a Division street tailor shop. On the night of the ball they languished in the Tombs, and the honor of the Batavia Street Gang was trailed in the dust by the elegant heroes of Cherry Hill.

CHAPTER XIII

THE PRINCE OF GANGSTERS

I

THE MOVING pictures and the stage have always portrayed the gangster as a low, coarse person with an evilly glinting eye, a chin adorned with a rank stubble of unkempt beard, a plaid cap drawn down over beetling brows, and a swagger which in itself was sufficient to inform the world that here was a man bent on devilment. It is true that there were many such, and in the lore of the gangs there are numerous tales of their mighty exploits, but in the main the really dangerous gangster, the killer, was more apt to be something of a dandy. He dressed well, he shaved daily, he kept his nails manicured and his hair oiled and plastered to his skull, and when his gang gave a racket he generally contrived to grace the festivities in all the glory of a dress suit. In the days of the Dead Rabbits and the Bowery Boys, and later when Dandy Johnny Dolan of the Whyos was the fashion plate of gangland, the gangster was a big man; but in the course of years the misery and congestion of tenement life took their toll, and police and prison records show that the average gang member of the time of the Gophers, the Eastmans and the Five Pointers was not more than five feet and three inches tall, and weighed between 120 and 135 pounds.

Such noted followers of Paul Kelly as Eat 'Em Up Jack McManus and Louis Pioggi, better known as Louie the Lump, who was but a slim and beardless boy when he acquired a reputation as a murderer, followed the fashions with great care; and even Biff Ellison, for all his hugeness and great strength, was a fop in matters of dress. Ellison dearly loved to sprinkle himself with scent, of which he had his own private blend especially compounded by a druggist sworn to secrecy. Johnny Spanish was always arrayed like a lily of the field, as were Kid Twist and Richie Fitzpatrick, the most famous of Eastman's lieutenants; and Razor Riley, a noted Gopher who weighed less than a hundred pounds, but made up for his lack of heft by an amazing proficiency in the use of revolver, blackjack, and a huge razor which gave him his nickname. And Paul Kelly, who is now reformed and honorably occupied as a real estate broker and business agent for labor unions, was a perfect example of this type of gangster. Throughout his long career as chief of the Five Pointers Kelly exercised power second only to that of Monk Eastman, yet he was a dapper, soft-spoken chap who seldom engaged in rough-and-tumble fighting, although in his early youth he had been a bantam-weight pugilist of more than local renown. He resembled a bank clerk or a theological student more than a gang chieftain, and his dive, the New Brighton, was one of the flashiest palaces of sin in the city. Unlike most of his fellows, Kelly was fairly well educated. He spoke French, Spanish, and Italian, and with his well-bred manner could have moved at ease in relatively cultured society.

The story is told of a woman who went to New Brighton in Great Jones street, under the protection of a Headquarters detective, for the express purpose of seeing Paul Kelly, who had been mentioned in the newspapers in connection with some particularly sensational gang affray. For some time they sat in the midst of thieves and gangsters, literally surrounded by the current of miserable humanity which boiled up in the Bowery and Chatham Square and swirled through Chinatown and the East Side. Meanwhile they chatted with a dark, quiet little man who had been sitting at a table when they entered. He entertained them for half an hour with a dissertation on art, and then the woman and her escort departed. As they stepped out of the place the woman said:

"I am sorry we did not get to see Paul Kelly."

"Why," said the detective, "that was Paul Kelly you were talking to."

"Good gracious!" she exclaimed. "I thought he was slumming, too!"

But no one would ever have mistaken Monk Eastman, a worthy successor to Mose the Bowery Boy and as brave a thug as ever shot an enemy in the back or blackjacked a voter at the polls, for a bank clerk or a theological student. So far as looks were concerned, and actions, too, for that matter, Eastman was a true moving picture gangster. He began life with a bullet-shaped head, and during his turbulent career acquired a broken nose and a pair of cauliflower ears, which were not calculated to increase his beauty. He had heavily veined, sagging jowls, and a short, bull neck, plentifully scarred with battle marks, as were his cheeks. He seemed always to need a hair cut, and he accentuated his ferocious and unusual appearance by affecting a derby hat several sizes too small, which perched precariously atop his shock of bristly, unruly hair. He could generally be found strutting about his kingdom very indifferently dressed, or lounging at his ease in the Chrystie street rendezvous without shirt, collar, or coat. His hobby was cats and pigeons—animals have always seemed to possess a fascination for gangsters; many of them, after they reformed, or had been compelled by the police to abandon the active practice of thuggery, opened bird and animal stores and prospered. Monk Eastman is said to have owned, at one time, more than a hundred cats and five hundred pigeons, and although they were offered for sale in his bird and animal store in Broome street, it was seldom that he could be induced to part with any of them. He sometimes went abroad, on peaceful missions, with a cat under each arm, while several others trailed along in his wake. He also had a great blue pigeon which he had tamed, and which perched on his shoulder as he walked.

"I like de kits and boids," Eastman used to say. "I'll beat up any guy dat gets gay wit' a kit or a boid in my neck of de woods."

When a reporter once asked Eastman, a few months before his death, how many times he had been arrested, the gang leader replied that he would be damned if he knew; and at Headquarters the police said that they had lost count of the number. "What difference does it make?" asked a detective who had often performed the thankless task. "The politicians always sprung him. He was the best man they ever had at the polls." Nor could Eastman number his marks of battle. He had at least a dozen scars from knife wounds on his neck and face, and as many more on other parts of his body. He boasted that he had been shot so often that when he climbed on the scales he had to make allowance for the bullets imbedded in his body. When he enlisted in the New York National Guard at the outbreak of the World War and stripped for examination, the physicians thought they had to do with a veteran of every battle since Gettysburg. They asked him what wars he had been in.

"Oh!" replied Eastman, grinning, "a lot of little wars around New York!"

During his career as a gang chieftain Monk employed a score of aliases, among them Joseph Morris, Joseph Marvin, Edward Delaney, and William Delaney, but it was as Edward Eastman that he was best known. His real name appears to have been Edward Osterman. He was born about 1873 in the Williamsburg section of Brooklyn, the son of a respectable Jewish restaurant owner. His father set him up in business before he was twenty years old with a bird and animal store in Penn street, near the family establishment, but the boy was restless, and dissatisfied with the monetary rewards of honest toil. He soon abandoned the store and came to New York, where he assumed the name of Edward

Eastman and quickly sank to his natural social level. In the middle nineties he began to come into prominence as Sheriff of New Irving Hall, and is said to have been even more ferocious than Eat 'Em Up Jack McManus, who was making history in a similar office at Suicide Hall and the New Brighton. Eastman went about his duties carrying a huge club, while a blackjack nestled in his hip pocket, and each of his hands was adorned with a set of brass knuckles. In the use of these weapons he was amazingly proficient, and in an emergency could wield a beer bottle or a piece of lead pipe with an aptitude that was little short of genius. He was also a skillful boxer, and was a formidable adversary at rough-and-tumble, although he was not more than five feet and five inches tall, and his weight never exceeded one hundred and fifty pounds.

Within a year after his career began Eastman had cracked scores of heads, and he boasted that during his first six months as Sheriff of the New Irving fifty men whom he honored with his attentions had required the services of surgeons; his clubbings became so frequent, indeed, that the jocose drivers of Bellevue Hospital ambulances referred to the accident ward as the Eastman Pavilion. But Monk was always a gentleman; he was proud of the fact that he had never struck a woman with his club, no matter how much she annoyed him. When it became necessary to discipline a lady for a lapse in manners, he simply blackened her eyes with his fist.

"I only give her a little poke," he exclaimed. "Just enough to put a shanty on her glimmer. But I always takes off me knucks first."

Naturally, Eastman became one of the most celebrated citizens of the East Side, and innumerable young men began to imitate him in speech and manner, so that there came into existence a Monk Eastman school of hoodlums and brawlers. They expressed their admiration for the great bouncer by their slovenly appearance, their clipped, slangy speech, and a willingness to fight anybody, any time, and anywhere. Practically all of them enlisted under Eastman's banner when he surrendered his post at the New Irving and embarked upon a career as a practicing gang leader, and by 1900 he felt powerful enough to claim sovereignty over the domain which later became his by right of might. Then began his feud with Paul Kelly of the Five Pointers over the strip of territory between the Bowery and Nigger Mike's place in Pell street. Scarcely a week passed in which the gang chieftains did not send patrols into this No Man's Land, armed with blackjacks and revolvers and with instructions to kill or maim every opposing gangster found within the disputed territory.

The merciless warfare between the great captains kept the Chatham Square, Bowery and Chinatown districts in an uproar of excitement and terror, for not all of the gangsters were good shots, and their wild bullets frequently injured non-combatants and smashed windows. Occasionally the police appeared in force and made spectacular pretence of clubbing both sides, but in general these were meaningless gestures, for both Eastman and Kelly had strong political connections and were in high favor with the Tammany Hall statesmen. Eastman, in particular, became an especial pet of the Wigwam; for years he served the Tammany organization in many ways, and was especially useful around election times, when he voted his gangsters in droves and employed them to blackjack honest citizens who thought to cast their ballots according to their convictions. Whenever Eastman got into trouble Tammany Hall lawyers appeared in court for him and Tammany bondsmen furnished his bail, which was promptly forfeited and the case expunged from the records. In the intervals between his political engagements Eastman did what may best be described as a general gang business. He became interested in houses of prostitution and stuss games, he shared in the earnings of prostitutes who walked the streets under his protection, he directed the operations of his pickpockets, loft burglars and footpads, and provided thugs for men who wished to rid themselves of enemies, graduating his fees according to the degree of disability desired. Eastman himself sometimes led selected members of his gang in raids upon the stuss games which flourished throughout the East Side, and also, on occasion, personally accepted a blackjacking commission.

"I like to beat up a guy once in a while," he used to say. "It keeps me hand in."

Eastman had frequently felt the thud of a fist against his flesh while officiating as Sheriff of the New Irving, but it was not until the summer of 1901 that he experienced his first contact with a bullet. Then, having ventured abroad without his body guard, he was assailed in the Bowery, near Chatham Square, by half a dozen Five Pointers who fell upon him with blackjack and revolver. Unarmed except for his brass knuckles and his slung-shot, Eastman defended himself valiantly, and had knocked down three of the attacking force when a fourth shot him twice in the stomach. They fled, leaving him for dead upon the sidewalk, but he scrambled to his feet and staggered to Gouverneur Hospital, closing a gaping wound with his fingers. For several weeks the gang leader lay at the point of death, but in conformity with the code of the underworld he refused to divulge to the police the name of the man who had shot him. Meanwhile the war with the Five Pointers proceeded with redoubled ferocity, and a week after Eastman had been discharged from the hospital the police found a dead Five Pointer lying in the gutter at Grand and Chrystie streets; he had been decoyed from his accustomed haunt by a woman and shot to death.

For more than two years the conflict between the Eastmans and the Five Pointers raged almost without cessation, and the darkened streets of the East Side and the old Paradise Square section were filled night after night with scurrying figures who shot at each other from carriages, or from that strange new invention, the automobile, or pounced one upon the other from the shelter of doorways, with no warning save the vicious swish of a blackjack or section of lead pipe. Stuss games owned by members of the Eastman clan were held up and robbed by the Five Pointers, and Kelly's sources of revenue were similarly interfered with by the redoubtable Monk and his henchmen. Balls and other social functions in New Irving and Walhalla Halls were frequently interrupted while the gangsters shot out their mutual hatred without regard for the safety and convenience of the merry-makers; and the owners of dives and dance halls lived in constant fear that their resorts would be the scene of bloody combat, and so subject them to unwelcome notoriety. But it was not until the middle of

August, 1903, that the crisis of the war was reached and the gangs met in the battle which marked the end of the feud, for it aroused the politicians to a realization of the needless slaughter of their most valuable assets, and awakened the general public to a knowledge of the power of the gangs.

There had been desultory fighting throughout the hot days of summer, and at eleven o'clock on a sultry August night half a dozen prowling Eastmans came upon a like number of Five Pointers preparing to raid a stuss game in Rivington street, under the Allen street arch of the Second avenue elevated railroad. The game was in Eastman territory and was known to be under Monk's personal protection, for it was operated by one of his friends who faithfully gave him a large percentage of the take. The indignant Eastmans promptly killed one of the invading Five Pointers, and after a flurry of shots the adherents of Paul Kelly sought refuge behind the pillars of the elevated structure, whence they emerged cautiously from time to time to take pot shots at the Eastmans, who had availed themselves of similar protection. After half an hour of ineffectual firing, during which two policemen who attempted to interfere fled down Rivington street with their uniforms full of bullet holes, messengers were dispatched to the headquarters of both gangs, and within a short time reinforcements began to arrive.

Eastman himself led a detachment of his thugs on the run from the Chrystie street dive, and from the shelter of an elevated pillar in the fore front of the battle directed the fire of his gangsters. The police were never able to learn whether Paul Kelly himself took part in the fight, but it is quite likely that he did, for he was never one to shirk danger, and whenever there was trouble he was generally to be found in the midst of it. At any rate, more than a hundred gangsters, about evenly divided between Eastmans and Five Pointers, had arrived by midnight, and were blazing away at each other with every elevated pillar sheltering a gunman. Half a dozen Gophers, wandering out of Hell's Kitchen into the East Side in quest of profitable adventure and honorable advancement, came upon the scene, and stayed not to learn the point at issue or even who was fighting, but unlimbered their artillery and went joyfully into action, firing indiscriminately at both Eastmans and Five Pointers. As one of the Gophers later explained:

"A lot of guys was poppin' at each other, so why shouldn't we do a little poppin' ourselves?"

While the battle raged storekeepers of the district barricaded their doors and windows, and dwellers in the tenements locked themselves in their rooms. Half a dozen policemen arrived after the fighting had been in progress about half an hour, but retired in disorder when the gangsters greeted them with a hail of bullets. It was not until the reserves from several stations charged down Rivington street with roaring revolvers that the thugs left the protection of the elevated railroad structure and fled into their dens. They left three dead and seven wounded upon the field, and a score were arrested before they could get away. One of the prisoners was Monk Eastman, who gave the name of Joseph Morris and said that he had just happened to be passing and heard the shooting. Naturally, he stopped to see what was going on. He was arraigned before a magistrate next morning and promptly discharged.

The politicians suffered excruciating pain when they opened their newspapers and read the accounts of the fighting under the elevated structure. Having provided burial for the dead and proper hospital care for the wounded, they called upon Eastman and Paul Kelly and impressed upon them the obvious fact that such wholesale combat jeopardized their usefulness. The gang chieftains were told that no one objected to an occasional murder or blackjacking if they were strictly in line of business, and that even a little fancy sniping now and then might be overlooked, for everyone knew that gangsters would be gangsters; but that engagements in force terrorized the East Side and must stop. A meeting between Eastman and Kelly was arranged, and a few days later the gang leaders came face to face in the Palm, an unsavory dive in Chrystie street near Grand, Kelly having been guaranteed safe conduct at the request of the Tammany politicians. Tom Foley, a notable figure in the councils of the Wigwam, who had employed Eastman to good advantage during a hot campaign in the Second Assembly district, acted as mediator, and after he had presented the case for peace, with covert threats that both gangs would be smashed if they continued their private feud, Kelly and Eastman agreed to stop the shooting and stabbing. It was further agreed that the disputed strip between the Bowery and Nigger Mike's should be neutral territory, subject to the operations of either gang. Foley then gave a ball to celebrate the truce, and just before the grand march Eastman and Kelly met in the center of the dance floor and ceremoniously shook hands. Thereafter they viewed the revels of their followers from a box, while the Eastmans and the Five Pointers danced with each others' girls under the benign eye of Tom Foley; and there was peace on earth and good will toward men.

So far as the actual number of men engaged was concerned, the battle of Rivington street was not to be compared with some of the earlier conflicts between the great gangs of the Bowery and Five Points. But it probably marked the heaviest concentration of firearms in gang history, for the old-timers were inclined to settle their differences with clubs, teeth, fists, and brickbats, and only an occasional gangster sported a pistol. But during the Eastman period there were few thugs who did not carry at least two revolvers; some lugged as many as four, besides the standard equipment of blackjacks and brass knuckles. Before the passage of the Sullivan law early in 1911, which made the possession of a firearm a prison offense, one or more guns was carried openly at the hip or thrust into the belt, while another could generally be found slung by a special harness under the gangster's armpit. This was a favorite device of the killers; a revolver so carried was easier to draw than if borne in any other position, and there was scant likelihood that it would be snatched by an adversary. Occasionally, when the police were on their infrequent rampages, a gang leader who was temporarily in bad odor with the authorities went about with his pockets sewed up, attended by a henchman who supplied him with cigarettes, matches and other articles which he might require. Prying detectives then not only failed to find a revolver on his person, but could not put one there and so send him to prison on manufactured evidence.

But such a gangster was by no means unprotected. Behind and before him marched his thugs with their pockets literally crammed with knives, blackjacks, and revolvers, and if trouble developed the chieftain found the proper weapon immediately ready to his hand. These gun-carriers were frequently arrested but they took the chance gladly in order that they might serve the Master and win favor in his eyes. Often a woman bore the revolver; she carried it in her muff, or in the huge hat of the period, or in a pocket of her jacket. The enormous coiffures called Mikado tuck-ups, which were popular in the nineties, offered excellent places for the concealment of a weapon; and when the pompadour came into vogue, the wire contrivance called a rat, upon which the hair was built up over the forehead, was replaced by a revolver. And sometimes the gangster's sweetheart carried his pistol smuggled against the bare skin of her upper arm, where it was held in place by elastic bands and was instantly available through a slit in her leg-of-mutton sleeve. Many of the gangsters kept reserve revolvers and blackjacks, which they called Bessies, in cigar and stationery stores throughout their districts.

2

DEBARRED by the terms of his agreement with Tom Foley from battling the Five Pointers, Monk Eastman sought an outlet for his restless spirits by increasing the frequency with which he attended in person to the various sluggings and blackjackings which had hitherto been largely carried out by his henchmen. Less than three weeks after the battle in Rivington street Eastman and two of his gangsters went to Freehold, N. J., where they assaulted James McMahon, a coachman employed by David Lamar, whose financial operations had earned him much fame as the Wolf of Wall street. McMahon was to have appeared in court against Lamar, but as he and his lawyers walked up the courthouse steps Eastman and his thugs fell upon them, and beat and stabbed McMahon so savagely that he was unable to testify, and the case was dismissed. The gangsters escaped in a cab, but were captured a few hours later and lodged in the Freehold jail, where Eastman gave his name as William Delaney.

The gang chieftain sent word of his plight to Kid Twist, his principal lieutenant, who promptly mustered fifty heavily armed gangsters and loaded them into a string of carriages, intending to storm the New Jersey prison. But before the vehicles could leave the Chrystie street rendezvous Inspector McCluskey swooped down upon them with a large force of patrolmen, and after a fierce fight forced the thugs back into their den. Kid Twist then notified Tammany Hall, and the next morning two of the Wigwam's most brilliant legal luminaries proceeded post haste to Freehold. There political wires were pulled and witnesses obtained, and when Eastman and his followers were arraigned on a charge of felonious assault they were discharged and returned to Manhattan in triumph. That night Monk held a levee in his headquarters to celebrate his escape from Jersey justice.

The truce between the Eastmans and the Five Pointers was scrupulously observed by both sides for several months, but in the winter of 1903 an Eastman named Hurst wandered into a Bowery dive and became involved in a weighty argument with a disciple of Paul Kelly, one Ford, the issue being the bravery of their respective chieftains. The dispute ended in a fight, and Hurst was badly mauled; it is related that his nose was broken in two places and one of his ears twisted off. Monk Eastman immediately sent word to Kelly that Ford's life was forfeit, and that if Kelly did not care to attend to the matter of putting him out of the way, the Eastmans would invade the domain of the Five Pointers and take summary vengeance. As Monk expressed it, "We'll wipe up de earth wit' youse guys." Kelly replied tartly that the Eastmans were welcome to Ford if they could take him, and both sides prepared for war. But again the anxious politicians interfered, and once more a meeting was arranged between Eastman and Kelly, who made no promises but agreed to talk the matter over in the presence of neutral persons. Accompanied by armed body-guards, the gang leaders again met in the Palm. They shook hands with great formality and then, each with a huge cigar between his teeth and a hand on his revolver, sat at a table and proceeded to discuss ways and means to retain their honor and at the same time keep their thugs from each other's throats. They recognized that something must be done, for the politicians had informed them that if another outbreak occurred protection would be withdrawn and the police permitted to wreak their will upon them. And there were many policemen who yearned for just such an opportunity, for the honest members of the force had long suffered at the hands of the gangsters.

After much discussion it was agreed that the issue of supremacy should be decided by a prize fight between Kelly and Eastman, the loser to accept the overlordship of the victor and be content to remain strictly within his own domain. On the appointed night the gang chieftains, each accompanied by fifty of his best fighters, repaired to an old barn in the farthest reaches of The Bronx. Because of his early experience in the professional prize ring, Kelly possessed superior science, but it was offset by Eastman's weight and greater ferocity. They fought for two hours without either gaining an advantage, and at length, after they had collapsed and lay one across the other still trying feebly to strike, their followers loaded them into carriages and hauled them to the East Side and the Five Points. The bout was pronounced a draw, and as soon as they had recovered from their wounds the gang chieftains marshalled their resources and prepared for war to the finish, despite the protests of the politicians.

There were a few unimportant skirmishes, but the end of Monk Eastman's rule was in sight, and great trouble was also brewing in the pot for Paul Kelly. Eastman's downfall came first. At three o'clock in the morning of February 2, 1904, he and Chris Wallace, having gone far afield to Sixth avenue and Forty-second street to blackjack a man who had annoyed one of the gang leader's clients, saw a well-dressed young man staggering uncertainly down the street. Behind him, at a distance of some few yards, was a roughly dressed man who the gangsters thought was a lush worker waiting for his victim to fall. Eastman and Wallace promptly held up the young man, but it developed that he was a member of a rich family, and that the rough-looking man was a Pinkerton detective hired to protect him while he sowed his wild oats. The Pinkerton method has always been to shoot first and then ask questions of criminals, and as soon as Eastman and Wallace had poked their revolvers under the young man's nose and begun to slip their nimble fingers into his pockets, the detective promptly shot at them. The surprised gangsters returned the fire, and then fled down Forty-second street, turning occasionally to send a warning bullet in the direction of the pursuing Pinkerton. But at Broadway and Forty-second street, in front of the Hotel Knickerbocker, they ran into the arms of a policeman. Wallace escaped, but the patrolman knocked Eastman down with his nightstick, and when the gang leader regained consciousness he was in a cell in the West Thirtieth street station, and had been booked on charges of highway robbery and felonious assault. Indictments were promptly procured, and although at first Eastman laughed at the efforts of the District Attorney to bring him to trial, he became frantic when Tammany Hall ignored his appeals for aid. He was abandoned by his erstwhile friends, and almost before he knew what had happened to him he had been tried, convicted and was on his way to Sing Sing Prison under a ten-year sentence. Paul Kelly professed profound grief when he heard of his rival's misfortune. "Monk was a soft, easy-going fellow," said Kelly. "He had a gang of cowards behind him, second story men, yeggs, flat robbers and moll-buzzers. But he was a game fellow. He fought everyone's battles. I'd give ten thousand dollars to see him out of prison." The politicians, however, would not give ten cents, and so Eastman donned the stripes, and was never more a power in the underworld.

The harassed East Side hoped that with Eastman imprisoned there would be peace among the gangs, and the police and politicians exerted every effort to bring about such a desirable condition. Paul Kelly was amenable to reason, for the political powers had told him flatly that a continuation of the trouble would find him in very hot water; they threatened, among other things, to close his New Brighton dive, which was not only a source of much revenue but the pride of his heart as well. For a year or so there were very few outbreaks, for the downfall of Eastman had demoralized his gang, and his chief lieutenants, Kid Twist and Richie

Fitzpatrick, were busy trying to hold the gangsters together. They succeeded to a very large extent, but inevitably became jealous of each other, and were soon at sword's points over the succession, each claiming the right to Monk's throne. There was little to choose between them as thugs. Kid Twist, whose real name was Max Zweibach, or Zwerbach, had killed six men and had been entrusted by Eastman with many important enterprises, but Richie Fitzpatrick was also a killer, and was not disposed to be the satellite of any star of a lesser magnitude than the great Monk himself.

Kid Twist finally proposed a conference to settle all differences and determine definitely who was to rule the gang, and Fitzpatrick foolishly assented, although he well knew Twist's treacherous nature. The pair met late at night in the back room of a Chrystie street dive, but scarcely had the conference begun when the lights were suddenly extinguished and a revolver blazed. When the police arrived the room was vacant except for Richie Fitzpatrick, who lay stretched upon the floor with a bullet in his heart and his arms carefully folded across his chest. The detectives came into possession of manufactured evidence implicating Kid Dahl, a warm friend of Kid Twist's, and Dahl was promptly arrested. But he was as quickly released, for he produced an iron-bound alibi, and obviously had played no part in the murder. Twist sent flowers to Fitzpatrick's funeral and adorned his sleeve with a mourning band, both of which were regarded in the underworld as very graceful gestures, and then assumed unquestioned dominion over the Eastman gang. It was necessary to reward Kid Dahl for his fortitude in submitting to arrest, and Kid Twist cast an envious eye upon the stuss game operated in Suffolk street by the Bottler, a Five Pointer whose sobriquet aptly described him. The Bottler was no fighter, but he was a genius at cheating, and his game was one of the most prosperous on the East Side. Paul Kelly had guaranteed him protection in return for frequent contributions to the war chest of the Five Pointers.

Twist and Dahl called upon the Bottler one hot summer evening, and the latter was informed that thereafter Kid Dahl would be his partner in the stuss game, and that all profits were to be equally divided. The Bottler protested, but perforce consented to the arrangement, for the alternative was death, and he knew that he would be defunct long before Paul Kelly could send his legions to the rescue. For several weeks the Bottler and Kid Dahl shared in the earnings of the game, and then Kid Twist sent word to the Bottler that his share of the stuss game had been allotted to the Nailer, who had performed some slight service for the gang leader and deserved reward. The Bottler was invited to seek new pastures immediately, but with the courage of desperation he barricaded his house and swore that he would defend himself and his stuss game against Kid Twist and all his minions. The indignant Kid Dahl immediately besieged the place, but as he strode back and forth waving his revolver and angrily inviting the Bottler to come forth and die, a detective interfered, and the next day he was fined five dollars for disturbing the peace. A similar fine was imposed upon the Bottler for being the cause of the disturbance.

Twist and his councillors now gave serious thought to the Bottler, and it was decided that only blood could wipe out the affront to the gang and the challenge to the chieftain's authority. But the police were aware of all the circumstances, and it was inevitable that there would be considerable danger should either Kid Twist or Kid Dahl attend in person to the Bottler's demise. In the emergency Kid Twist sent to Brooklyn for Vach Lewis, otherwise Cyclone Louie, a professional strong man who occasionally appeared at Coney Island side shows and thrilled the tourists by bending iron bars around his neck and twisting them about his arms. Cyclone Louie agreed to kill the Bottler out of friendship for Kid Twist and Kid Dahl, and the time for the murder was fixed at nine o'clock of a certain evening. At that hour Kid Twist was in the Delancey street police station arguing with the desk sergeant about the release of a gangster who had brought about his own arrest for just such a purpose, while Kid Dahl was in a Houston street restaurant, quarrelling with the proprietor over the time. And while alibis were thus being arranged, a man with his hat drawn down over his eyes entered the stuss game, walked up to the Bottler and shot him twice through the heart in the presence of twenty men. But when the police came there was only the dead Bottler. A few days later the game reopened with Kid Dahl and the Nailer in charge. Kid Dahl loudly bemoaned the unfortunate death of his partner, and hung crêpe on the door of the stuss house.

While Kid Twist was concerned with the affairs of the Bottler, and was otherwise consolidating his position as successor to Monk Eastman, the fates were shuffling the cards for Paul Kelly, and finally chose Razor Riley and Biff Ellison as the instruments wherewith to accomplish the downfall of the king of the Five Pointers. Ellison's first appearance in New York gang circles had been as bouncer in Fat Flynn's resort in Bond street, where he earned his sobriquet. Later he became sheriff of a Chrystie street resort, and attracted much favorable attention by knocking a policeman unconscious with a beer bottle and then stamping him. The cause of the enmity which in time arose between Kelly and Ellison was never known, although some of the detectives believed that it may have been Kelly's reputed refusal to bestow upon Ellison the honorable post of Sheriff of the New Brighton, made vacant when Eat 'Em Up Jack McManus was tapped on the head with a piece of lead pipe.

But whatever the cause, the undoing of Paul Kelly became an obsession with Biff Ellison, and Razor Riley saw eye to eye with him in his hatred, for Riley had once been ejected from the New Brighton by Paul Kelly in person, and never forgot the indignity. Also, as a Gopher of distinction, Riley was at all times prepared to undertake any project which might disturb or demoralize another gang. So there came at length a winter's night when Ellison and Riley, both half drunk, sat at a table in Nigger Mike Salter's place in Pell street and debated the feasibility of a raid upon the New Brighton. The more they drank the more attractive the enterprise appeared, for they conjectured that they might be able not only to kill Paul Kelly, but to win great renown in gangland by such a daring adventure. About half an hour before midnight they left Nigger Mike's and went northward through the softly falling snow along the Bowery to Great Jones street, and so to the New Brighton, where the flower and chivalry of the gangs were assembled in their nightly revels.

When Ellison and Razor Riley strode into the resort, Paul Kelly sat at a table in the rear, talking to Bill Harrington, Rough House Hogan, and Harrington's sweetheart, who was variously known as Goldie Cora and Cora the Blonde. For a moment the raiders stood just inside the doorway, and then, each hand clutching a revolver, they rushed upon the dance floor, while the music ceased abruptly and the dancers spread out before them like a fan, for there was murder in their hard eyes and in the cold glint of the guns. Harrington cried a warning when they were yet twenty feet from Paul Kelly, whereat Razor Riley turned and shot him through the brain. A bullet from Ellison's revolver ripped through Paul Kelly's coat sleeve, and the gang leader promptly dived under the table, coming up on the other side with a revolver in each hand, and with both guns spitting bullets at the onrushing Ellison and Riley. The next instant someone switched out the lights, and for five minutes revolvers blazed in the darkness, and the gangsters and their ladies who were not concerned in the fighting left the New Brighton by doorway and window. It was half an hour later that a policeman wandered in, and the dive which only a little while before had blazed with light and merriment was now dark, and deserted save for the dead body of Harrington sprawled upon the floor.

Neither Riley nor Ellison was injured, but three bullets had crashed into Paul Kelly's body, and he was carried by his friends into the street, and hurried northward into Harlem. There he lay in seclusion for a month, while political wires were pulled and arrangements made for his safety. He then surrendered to the police, but was never brought to trial, for his plea of self-defense was accepted. Razor Riley fled into the fastnesses of Hell's Kitchen, and died of pneumonia before the police could search him out, while Biff Ellison went to Baltimore. He was not caught until 1911, when he ventured into New York. He was promptly convicted and sent to Sing Sing for from eight to twenty years, but long before he had completed his sentence he was a mental and physical wreck.

The New Brighton was never reopened after the raid by Ellison and Razor Riley, but when he had recovered from his wounds

Paul Kelly started another place in Great Jones street which he called Little Naples. Misfortune, however, had marked him for its own, and the new venture came under the displeasure of the reform elements and was closed during the latter part of 1906. Thereafter the Five Pointers dwindled in membership and in prestige and Kelly's power gradually declined, although for several years he retained under his leadership some of the hardiest thugs and the quickest shooting gunmen of the underworld, all of whom were eager to find favor in his eyes and carve for themselves permanent niches in gangland's hall of fame. And not the least ambitious was Louis Pioggi, better known as Louie the Lump, who joined the Five Pointers in 1906 as a dapper, undersized youth of seventeen, and two years later became an important figure because it fell to his lot to avenge the unfortunate Bottler and complete the breakup of the old Monk Eastman gang.

It was the custom of the gang leaders and their more important followers to take their ease in the drinking and dancing places of Coney Island during the early part of a summer evening, returning later to the dives of Chinatown and the Bowery. On the night of May 14, 1908, both Kid Twist and Louie the Lump decided to grace the Island with their presence, neither knowing that the other was to be there. Louie the Lump wandered about the resort for a while, and then went to the dance hall where Carroll Terry, a lovely dancing girl, was employed, although she had already given him to understand that she preferred the attentions of the more illustrious Kid Twist. He danced with her, and after much pleading induced her to promise that she would return to Manhattan with him after her night's work had ended. Half an hour later Kid Twist and Cyclone Louie entered the dance hall and sat at a table, where Carroll Terry joined them. They were drinking beer when Louie the Lump passed some time later. He looked in and saw them, and went away with rage and jealousy in his heart, for he knew that the girl would not go with him now that Kid Twist had arrived. He wandered off Surf avenue into a saloon, and there began to drink straight whiskey as rapidly as he could pour it down his throat. But he had not been thus engaged more than a few minutes when Kid Twist and

Cyclone Louie came in. They joined him, despite his glowering frown and his very evident distaste for their company.

"I just seen Carroll, Louie," said Twist, with a grin, "an' she says youse is the biggest bum she knows."

Louie the Lump writhed in agony, but said never a word.

"She says you was an active little cuss," Twist continued, "always jumpin' aroun'. Let's see how active youse is, kid. Take a jump out of the window!"

Louie the Lump hesitated, and Kid Twist's hand crept menacingly toward his pocket. So Louie jumped. He landed on all fours, and scrambling to his feet stood for a moment beneath the window listening to the boisterous merriment of Kid Twist and Cyclone Louie. Then he went to a telephone. He called a man high up in the councils of the Five Pointers and stated his case. He had to kill Kid Twist and he had to kill him immediately, for by all the standards of gangland, he had been outrageously insulted and humiliated.

"I got to cook him," said Louie the Lump.

"Sure you got to cook him," agreed the man higher up. "You tail these birds and I'll send a fleet down. When the boys get there you get these bums into the street and open up wi' your cannisters. The boys'll take care of Twist's mob an' the bulls."

Half a dozen Five Pointers hurried to Coney Island as rapidly as the trolley cars would carry them. When they reached the resort from which Louie the Lump had made such an inglorious exit they found Kid Twist and Cyclone Louie still sitting at a table chuckling over the tale which would ring up and down the Bowery on the morrow. Louie the Lump, white hot anger blazing from his dark eyes, lounged in an ancient coupé which had been drawn up at the curb. The leader of the Five Pointers spoke briefly to the driver of the vehicle, money changed hands, and a gangster mounted the box and took the reins, while the owner of the coupé vanished in the crowd. A few minutes later a thug unknown to Kid Twist walked into the dive and timidly approached the gang leader.

"Say, Kid," he said, "Carroll Terry wants to see you outside a minute."

THE PRINCE OF GANGSTERS ■ 273

"Sure," replied Twist. "I'll be right out. Come on, Louie."
They stepped into the street and a voice cried:
"Over this way, Kid!"
Twist turned and saw enemies on all sides of him. But before he could draw a revolver Louie the Lump crashed a bullet through his brain, and then shot him in the heart as he toppled to the sidewalk. Cyclone Louie started to run, but the guns of the Five Pointers blazed and cracked, and the strong man fell across the body of his chieftain, shot through and through. Carroll Terry, on her way to meet Kid Twist, reached the scene just in time to receive a bullet through her shoulder from the spitting gun of Louie the Lump. She too, fell across the dead body of the gang leader.

These things happened within a few seconds, and with their victims lying upon the sidewalk, the Five Pointers scattered. Louie the Lump leaped into the coupé, sent a bullet through the helmet of an inquisitive policeman, and having thus discouraged pursuit, set out for Manhattan. There he remained in hiding until certain political movements had been made, and then he went into court and pleaded guilty to manslaughter. He was sentenced to eleven months in the reformatory at Elmira, but he was not impressed.

"What's eleven months?" he sneered. "I could do that standin' on me head!"

3

ABOUT a year after the murder of Kid Twist, in June, 1909, Monk Eastman was released from Sing Sing by the State Board of Parole under the law which made a convict sentenced for the first time eligible for parole after he had served one-half his sentence. Eastman immediately returned to the East Side, but found himself a king without a kingdom and a general without an army. The death of Kid Twist had completed the demoralization of the Eastman gang, and it had begun to break up into factions, many of them at war with each other. Humpty Jackson and other leaders were in jail, still others had been killed, and some of the smaller gangs had vanished altogether. Even Paul Kelly had seen the hand-writing on the wall in the increased activity of the Committee of Fourteen and other reform agencies, and, although he retained many of his downtown connections and was a power there for sev-eral years, had transferred his principal headquarters to Harlem. There he made his first experiments in handling labor, an occu-pation which was to become an important source of revenue for him after he had reformed. He organized the ragpickers on the dumps at East River and 108th street, and became their business agent and walking delegate. Within a few months he called a strike, and three men were murdered in the fighting which fol-lowed the attempt of the employers to break the strike by import-ing downtown gangsters. Members of the Kelly gang then accept-ed commissions from a clique of real estate agents who coveted the fine old mansions which were still scattered through the dis-trict north of Yorkville, along the upper East Side, in the vicini-ty of 111th street. When the owners would not sell the gangsters began a campaign of systematic destruction and terrorization. They first stole the lead pipe and the outside trimmings; then they punched holes in the roofs, broke windows, destroyed porch-es and doors with bombs, and in obstinate cases resorted to beat-ing and shooting. After a few weeks of this sort of treatment the property owner was generally glad to sell at whatever price he could get and leave the neighborhood, and the clique immediate-ly remodelled the houses into cheap tenements and filled them with the hordes of Italians that had begun to swarm into the upper East Side.

Eastman tried desperately to reorganize his gang and regain his old position of importance, but he was unable to enlist under his banner more than half a score of his old followers, and so he became a sneak thief, a burglar, a pickpocket, and a dope ped-dler. He worked quietly for some three years, but in 1912 detec-tives invaded his apartment in East Thirteenth street and found him smoking opium, and in possession of a complete outfit for the manufacture of the drug. He was sent to prison for eight months by Judge Mayer of the United States District Court. In

September, 1914, Eastman was again arrested in Buffalo and accused of burglary, but was discharged. In June of the following year, however, he was convicted of a robbery in Albany and sent to Dannemora Prison for two years and eleven months. In September, 1917, he was arrested for fighting, but was discharged upon arraignment in Magistrate's Court. The next day the former gang leader went to Yonkers and enlisted in the 106th Infantry of the New York National Guard under the name of William Delaney. Within a few months he went overseas with his regiment.

The man who had ruled a thousand thugs with an iron hand submitted readily enough to the rigorous discipline of the Army, and served throughout the World War with honor and distinction. Bullets in the mass held no terrors for him after the gun fights of the East Side, and whenever his platoon went over the top Eastman was always in the forefront of the charge. Once when his company was relieved after holding a particularly hot part of the line, Eastman asked his commanding officer for permission to remain with the relieving troops as stretcher bearer; and while the other men of his regiment were resting he served in the front line, carrying wounded men to the rear. Again, when he had been wounded, he eluded his nurses after three days in the hospital and, unarmed and half-clad, made his way to the front and joined his command. Monk Eastman received no decorations for valour, but he won the esteem and confidence of his fellow doughboys and his officers, and when the regiment returned to America the latter signed a petition to Governor Alfred E. Smith to restore the gangster's citizenship. The captain of his company wrote to the Governor that Eastman "was a quiet and disciplined soldier, and toward all his comrades he evinced the greatest kindness and devotion."

On May 3, 1919, Governor Smith signed an executive order restoring Monk Eastman to full citizenship, and the former king of the gangsters said that he would go straight. The police obtained a job for him, and he did not again come to their attention until the morning of December 26, 1920, when his body was found lying on the sidewalk in front of the Blue Bird Café at No. 62 East Fourteenth street, near Fourth avenue. He had been shot five times and was dead. A few days later Eastman was buried with full military honors, and in December, 1921, Jerry Bohan, a Prohibition Enforcement Agent, pleaded guilty to manslaughter in the first degree and was sentenced to prison for from three to ten years. He was paroled late in 1923. Bohan said that he had quarrelled with Eastman over tipping a waiter, but when detectives began to investigate they found that Monk had been bootlegging and selling dope.

CHAPTER XIV

THE WARS OF THE TONGS

1

DOYERS STREET is a crooked little thoroughfare which runs twistingly, up hill and down, from Chatham Square to Pell street, and with Pell and Mott streets forms New York's Chinatown, of which it has always been the nerve center and the scene of much of the turbulent life of the quarter. It is an orphan street, ignored by the handbooks and histories of early New York, and there appears to be no record of how and for whom it was named. Perhaps the best guess is that it honors the memory of Anthony H. Doyer, who built a house at No. 3 in 1809, and after living there several years removed to Hudson street. In the beginning the thoroughfare was probably Doyer's Lane or Doyer's Road, and then it was listed as Doyer's street. Eventually a careless sign painter omitted the apostrophe and it became Doyers street, as it is today. A preposterous legend has it that one of the early Doyers buried a treasure of thirty-five million dollars in gold in the walls of his house, and there has been much tapping and digging for hidden chambers, but without success. The vastness of the sum belies the tale, yet it persists, and every few years a claimant to the mythical Doyer fortune appears, speaks his little piece and vanishes when he learns that the records of the Public Administrator do not show the existence of such an estate.

There has never been much reason for Doyers street, although in the early days of the city it may have been of some use as a lane or an alley. It is true that it forms a connecting link between Chatham Square and Pell street, but Pell street itself is but two blocks long and runs into the Bowery a few yards north of the Square. Doyers street is no good for traffic; it is too narrow; it resembles one of those mean byways in what the A.E.F. used to call the foreign sections of French cities. It is little more than two hundred feet in length, and it curves and twists so much that to get from one end of it to the other one could almost follow the directions for reaching the house of Kassim Baba—first to the right and then to the left, and again to the right and again to the left. But instead of the blue cross emblazoned upon the stone pillar of Kassim's palace there is at the Pell street end of Doyers street the high side wall of the Hip Sing Tong House, plastered over with red and white posters covered with Chinese writings in orange and black. This wall is the community billboard of Chinatown. It was there, during the tong conflicts, that the declarations of war were posted that all men might read save the stupid white devils. Likewise it held the edicts of the Gamblers' Union, the Bin Ching, a very efficient supervising agency for the tongs in the days when gambling was the principal diversion of the quarter.

A hundred years ago the section now called Chinatown was a district of brick dwellings inhabited principally by solid German families, with a sprinkling of respectable Irish who had little in common with their brawling brethren of the Five Points. But in 1858 a Cantonese, by name Ah Ken, came to New York and made his home in Mott street and put his slender capital in a small cigar store in Park Row. He prospered, and ten years later appeared Wah Kee, who established a shop at No. 13 Pell street, half a block from Doyers, where he did a good business in curios, vegetables, and preserved fruits and sweets. Most of Wah Kee's profits, however, came from gambling games and an opium-smoking dive which he operated above his store. Almost immediately he attracted the riff-raff of the Bowery and Chatham Square, and the character of the neighborhood began to change.

Wah Kee's graft was so excellent, and the police viewed his activities in such a tolerant and reasonable light, that word of his success spread abroad and in two years another Cantonese had set up a shop as a blind for a gambling hell and opium resort at No. 4 Mott street. In 1872 there were twelve Chinamen in the district, and by 1880 the number had increased to seven hundred. Then they came in droves, and it was not long before they had driven out the Irish and Germans and usurped the tenements in Doyers, Mott and Pell streets, while the overflow spread into the Bowery and along the streets southwest of Chatham Square, toward Five Points. In 1910 it was estimated that there were between ten thousand and fifteen thousand Chinese in New York, but now there are probably not more than half that number, for in recent years the colony has been considerably reduced by migrations to New Jersey towns, especially Newark, which has a larger Chinese settlement than the metropolis.

The tong wars appeared to have begun about 1899, and, with the exception of one or two which started over women, were all caused by conflicting gambling interests. The tongs are as American as chop suey—the latter is said to have been invented by an American dishwasher in a San Francisco restaurant, while the first tong was organized in the Western gold fields about 1860— and finally they became little more than associations for parcelling out gambling and opium smoking privileges. During the height of their power fan tan and pi gow games ran wide open throughout the lengths of Mott, Doyers and Pell streets; practically every store harbored a game of chance, and on quiet nights the fumes of opium, smoked in the basements and in the dingy rooms above the gambling places, floated down to the streets and mingled with the odors of stale beer, raw whiskey and unwashed men of all races. In the middle nineties there were two hundred gambling games in the small triangular area formed by the three streets of Chinatown, and almost as many opium dens. These dives paid an average of $17.50 a week each to the police, and smaller sums directly to the heads of the tongs, as well as a percentage of winnings to the Gamblers' Union. The latter sum came out of the pockets of the players and went to the tongs, but was in addition to the regular tribute exacted from the owner of the game. The efficiency with which the Union operated is shown by the following placard which was distributed in Chinatown in 1897, after the police, in a sudden spasm of virtue, had closed the gambling dens for a few weeks:

NOTICE TO FORTUNE SEEKERS

The gambling houses are reopened again. As extra expenses must be paid, a new rule has gone into effect. Instead of the old percentage of seven per cent., deducted from all winnings of over fifty cents, a new percentage has been established. Henceforth a percentage of seven per cent. will be deducted from all winnings, and a percentage of fourteen per cent. from all winnings over $25.

Every gambling place must post this notice on the wall where it can be easily seen.

Inspectors of the Gamblers' Union shall visit all gambling houses to see that this law is enforced, and any failure to comply with said law shall be punished by a fine of $10, half of which shall go to the informer.

Given under our hand and seal in the 17th year of Quong Soi, King, and the 9th month (October).

New York Bin Ching Union.

During this golden age of fan tan and pi gow Tom Lee was head of the On Leongs and boss of all the gambling; the Hip Sings were meek and lowly, and were permitted to operate only a few games. Moreover, Tom Lee controlled the only Chinese votes in New York City, six in number, and when occasion required voted them early and often, so that he was lord of the district and beloved of the politicians. In proof of their high regard they called him Mayor of Chinatown and invested him with the office of Deputy Sheriff of New York County. Thereafter the chieftain of the On Leongs pompously strode the streets with his splendidly burnished star glistening on his blouse, his great body encased in a suit of chain mail, and his hands resting on the shoulders of two retainers who walked by his side. Life was very pleasant for Tom Lee in those days; he was rich and powerful and there was no fly in his ointment save Wong Get, a mild and affable Chinaman who strove for ten years to topple Tom Lee from his pedestal. But Wong Get failed dismally; perhaps because Chinatown laughed at him, for he was a dude. He had cut his hair and wore white man's clothing, and his countrymen felt that he could not be trusted.

But early in 1900 the quiet and peaceful flow of Tom Lee's power was rudely interrupted by the appearance of Mock Duck, a bland, fat, moon-faced little man who was ambitious to rule the district as Emperor, and so became the terror of Chinatown. Mock Duck was a curious mixture of bravery and cowardice. He wore the shirt of chain mail with which all of the tong killers of the period protected their precious bodies, he carried two guns and a hatchet, and at times he would fight bravely, squatting on his haunches in the street with both eyes shut, and blazing away at a surrounding circle of On Leongs with an utter disregard of his own safety. He seldom hit what he aimed at, or anything else for that matter, but so long as he could pull the trigger he was dangerous to anyone up, down or sideways within range. At other times Mock Duck got the wind up, and fled pell mell to San Francisco or Chicago—but he always came back, filled with new schemes for the discomfiture of the On Leongs. However, these flights may have been strategical; it is not improbable that in reality Mock Duck was afraid of no one but his wife, Tai Yu. Once she invaded the flat of a Chinese woman in Division street, and finding Mock Duck there led him home by the scruff of the neck, stopping at every street corner to kick and slap him. He had to go blazing away with his two guns for a long time before he could quiet the laughter that this disgraceful incident inspired.

Flag of Truce on the On Leong Tong House in Mott Street

Mock Duck was a notable gambler in a race of gamblers. He would bet on anything; he has been known to wager his entire wealth on whether the number of seeds in an orange picked at random from a fruit cart was odd or even. He even gambled with his religion; hearing much of the power of the Christian God, and, indeed, seeing evidences of it in the prosperity of poorly paid policemen, he emblazoned over the head of his personal joss in his own house the motto from the American dollar, "In God we trust." Some years later, after the Society for the Prevention of Crime had unwittingly aided him in his schemes against the On Leongs, he replaced the joss in the Hip Sing Tong House with a huge crayon portrait of Frank Moss, counsel for and aid to the celebrated Dr. Charles H. Parkhurst in his pursuit of the devil.

Wong Get was fast growing discouraged with the progress of his fight against Tom Lee when Mock Duck arrived in New York, but he remained a power in the councils of the Hip Sings, and Mock Duck formed an alliance with him. Within a year Mock Duck had obtained control of the tong, and had increased its membership so that he felt strong enough to beard the lord of the On Leongs. He calmly demanded that the potentate of the quarter give him a half interest in the gambling privileges of Chinatown, or prepare to fight. Tom Lee laughed, and all of Chinatown except the men of the Hip Sing tong joined him. But there was no laughter a few weeks later when two of Tom Lee's votes burned to death in an incendiary fire that destroyed an On Leong boarding house in Pell street, which was not then the street of the Hip Sings as it became later, after the On Leongs had retired into the fastnesses of Mott. Although Mock Duck indignantly disclaimed all knowledge of the catastrophe, it was obvious that he was a power to reckon with, and to teach him a lesson an On Leong hatchet man sallied forth and slew the first Hip Sing he met in Doyers street.

Mock Duck immediately flung out the flag of the high-binder from the Hip Sing Tong House, and for several years it was literally war to the death. The Four Brothers joined the Hip Sings, and Mock Duck's hatchet men made strenuous efforts to kill Tom Lee. They very nearly succeeded, one of them firing a bullet through a window so close to the On Leong chieftain that it shattered an alarm clock on a shelf beside his head. In the midst of the killing Mock Duck went to Dr. Parkhurst's Society and virtuously gave Frank Moss the addresses of the principal On Leong gambling places—and Moss did the rest. He compelled the police to raid the houses; and as rapidly as they were closed Mock Duck and Wong Get reopened them with Hip Sings in charge and the games running as merrily as ever, the difference being that the profits went to Mock Duck and the Hip Sings instead of Tom Lee and the On Leongs. Then it was that Mock Duck proclaimed Frank Moss a very powerful joss, indeed, for both Moss and Dr. Parkhurst turned a deaf ear to Tom Lee's protests. This particular war continued until 1906, when Judge Warren W. Foster of the Court of General Sessions invited the leaders of the

Hip Sings and On Leongs to his home and induced them to sign a
treaty of peace, under the terms of which the On Leongs were to be
supreme in Mott street and the Hip Sings in Pell, while Doyers
street was to be neutral territory. A great celebration was held in the
Port Arthur Restaurant at Mott street and Chatham Square, and in
honor of the occasion Tom Lee drank 107 mugs of rice wine. But
the ink had scarcely dried on the treaty when a Hip Sing gunman
shot at an On Leong man in the crook of Doyers street, and within
a week the rusty revolvers were whanging away again and the hatchets and snickersnees had been brought out and sharpened. It was
not until another six months that Judge Foster, with the help of the
Chinese government, negotiated another truce which remained in
effect until the great war of 1909.

During the height of Mock Duck's prosperity the agents of the
Gerry Society began snooping about his home, investigating the
report that Ha Oi, the adopted daughter of the tong leader, was a
white child. The courts found that she was the daughter of one
Lizzie Smith, who married Wu Ching Mung of San Francisco after
the death of her white husband. When Lizzie Smith died Wu
Ching married Tai Yu, and when Wu Ching Mung died Tai Yu married Mock Duck, and so Ha Oi came to the house of the Hip Sing
chieftain. The child was taken away from him when agents of the
Society found her asleep at the foot of a couch on which lay Mock
Duck and his cousin with an opium layout between them.

Mock Duck, frantic, went about the streets of Chinatown with
tear-filled eyes, begging for help. He took the case to the Appellate
Division of the Supreme Court, but lost, and then in despair he
turned his gambling interests over to Wong Get and went on a tour
of the American continent. He gambled feverishly in Chicago, San
Francisco and throughout the West, and within a year came back
to Chinatown with his shirt front blazing with diamonds and thirty thousand dollars in his pockets, and dazzled the quarter by
changing his suit three times a day. But prosperity could not
quench his thirst for power; guns began to roar and hatchets to
flash almost as soon as he returned. He was arrested many times
for murder and for gambling, but he was never convicted until
1912, when he was sent to Sing Sing for operating a policy game.

Few men have been shot at oftener than Mock Duck, yet despite the whirl of bullets in which he lived for more than ten years he was never injured but once. That was on November 4, 1904, when three On Leongs suddenly appeared in Pell street as he was taking the air in front of his home. They squatted on the ground, shut their eyes and blazed away, and Mock Duck went down with a bullet in his hip. Policemen came running from Doyers street and from either end of Pell street, but they caught only one of the On Leong gunmen. Him they protected by forming a square with their bodies, and then moved slowly toward Chatham Square and the patrol wagon, surrounded by Hip Sings waving hatchets and pistols and striving desperately to find an opening in the wall of cops through which they could shoot or hack.

Mock Duck was in the Hudson Hospital for three weeks, and then came out whole and healthy and filled with a craving for revenge. And he obtained it. Doyers, Pell and Mott streets echoed to the shots that infuriated Hip Sings fired at fleeing On Leongs, and Mock Duck was in the forefront of every foray until his arrest in 1912. There was not a great deal of evidence against him, and he always insisted that he had been framed, but the courts apparently decided that it was high time something was done about him, so they sent him to prison. Since his imprisonment Mock Duck has not been active; he went to Brooklyn when he was released, and has remained there. In 1918 he made formal proclamation that he was done with tongs and wars; that he had acquired sufficient wealth and adventure and that his face would never again be seen in Chinatown. So far he has kept his word.

2

MUCH of the history of Doyers street and Chinatown has been enacted around the old Chinese Theater and the Bloody Angle, the latter a sharp bend in Doyers street opposite the old Arcade, which once led to Mott street and was closed by the police because it offered too easy an avenue of escape to the hatchet men of the On Leongs. The police believe, and can prove it so far as such proof is possible, that more men have been murdered at the Bloody Angle than at any other place of like area in the world. It was, and is, an ideal place for ambush; the turn is very abrupt, and not even a slant-eyed Chinaman can see around a corner. Armed with snickersnee and hatchet sharpened to a razor's edge, the tong killer lay in wait for his victim, and having cut him down as he came around the bend, fled through the Arcade, or plunged into the theater and thence into Mott or Pell street through one of the underground passageways.

The Theater is now a mission of the New York Rescue Society, with hymns and sandwiches for the bums instead of the witticisms of the comedian Ah Hoon and the dramatic goings-on of the tragedian Hom Ling, who made special pilgrimages from Canton to play in New York and San Francisco. It was originally opened in 1895, and was the first Chinese theater east of San Francisco—and the last, except for occasional performances by travelling troupes in one of the old Bowery houses under the patronage of the companies which operate the sight-seeing buses. The playhouse became the property of the Rescue Society in August, 1910, after Raymond Hitchcock, the actor, and Joe Humphreys, who officiates as announcer at important prize fights, had taken it over and tried in vain to subject Chinatown to the civilizing influence of the moving picture. The Society investigated only slightly the current tale that the basement had been used for years as a burying ground for tong war victims, and made no alterations in the building except to give it a bath, wall up the entrances to the tunnels and remove the opium bunks from the cellar. The hooks from which the bunks swung are still embedded in the masonry. The paintings on the walls of the auditorium, frescoes depicting scenes of dragon hunting and the triumph of virtue, also remain, and are frequently pointed out by gabby guides as fine examples of Chinese art which had been removed from an ancient temple and brought to America for the delectation of the transplanted Cantonese in the New York colony. As a matter of truth, the pictures were painted by Chin Yin, who lived next door and was calligrapher, house painter, artist and janitor. He received thirty-five dollars for the job.

The original promoters of the theater were hard put to it to make their enterprise pay, for they charged only twenty-five cents admission and required a packed house at every performance to meet their pay rolls. Then, too, they were troubled by the fact that after the tong wars began the On Leongs, Hip Sings and Four Brothers became enamoured of the theater as a place to stage their fights and killings. Frequently the great Hom Ling was compelled to abandon his rantings and flee because an eager Hip Sing had slipped the keen blade of his hatchet across the throat of an On Leong as that worthy sat enjoying the play. Frequently, too, the performance was interrupted by the bark of revolvers, for eventually the Chinese went in for the white devil's weapons, even if they continued to ignore his law. But they were never good shots; their procedure was to point their guns in the general direction of their intended victim, close their eyes and pull the trigger until there were no more explosions.

Ah Hoon, who is said by Chinese critics of the drama to have been a really gifted comedian, was killed because he insisted upon interpolating in his performances comment on the activities of the quarter; and since he was a member of the On Leong tong and intensely partisan, his quips and pleasantries were generally at the expense of the Four Brothers and Hip Sings. These things rankled, and the Rev. Huie Kim, a Christian and head of the Morning Star Mission in Doyers street, warned Ah Hoon that he was treading on dangerous ground, and publicly said the comedian was a bad man. But Ah Hoon persisted, and when the Four Brothers and Hip Sings declared war upon the On Leongs for other reasons, he put no limit to his jests about the enemies of his tong. So the Hip Sings and Four Brothers decided to kill him, and desiring to be fair, dispatched an emissary who gave him notice; he was told the exact hour and minute he would die, and further, that since he had been so insulting in his remarks, he would be murdered on the stage where he had made them.

On December 30, 1909, after Tom Lee had temporarily abdicated as chief of the On Leongs and had left town for a rest and to escape Hip Sing bullets, a Chinese woman who lived on the floor beneath Ah Hoon went to the police and asked protection for the threatened comedian. Sergeant John D. Coughlin, now Chief Inspector, and two patrolmen accompanied Ah Hoon to the theater, and sat on the stage during the performance, curiously out of place in their blue uniforms. Ah Hoon went through his act in fear and trembling, cutting his lines and cracking no jokes whatever about the Hip Sings and Four Brothers. The theater was crowded, for word of the impending tragedy had spread throughout Chinatown, and outside in the street surged a vast crowd which had come to see the fun and had not been able to buy even standing room. But fearing the police, the Hip Sing killers went back on their sworn word and did not kill Ah Hoon, and at the end of the show the patrolmen escorted the actor through an underground passageway to his home in Chatham Square. He went to bed, his door locked. The only window of his chamber faced a blank wall, and On Leong hatchet men, heavily armed and clad in their shirts of mail, stood guard in the doorway of the house, while others patrolled the streets. Yet when morning came Ah Hoon was dead. He had been shot through the heart by a Hip Sing killer who was lowered in a boatswain's chair from the roof, and had got at him through the window. The comedian's body was found by Hoochy-Coochy Mary, who lived on the floor below and had heard the shot.

The death of Ah Hoon caused the flashing of hatchets and blazing of revolvers all through the Chinese quarter, and added to the woes of the theater owners, for the comedian was popular and had a great following. The climax of the war came on New Year's Night. The house was filled with spectators, for this was the great Chinese celebration of the year, and a report had been industriously circulated that the warring tongs had arranged a truce. The performance went with verve and fire, but suddenly someone threw a bunch of lighted fire-crackers into the air over a row of orchestra seats. They snapped and popped, and the crowd milled about in a panic. But pistols snapped and popped also during the excitement and when the audience left the building five On Leong men did not move; they had been killed quickly and efficiently under cover of the exploding fireworks. Mock Duck and others of the Hip Sing highbinders were arrested, but no proof was found and they were not punished.

Annoyed that such things should happen in their house of entertainment, the owners of the theater announced that they would close the place. There were conferences, and finally, early in 1910, it was agreed that the truce of 1906 should be again put into effect so far as the theater was concerned, and that it would not be sporting to do any more killing within the building. But the Bloody Angle and the remainder of Doyers street were not mentioned, and the hatchet and gun men who had been making a shambles of the playhouse now waited outside for their victims, so that the audiences were as small as ever. Then various white devils took over the theater, and when Hitchcock and Humphrey failed to prosper with a motion picture show it was evident that the Chinese playhouse could no longer endure. So it became a mission and the home of the white man's god, and therefore of no further interest to the Chinese.

The tong war in which Ah Hoon was killed, and which brought about the abandonment of the theater by the Chinese, was caused by the murder of little Sweet Flower, otherwise Bow Kum, a slave girl who had been sold by her father in Canton for a few dollars and brought to the United States, where she brought three thousand dollars in the open market in San Francisco. Low Hee Tong, high in the councils of the Four Brothers and their allies the Hip Sings, was the purchaser, and lived with the girl for four years. Then he got into trouble with the police, and when he could not produce a marriage license Bow Kum was taken away from him and put in a Christian mission to be saved from sin. Then came Tchin Len, an industrious truck gardener, who married her and brought her to New York. Low Hee Tong pressed Tchin Len to return the money which he had invested in the girl, but the gardener refused to pay, whereupon Low Hee Tong set forth his grievances in a letter to the Four Brothers and Hip Sings in New York. His tong leaders felt that the claim was justified, and in his behalf made solemn demand upon the On Leong tong, of which Tchin Len was a member. The On Leongs ignored the demand, and the Four Brothers and Hip Sings immediately broke out the red flag of the highbinder from the tong houses in Pell street and declared war in posters of violent hue emblazoned upon the billboards. A few days later, on August 15, 1909, a hatchet man slipped into the home of Tchin Len at No. 17 Mott street and stabbed Bow Kum to the heart, also cutting off her fingers and slashing her innumerable times across the body.

Then the killing began. This was probably the most disastrous war the tongs ever fought in New York, with a casualty list of about fifty dead and several times that number wounded, and with considerable destruction of property by bombs, for by that time the Chinese had begun to experiment with dynamite and the results were fearful. Old Tom Lee counseled peace before the white devils interfered and drove both tongs out of the city, but the younger, hot-blooded Hip Sings, Four Brothers and On Leongs swore by the bones of their ancestors that they would not stop until they had exterminated their enemies. Finally Captain William Hodgins of the Elizabeth street station, backed by Chinese merchants who were members of none of the warring tongs, induced the chieftains to listen to peace proposals. He went first to the On Leongs, and they told him that nothing would please them more than to make peace with their brethren, but first the Hip Sings and the Four Brothers must give them a Chinese flag, a roast pig and ten thousand packages of fire-crackers. This was about the same as if the Ku Klux Klan were required to celebrate Yom Kippur, give their nightgowns to the Knights of Columbus and grovel before the Pope, so the Hip Sings and Four Brothers squawked with rage and the shooting and cutting went merrily on for another year. Late in 1910 the trouble was finally settled by a committee of forty appointed by the Chinese Minister in Washington, and composed principally of Chinese merchants, teachers and students. The truce thus arranged granted no humiliating demands from either side, and although it was rejected by the Four Brothers, it remained in effect until 1912, when a new tong, the Kim Lan Wui Saw, appeared in Chinatown and declared war on both the On Leongs and the Hip Sings, who vowed that the Four Brothers had foment-ed the disturbance. The ancient rivals combined to exterminate the upstarts, and were proceeding satisfactorily when the Chinese government again interfered, and with the aid of the New York

The Bloody Angle of Doyers Street

The Old Chinese Theatre

Chuck Connors in One of His Fake Opium Dens

police compelled the tongs to agree to a new treaty. It was signed on May 22, 1913, by the Chinese Merchants' Association, the On Leong tong, the Hip Sing tong and the Kim Lan Wui Saw, but not by the obstinate Four Brothers.

This treaty kept Chinatown in peace, to the great profit and prosperity of all factions, until 1924, when another war began because several members of the On Leong tong, expelled from that organization, found refuge with the Hip Sings, taking with them, according to the On Leongs, a considerable sum of On Leong money. The fighting continued sporadically for several months, but never reached the proportions of the earlier conflicts. So far as New York was concerned, most of the killing was not in Chinatown, but among Chinese laundrymen and restaurant owners in the Bronx and Brooklyn. Only a few men were murdered in Mott, Doyers and Pell streets. There was also a big war in the West in 1921, in which the Suey Ying, Bing Kong, Suey Don and Jung Ying tongs participated, but none had members in the east and New York was not affected.

3

THE gangs did very little fighting in Chinatown, but the quarter was thickly sprinkled with resorts run by white men, wherein the gangsters found repose and recreation. Scotchy Lavelle, who had abandoned the arduous life of a river pirate to become bouncer at Callahan's Dance Hall at Chatham Square and Doyers street, opened his own dive at No. 14 Doyers street about the time Monk Eastman appeared in gangland. Across the street from Callahan's was the place operated by Barney Flynn, who became very popular with his Irish customers when, having commissioned an artist to paint a portrait of George Washington, he refused to accept the work until several dead Englishmen had been painted at the General's feet. At No. 6 Doyers street was the Chatham Club, where Irving Berlin occasionally sang and waited on table, coming by special permission of Nigger Mike Salter, in whose resort at No. 12 Pell street he worked as a singing waiter in the days before he discovered ragtime. Lavelle's is said to have witnessed the birth of the familiar phrase, "Who wants the handsome waiter?" A curio store now occupies the front room of the old Chatham Club, but the exterior of the building remains unchanged; it is a curious, many-gabled structure, unbelievably dingy and dirty and tricked out in amazing architectural doodads.

These dives, especially the Chatham Club, Barney Flynn's and Nigger Mike's, were also the headquarters of the white parasites who had drifted into Chinatown and earned precarious livings as Lobbygows, or guides to the quarter. Big Mike Abrams was one of the notorious figures of the district during the late nineties. Big Mike had formerly operated opium smoking dens in Pell street and at Coney Island, but in his later years he roamed the Chinese area and devoted himself principally to beating Chinamen occasionally accepting slugging and shooting commissions and acting as stall for a gang of pickpockets. It was Big Mike's proud boast, a short while before he died, that no fewer than ten Chinamen had met death at his hand. Three he had decapitated with a clasp knife in Pell street before a horrified assemblage of their own people. But Big Mike lost much of his fearsomeness when a Hip Sing hatchet man known as Sassy Sam, fortified by rice brandy and rose wine, chased him the length of Pell street with a long, curved sword. Soon afterward Big Mike removed the head of Ling Tchen and the Hip Sings took counsel on the affair, for Ling Tchen was one of the chief men of the tong and his murder called for action. Within a month Big Mike was found dead in bed, his room filled with gas which had seeped through a line of slender garden hose that stretched from an opened jet in the hall to the keyhole of the sleeping chamber.

The most celebrated of all the white hangers-on in Chinatown was Chuck Connors, who was born in Mott street of a respectable Irish family and christened George Washington Connors. He acquired his sobriquet by his fondness for chuck steak, which in the wild days of his youth he cooked on a stick over gutter fires. A great deal was written about him in the newspapers of the period, especially after he had become the acknowledged King of the Lobbygows, and he was variously called the Sage of Doyers street and the Bowery Philosopher. He was one of the originators of the dese, dem and dose school of linguistic expression, and achieved a considerable reputation as a wit and story teller. In his teens and early twenties Chuck was a lightweight pugilist of much promise, but in his later years he became a bar fly and a tramp; he used to sit absolutely motionless for hours at a time in a chair tilted against a wall of the Chatham Club, while crowds of tourists gaped at him in awe.

It is very likely that most if not all of the smart sayings attributed to Chuck Connors had their inceptions in the brains of Frank Ward O'Malley and Roy L. McCardell, then writing for the *Sun* and the *World*. They found Connors a prolific source of copy; he would stand for anything, and he was always careful to read the newspapers and find out exactly what he was doing and thinking. When there was nothing else on which to build a feature story, there was always Chuck Connors, and with almost continuous publicity he was soon built up into a nationally known figure. His talk, or at least the talk that O'Malley and McCardell ascribed to him, found its way onto the stage, and even today is accepted as the sort of stuff that is spoken on the Bowery. Here is a typical specimen, published after Chuck had consented to grace the American theater in an act with Nellie Noonan, Queen of the Seventh Ward:

> To de woods fer mine. I bit so easy de jay must a t'ought he had a dead one on de string. Anyhow he had de show all fixed up an' me in a sleepin' car before even I turns me mind to de wagis for yours truly. Th' first time I goes to de box offis fer me dough I near drops dead. De guy behin' de bars passes me out a envelick wit' $15 in it.
>
> "W'at t' 'ell?" says I. "W'at t' 'ell is dis?" says I, like dat, to de bloke in de windy.
>
> "Dat's your wagis," says de guy.

Probably the only work that Chuck Connors ever did was during the year he courted the girl who later became his wife. He obtained a job as fireman on one of the little locomotives which hauled the elevated railroad trains before the lines were electrified, and remained a useful citizen until his wife died. Then he reverted to his former status and became a notable ornament of Chinatown. She had taught him to read and write, though imperfectly, and he delighted in displaying his erudition at the Chatham Club, reciting the alphabet backwards and answering questions about the multiplication table. Frequently he appeared in a Bowery skit at various theaters, and with road companies, and once was on the bill at Oscar Hammerstein's famous variety theater, the Victoria, on Broadway. Not long after the death of his wife Chuck was shanghaied by a Water street crimp, and voyaged to England as an unwilling fireman. He promptly deserted when the ship docked, and remained for two weeks in Whitechapel, where he became enamoured of the manners and customs of the costermongers. He was particularly impressed by their dress, and when he returned to New York he had a Division street tailor fashion a pair of wide sailor pants and a blue, square cut pea jacket, adorned with two rows of very large pearl buttons. These he wore with a blue shirt and a sailors' silk scarf of vivid hue. He attempted to introduce a costermonger's pearl buttoned cap as an article of gentlemen's wear in Chinatown and along the Bowery, but it failed to meet with favor and he soon abandoned it for the low-crowned black or brown derby which was then in vogue.

When he had been exploited by the newspaper reporters so that he had become well known, Chuck Connors organized the Chuck Connors Club and gave rackets at Tammany Hall several times a year. He became a power in the politics of Chinatown and the Bowery, controlling the votes of lesser Lobbygows, and was frequently consulted by such shining lights of Tammany Hall as Big and Little Tim Sullivan. Both of these statesmen were honorary members of the Chuck Connors Club, as were also Al Smith, now Governor of New York; Richard Mansfield, the actor; John L. Sullivan, champion pugilist; Honest Johnny Kelly, the gambler; Walt B. McDougall, the cartoonist, Jim Corbett, Bob Fitzsimmons and many others. For many years during the latter part of his life Chuck Connors lived in a two-room apartment at No. 6 Dover street, near the East River, in a tenement house which was called Fox's Flats because it had been constructed by

Richard K. Fox, owner of the *Police Gazette*. He never paid any rent, and the fact that Fox made no effort to dispossess him gave rise to the report that the publisher had given him the flat rent free so long as he lived. But Chuck was seldom at home, except to sleep there occasionally; he spent his entire time in Chinatown, and generally could be found in the Chatham Club at any hour of the day or night.

At the age of sixty-one, in 1913, Chuck Connors died in the Hudson Street Hospital. The doctors said he had heart disease, but really it was neglect that killed him. He became old and garrulous and uninteresting; he complained of rheumatism, and frequently had to stay away from his accustomed haunts for several days at a time. The reporters, having exhausted him as a source of interesting copy, dropped him, and without publicity Chuck Connors was soon forgotten. The final nail was driven into his cross when Frank Salvatore, an Italian bootblack known as Mike the Dago, began to call himself Young Chuck Connors and organized the Young Chuck Connors Association. He acquired political influence as the prestige of the original Chuck declined, and when he announced that he would give a grand ball in opposition to the affair of the old Chuck Connors Club, the one time King of the Lobbygows consented to abdicate, or at least share his throne with the newcomer. It was agreed that on the program of Young Chuck's ball the name of Chuck Connors should appear as a patron immediately after that of Jim Jeffries, then heavyweight champion of the world, and before the name of Jim Corbett.

Chuck lingered on for several years after that, but his heart was not in his work, and finally he died. He was buried by members of the Press Club, and of the thousands upon thousands of persons who had known him fewer than forty attended his funeral.

4

WHILE Chinatown was becoming notorious as the battleground of the tongs and a place of evil resort, the Bowery was undergoing one of its frequent metamorphoses, and was rapidly descending to depths of vice and misery such as it had not known since the palmy days of Billy McGlory and Owney Geogheghan. From Astor Place to Chatham Square the beer gardens, concert saloons, dance halls and theaters which had continued the struggle to make the Bowery a place of entertainment, gave way to dives as low as those of the old Bowery and the Fourth Ward when Kit Burns' rat pit, the Hole-in-the-Wall and John Allen's house were in the heyday of their glory. And places of equal meanness throve in Park Row southward from Chatham Square to City Hall Park, in the streets which crossed the Bowery, and along the thoroughfares of Cherry Hill. Probably no American City has ever been able to boast of resorts as depraved as the Doctor's, the Plague, the Hell Hole, the Harp House, the Cripples' Home, and the Billy Goat, all in Park Row; the Dump, the Princess Café and Johnny Kelly's dive, in the Bowery; the Inferno in Worth street; the Workingman's Friend in Mott street, Union Hall in Elizabeth street; the Cob Dock in Hester street, and Mother Woods' in Water street. Of only a slightly higher class were Chick Tricker's Fleabag and McGuirk's Suicide Hall, both on the Bowery. McGuirk's and Mother Woods' were the favorite haunts of the prostitutes and women thieves of the Bowery and water front districts, and McGuirk used to boast that more women had killed themselves in his establishment than in any other house in the world. In later years the building became the home of the Hadley Rescue Mission.

Not only were these places frequented by the gangsters at such times when their finances were low, and by pickpockets, burglars, and thieves of every description, but they particularly swarmed with panhandlers, beggars, cocaine and morphine addicts, and those homeless dregs of humanity who have never been known otherwise than as Bowery Bums. Whiskey, compared to which the modern bootleg product is nectar, was sold for five cents a large glass, and for those whose jaded palates failed to respond to the raw liquor there was a villainous mixture of water and liquid camphor, an even fiercer beverage than the concoction once sold by Johnny Camphine. There was also a hot punch compounded of whiskey, hot rum, camphor, benzine, and cocaine sweepings, which generally sold for six cents and was guaranteed to contain a case of delirium tremens in every drop. In some of the dives, notably the Doctor's, a premium check was given with every drink, six checks entitling the holder to one drink free. In the Billy Goat two drinks were sold for a nickel to every person who appeared between 5 and 5:30 o'clock in the morning. Sometimes such a long line would form to take advantage of this generosity that police reserves were called to hold the struggling bums in check.

Many of the habitués of the Bowery and Park Row dens had once been men of substance and standing in their communities— in 1910 a reporter for the *New York World* who spent an hour at the Doctor's met a man who had been a wealthy merchant in Baltimore, another who was the scion of a distinguished Boston family and a graduate of Harvard, and still another, called the Scholar, who claimed Yale as his Alma Mater. The Scholar scorned to panhandle; he utilized his learning by writing, for a drink or a small sum of money, piteous appeals for the use of professional beggars. For two drinks he would produce a poem. One of his masterpieces, which was used with great success by panhandlers whose graft was pretended blindness, was:

> Help a poor blind man and don't turn him away,
> Just give him a dime and for you he will pray;
> You may get afflicted the same way some day,
> Help a poor blind man and don't turn him away.

The Doctor's was also a favorite resort of the panhandlers who preyed upon the public by simulating cripples, and the owner of the dive, Burly Bohan, thoughtfully provided a locker wherein crutches and canes were stored while the owners spent their gains for whiskey, rum and liquid camphor. One of the most successful of this type was old Tom Frizzell, a noted Bowery character who succeeded to the title of King of the Panhandlers after Jim Farrell, blinded by the fiery concoctions which he had been imbibing for many years, had been carried screaming out of John Kelly's dive at No. 10 Bowery to die in the alcoholic ward of

Bellevue Hospital. Old Tom generally sat at a table from which he could see the engraved portraits of fourteen Presidents of the United States which hung above the bar; he said that the sight of the statesmen always gave him courage, and that it was owing to their inspiration that for twenty years he had never been caught without pad money, that is, a nickel or a dime for lodging.

Against the rear wall of the Doctor's were two long tables. These were the rooms of the hotel, and sleeping places on and beneath them were sold for five cents. But the darkest corner under the table was reserved for Jack Dempsey, an ancient panhandler who earned his lodging by washing glasses and scattering sawdust upon the floor. Dempsey was probably the lowest of all the Bowery Bums. It was his proud boast that he had not owned a suit of underwear or a pair of socks in five years—this was in 1910—and that for eight years he had not slept in a bed. He was a camphor fiend and a cocaine addict, and when he obtained a drink of whiskey always added to it some eight to fifteen drops of liquid camphor; and while his body was still racked by the crash of the beverage he plunged a hypodermic needle laden with cocaine into his arm. Dempsey was a needle jabber, an aristocrat of the drug addicts. Lower in the scale were the sniffers, who inhaled the drug through the nose, and lowest of all were the ice cream eaters, who chewed the crystals of cocaine, morphine, or heroin. The ice cream eaters generally obtained a quicker result, but were scorned as greedy, and lost many of the delightful preliminary sensations.

The Dump at No. 9 Bowery, run by Jimmy Lee and Slim Reynolds, was a favorite resort of the panhandlers for many years, and it was there that many of their schemes were hatched. Goat Hinch and Whitey Sullivan, who eventually expiated their crimes in the electric chair, were among the noted patrons of the Dump; the former is said to have originated the practice of swallowing a concoction which would make him temporarily ill and so arouse the sympathies of people in the street. Sometimes the Goat chewed a cake of evil-smelling soap, producing fearful symptoms which invariably brought a shower of nickels and dimes. In common with other dives, the Dump provided sleeping quarters, but

Reynolds and Lee were more ingenious in their arrangements. They screwed short iron stanchions into the floor about seven feet from the rear wall, and into the wall affixed an iron framework. From the latter to the stanchions was a net of coarse rope, and when a bum passed out from dope or the effects of whiskey and camphor, he was simply tossed into the net to sleep it off.

Frequent raids by the police during the few years immediately preceding the World War, together with improved economic conditions, compelled the passing of a majority of the low Bowery dives and the gradual disappearance of the old time Bowery Bum. A few of the latter remain, and a few of the former also, but they are now speakeasies and drinks can no longer be obtained for a nickel. They generally cost from fifteen cents to a quarter. One of the last of the Bums is the Hoakie, who says he is a graduate of the University of Heidelberg, and points with pride to several scars on his face, which he vows were received in duels with other German students. Summer and winter the Hoakie wears a long, heavy overcoat tied under his chin with a string and girt with a heavy cord. When he walks he rattles and clanks, for beneath the overcoat, about his waist, dangle a skillet, a tin cup, a can of solidified alcohol, a spoon, knife and fork, and odds and ends of food, most of which he obtains by a skilful searching of garbage pails. With these utensils the Hoakie cooks his meals beneath the East River docks, and is beholden to no man.

CHAPTER XV

THE LAST OF THE GANG WARS

1

WHEN LOUIE the lump put a sudden and dramatic end to the earthly career of Kid Twist in the midst of a gaping Coney Island crowd, control of the three most important remnants of the old Monk Eastman gang fell into the hands of Big Jack Zelig, Jack Sirocco and Chick Tricker. But only Zelig achieved lasting renown as a gang chieftain, for Tricker and Sirocco were primarily saloon-keepers, and for the most part subordinated leadership of their gangs to more legitimate affairs. Sirocco, whose appearance was almost as awe-inspiring as that of Monk Eastman himself—he invariably wore a plaid cap drawn down over his eyes and seldom shaved—operated a prosperous gin-mill in the Bowery which became a favorite haunt of the gangsters after some of the

Chinatown dives had been closed. Tricker's place in Park Row was closed on complaint of the Committee of Fourteen in 1910, but a year before the reformers descended upon the resort he had begun to transfer his principal interests to the district which in earlier times had been celebrated as Satan's Circus. There he purchased Dan the Dude's old Stag Café in West Twenty-eighth street near Broadway, renamed it the Café Maryland, and speedily converted it into one of the wickedest dives in a notoriously wicked neighborhood. His gangsters, numbering probably thirty choice thugs, made their rendezvous in the Maryland, and busied themselves with burglaries, dope peddling, holdups, and blackjackings, and otherwise conducted themselves according to the standards of the underworld. Tricker retained a connection with the lower East Side by acquiring an interest in Jack Pioggi's drinking den in Doyers street, near the Bloody Angle, and a year or so later became the owner of the Fleabag, a fragrant dive at No. 241 Bowery.

Misfortune frequently beset the Café Maryland during the few years it was in operation. Three men were shot to death there late in 1909, when several of Tricker's own followers quarrelled over a woman, and about a year later the gang chieftain made the serious mistake of flouting the Gophers. It may be that Tricker underestimated the strength and ferocity of the terrors of the West Side, or that he credited the reports that the Gophers were embroiled in internecine strife; whatever the reason, he made no objection when one of his thugs ventured into Hell's Kitchen, captured the impressionable heart of Ida the Goose, and bore her in triumph to West Twenty-eighth street, where she was formally installed as belle of the Maryland. Ida the Goose was a noted beauty of the underworld and had been the beloved of a long succession of Gopher captains, so that her defection caused much comment. The Gophers indignantly demanded that she return forthwith to Hell's Kitchen, and when she refused to desert her new lover they sent an emissary to deal with Chick Tricker, and threatened to regain the lady by force of arms. Tricker refused to interfere, and the West Side ambassador retired from the conference seething with anger. Preparations for war immediately went forward in the

Kitchen, but for several weeks nothing happened, and the Tricker gangsters, who had been going about heavily armed in anticipation of an attack, relaxed their vigilance, and the garrison of the Maryland was considerably reduced. Then, on an October night which saw the first snowfall of the year, four of the most noted of the Gopher fighters, including the thug who had been the favored of Ida the Goose, entered the café and approached the bar in the manner of customers. They ordered beer, while half a dozen Tricker gangsters who lounged at the tables eyed them nervously, so amazed at the audacity of the Gophers in thus invading the rendezvous of an avowed enemy that it never occurred to them to launch an immediate attack upon the intruders. None spoke save Ida the Goose.

"Say!" she cried, indignantly. "Youse guys got a nerve!"

The Gophers ignored her. They calmly drank their beer, and when the mugs had been drained one said:

"Well, let's get at it!"

They whirled from the bar and eight revolvers flashed from as many pockets; and before the dazed henchmen of Chick Tricker could draw their weapons a hail of lead sprayed against the bar fixtures and splashed among the tables. The two bartenders, who were not members of Tricker's fighting forces, promptly dived headlong to the floor, and five of the six Tricker gangsters fell with disabling wounds. The sixth, the same young Lochinvar who had galloped out of Hell's Kitchen with Ida the Goose, flung away his gun, hastily scrambled across the floor, and found shelter behind the voluminous skirts of his inamorata. The Gophers made no effort to shoot him; they waited with ready revolvers to see what Ida the Goose would do. And that lady responded nobly to the best tradition of Hell's Kitchen. For a moment she stared at the craven wretch who had won her affections and lured her from the Gopher domain, and then with a contemptuous shrug of her shoulders she reached down and plucked him from his refuge.

"Say, youse!" said Ida the Goose. "Come out and take it!"

She shoved him into the center of the floor, where he sprawled tremblingly on hands and knees. And there he took it. Four guns blazed, and the gangster collapsed with four bullets in his body.

The Gopher who had been the sweetheart of Ida the Goose then stepped forward, and as was his right according to the niceties of gang procedure, put the finishing touches to the job with a bullet through the brain. Then the four Gophers turned on their heels and went into the street. And behind them, at a respectful distance, walked Ida the Goose, glowing with pride that such a great battle had been fought for her favors. And nevermore did she stray from Hell's Kitchen.

Big Jack Zelig's name was William Alberts. He was born in Norfolk street in 1882 of respectable Jewish parents, and began his criminal career at the age of fourteen, when he ran away from home and became one of Crazy Butch's fleet of juvenile pick-pockets. He was an apt pupil with a real gift for thievery, and made such rapid progress that within a year he had deserted the Fagin and was operating with great success on his own account, rolling lushes and deftly lifting pocket-books and jewelry from the crowds which thronged the Bowery and Chatham Square. He was a slight, thin-faced little boy, with enormous brown eyes which filled with tears and such a look of horror when he was arrested that his accuser's heart was melted and the complaint withdrawn. One man from whom Zelig had stolen a pocketbook and a valuable diamond ring was so overcome with remorse at having accused the innocent-appearing lad that he bought the young thief a new suit of clothing, and pressed money upon him. Zelig retained his childish appearance until he was in his early twenties, but when he had grown tall and lanky and his tear-filled eyes were no longer effective, he devised another scheme to thwart justice. Whenever he was arraigned a frail girl came timidly into the court room and wept, and pleaded with the Magistrate:

"Oh, Judge, for God's sake, don't send my boy husband, the father of my baby, to jail!"

Few hearts in the lower strata of the judiciary were hard enough to resist the tears and the agony in the girl's voice, and Zelig was invariably released with a warning; he was advised to be a good boy and go home to his wife and baby, of which he had neither. But at length Zelig came before Recorder John W. Goff, later a Justice of the Supreme Court and a jurist of exceptional balance. The

Recorder listened patiently until the girl had finished, then gently ordered her removed from the room and gave Zelig the first of his many jail sentences. Having served her purpose, the girl thereafter dropped out of sight, and to procure the protection which he required Zelig joined Monk Eastman's gang. He soon became a prominent figure throughout the underworld, and was noted for his proficiency in the use of revolver and blackjack. When Eastman was sent to prison Zelig probably ranked next to Kid Twist and Richie Fitzpatrick in the chieftain's confidence. Zelig was loyal to Twist during the latter's war with Fitzpatrick over the succession, and after Twist's death he proposed to Jack Sirocco and Chick Tricker that they divide the gang into three factions and permit the gangsters to make a choice of leaders. The most eminent of the Eastman thugs and killers cast their fortunes with Zelig, and as his fame increased his following was augmented by ambitious youths anxious to display their prowess as sluggers and gunmen. Perhaps the most celebrated of the newcomers were Gyp the Blood, Lefty Louis, Dago Frank and Whitey Lewis, who won enduring renown as the gunmen in the Rosenthal murder case. Their real names were Harry Horrowitz, Louis Rosenberg, Frank Cirofici and Jacob Siedenshner. Horrowitz's comrades originally called him Gib the Blood, but Gib had a harsh sound and the reporters soon changed it to Gyp, and it was as Gyp the Blood that he went hurtling down the corridors of gang history.

What time he was not working on commissions for Jack Zelig, or robbing drunken men in the Bowery dives, Gyp the Blood was a sheriff and gorilla at the cheap dances of the East Side; he soon became known as the best bouncer since Monk Eastman, which was no light praise. He possessed extraordinary strength, and frequently boasted that he could break a man's back by bending him over his knee. Moreover, he performed the feat several times before witnesses; once, to win a bet of two dollars, he seized an inoffensive stranger and cracked his spine in three places. He also became an expert revolver shot, and was extremely accurate at throwing a bomb, a task in which he delighted. "I likes to hear de noise," he explained. As an independent venture Gyp the Blood captained the Lenox Avenue Gang, a small band of burglars and pickpockets who operated uptown around 125th street. Whitey Lewis had been a third-rate pugilist, but under Big Jack's tutelage he became a blackjack artist of rare merit and a gunman of distinction. Lefty Louis was primarily a pickpocket, although he never hesitated to accept a gun job, while Dago Frank was proud of his wide reputation as a killer, and sneered at any task which did not hold a promise of bloodshed. He is said to have had six notches on his gun before the Rosenthal murder, and Val O'Farrell, a noted Central Office detective who was widely known in the underworld as one of the Three Musketeers—the others were his partners, Kinstler and Duggan—once described him as the toughest man in the world. Dago Frank had been a member of the Chick Tricker faction, but Tricker failed to provide sufficient action to satisfy his turbulent spirit, and he withdrew and enlisted under Zelig. He had a girl called Dutch Sadie, who was also a noted fighter; she carried a huge butcher knife in her muff, and frequently employed it to good effect when her lover was hard pressed.

With such gifted thugs as these at his command, Big Jack Zelig carried on his various activities with great success, and for several years did a big business in slugging, stabbing, shooting, and bomb throwing. He was very reasonable in his demands upon his clients; his range of prices was very wide, and occasionally, if the person to be assaulted was not prominent and there was slight chance of an extensive police investigation, he waived his fee and repaid himself by confiscating whatever valuables the victim might possess. One of Zelig's henchmen once told a detective that these were the rates quoted by the gang leader, although they were increased slightly for work of great danger:

Slash on cheek with knife	$1 to $10
Shot in leg	1 to 25
Shot in arm	5 to 25
Throwing a bomb	5 to 50
Murder	10 to 100

But even with murder and mutilation so cheap, there were slack seasons, and Zelig's pockets were not always lined with gold. Finding himself short of cash on a night late in 1911, when he wished to make an impression upon a new sweetheart, he invaded an East Side bordello and robbed the landlady of eighty dollars. Contrary to custom, she complained to the police, and the detective who was sent to remonstrate with Zelig and urge him to exercise greater caution found the gang chieftain in a sullen and fractious mood. A quarrel followed and Zelig was arrested, and when the sergeant at the police station found a loaded revolver in his pocket he was charged not only with robbery but with carrying concealed weapons as well. Facing the possibility of a long jail sentence because of his previous convictions, Zelig asked Tricker and Sirocco to call upon the woman whom he had robbed, return the eighty dollars and put the fear of hell into her heart, so that she would not testify against him. This Tricker and Sirocco failed to do, but the woman was finally threatened by an emissary of Jimmy Kelly, who owned a dive in the Bowery and captained a small gang. When she confronted Zelig she swore that she had never seen him before, and that he did not even resemble the man who had robbed her. The accusation of robbery thus collapsed, and the gangster's political connections quickly procured the dismissal of the charge of carrying concealed weapons. Within a few days Zelig was back in his old haunts, swearing vengeance upon Tricker and Sirocco. He had not been out of jail more than a few hours when he met Tricker in the street, and backing him into a doorway pressed a revolver against his stomach:

"I'll get you for not helping me," said Zelig.

Less than two hours later he made the same threat to Sirocco, emphasizing it by rubbing the barrel of his revolver against Sirocco's nose.

"Inside of a week," said Zelig, "you and Tricker will be cooked."

Tricker and Sirocco promptly took measures for their protection, and the word went forth that there would be great rejoicing if Big Jack Zelig should depart this life suddenly in a proper atmosphere of mystery. Early in the evening of December 2, 1911, Julie Morrell, an independent thug with a reputation as a killer, wandered into a Fourteenth street saloon and got into conversation with Ike the Plug, ostensibly a pickpocket, but in reality Zelig's secret agent and spy, and the source of much of the gangleader's information as to what went forward in the enemy's camp. Morrell's tongue had been loosened by heavy drinking, and he confided to Ike the Plug that he had a commission to kill Big Jack Zelig, and that he intended to perform the task that very night in a very spectacular fashion.

"I'll fill that big Yid so full of holes he'll sink!" boasted Morrell.

Down at Stuyvesant Casino in Second avenue the Boys of the Avenue were giving their annual grand ball and entertainment, an important social function sponsored by Jack Zelig and attended by his gangsters in force, wearing their dress suits and with their ladies on their arms. Thither hurried Ike the Plug and informed Zelig that Julie Morrell was gunning for him, and would doubtless be along presently. Zelig had been sitting near the door, graciously greeting his henchmen as they entered the hall, but as soon as Ike the Plug had reported, the chieftain moved to a table across the dance floor, where he had a clear view of the entrance. At one o'clock in the morning Julie Morrell appeared, but he had been drinking steadily to nerve himself to his task, and when he rolled into the Casino he could scarcely stand, and his revolver dangled loosely from his hand. Nevertheless, he staggered onto the dance floor and stared about him.

"Where's that big Yid Zelig?" he shouted. "I gotta cook that big Yid!"

Zelig spoke sharply, and the dancers scattered. The next instant the lights were extinguished. There was one shot, and when the police came Julie Morrell lay on the floor with a bullet in his heart. Zelig had vanished, and was not found for two weeks, when detectives lured him to an East Side corner by signing his sweetheart's name to a decoy letter. He was arrested, but was promptly released. With another notch in his gun—at least in the opinion of the underworld, where he was given credit for killing Morrell—he proceeded to make things interesting for Tricker and Sirocco. Several times during the next week he sent detachments of his gangsters into territory which was considered the especial province of the Sirocco gangsters, and held up their saloons and gambling houses. Raids were also made upon Tricker's dives, while Tricker and Sirocco retaliated in kind by invading the Zelig district and interfering with the conduct of Big Jack's business affairs. Whenever a Zelig gangster met one of a rival clan there was a fight, and within two weeks half a dozen men had been shot or stabbed. A Sirocco gangster was killed during a battle in the lower Bowery, and when there was no immediate punitive expedition the Zeligs became bolder, and with great daring forced their way into Jack Pioggi's dive in Doyers street, in the very heart of the enemy territory.

Chick Tricker had come downtown that night to look after some of his East Side interests, and was in Pioggi's when Zelig and half a dozen of his thugs rushed in, each man with a blazing revolver in either hand. They emptied their weapons, but their haste was great and their aim inaccurate, and no one was hurt. The arrival of reinforcements for Tricker and Sirocco forced Zelig to retreat without accomplishing anything except the smashing of windows and bar fixtures. The next morning policemen arrested Zelig and half a dozen of his henchmen, but they were quickly bailed out by professional bondsmen procured by the politicians. But Zelig had scarcely left the Criminal Courts Building when a gangster who had been lurking in the shadow of the Tombs rushed across the street and fired three shots at him. Zelig fell with a bullet behind his ear, and detectives promptly seized Charley Torti, a member of the Sirocco gang. A desperate fight ensued when Torti's companions attempted to rescue him, but the police wielded their clubs with great vigor and held on to their prisoner.

But even the shooting of Zelig and the arrest of Torti did not halt the war. Next evening, while Zelig lay at the point of death in a hospital, eight of his thugs piled into two taxicabs and swept past Chick Tricker's saloon in the Bowery, firing shot after shot at him when he came to the door in response to a yell. Tricker dropped flat on his stomach and emptied two revolvers at the rapidly moving automobile. He was not injured, but Mike Fagin, a hanger-on about the dive, was shot in the leg, and every window and glass panel in the resort was shattered. Tricker and Sirocco immediately mobilized their gangs, and the fighting continued throughout the night, the almost constant crack of revolvers and the shouts of the struggling gangsters throwing the whole East Side into confusion. Four Zelig men shot a Sirocco thug in the doorway of a Bowery saloon at midnight, and two hours later a dozen of Zelig's henchmen and as many Tricker and Sirocco gangsters clashed at Ninth street and Second avenue. There was a wild fusilade of shots, and one of either side fell to the sidewalk with serious wounds. Before dawn the gangs had engaged in nine pitched battles in which revolvers were used, while at a score of places individual thugs met and fought desperately with knives and blackjacks. Alarmed by the extent of the conflict, Police Headquarters stationed detectives at all of the known haunts of the gangsters early next morning, and every man who entered was searched for weapons, and some of the lesser thugs were hustled off to police stations. Chick Tricker himself was taken into custody, but was released almost immediately. Despite these measures and the appeals of the politicians, the fighting continued for about a week longer, when the police arrested nineteen of the thugs and confiscated a cartload of revolvers, daggers, blackjacks, brass knuckles, stilettos, and other weapons. Such unusual activity frightened the gang leaders, and they abandoned their feud in the interests of self-preservation.

2

SEVERAL years before his war with the Jack Sirocco and Chick Tricker gangs, Big Jack Zelig began to exploit an ancient source of gang revenue in a manner which was to have far-reaching consequences; it resulted in his downfall and eventually became an important factor in the overthrow of the gangs. Zelig continued to rob the cheap stuss and dice games of the lower East Side, for these places were the pariahs of the underworld and had scant police and political connections; but he formed alliances with the

owners of the more pretentious houses and furnished gunmen for
their protection; on their behalf his gangsters blackjacked proprietors of rival places, wrecked their establishments with bombs,
informed against them to the District Attorney and honest police
officials, and cowed their customers by frequent raids and displays of force. Although he retained his hold upon the lower part
of Manhattan, these new activities compelled Zelig to spend considerable time in the Times Square district, for the Roaring Forties
just north of the old Tenderloin had become the center of the
gambling industry; there was scarcely a street from Fortieth to
Fiftieth and from Fifth to Eighth avenues which could not boast
of at least half a dozen first-class gambling houses.

This area was also the heart of the theatrical and night life of
the city, and contained many famous places of varying degrees of
respectability. Jack's Restaurant, famous for its Irish bacon and
its flying wedge of waiters who ejected obstreperous customers
with a minimum of motion and a maximum of efficiency, was
open day and night at Sixth avenue and Forty-third street, and
was a favorite resort of writers and newspaper men, who also fore-
gathered at Joel's, a *chili con carne* place in West Forty-first street
near Seventh avenue. Rector's celebrated restaurant and cabaret
was at Broadway and Forty-fourth street, while a block south, on
the other side of Broadway, was Shanley's, where the noted
Bat Masterson could be found each night in the grill spinning
yarns of the Western plains in the days when he and Wild Bill
Hickok were boon companions and fellow man-hunters. The
Knickerbocker Hotel Bar, with Maxfield Parrish's famous painting of Old King Cole above the shining mahogany and the glistening bar glass, was at Broadway and Forty-second street, while
across Broadway was Considine's Café, much frequented by rac-
ing men and pugilists. It was there that the contracts for all the
big prize fights were signed amid an imposing array of cham-
pagne bottles. Just below Considine's the Opera Café was striving
unsuccessfully to enforce a rule requiring all customers to wear
evening dress, and farther south, in Thirty-ninth and Thirty-
eighth streets, Bustanoby's, the Normandie Grill, and the Café
Maxim maintained the tradition of Satan's Circus. During a part

of this period, until December, 1913, the Haymarket was still in operation, but was a sad relic of its former splendour, while another similar dive was the German Village, in Seventh avenue. Many assignation houses and places of prostitution remained in the Hay-market area, around Sixth and Seventh avenues in the twenties and thirties. Some of these resorts were very up to-date; they were equipped with cash registers, and the inmates received brass checks which they cashed at the end of each week.

On Broadway between Forty-second and Forty-third streets was Redpath's Café, where gifted bartenders concocted extraordinary Ramoz fizzes and Sazerac cocktails. The Astor Hotel Bar at Forty-fourth street, now, alas, occupied by a shirt shop and a drug store, was justly famous for its Astor Hotel No. I, a potent mixture of grape juice and Swedish rum, while during the Christmas holidays great bowls of eggnog and Tom and Jerry sat on the bar ready for serving. Churchill's, at Broadway and Forty-eighth street, was one of the best restaurants in the city, and also offered an excellent cabaret performance; its owner, Captain Jim Churchill, was a noted figure of the time. At Seventh avenue and Fiftieth street, some three blocks north and east of Churchill's, was the Garden, a favorite resort of college boys and visiting buyers, for it had the hottest show in town. Scores of cabarets, lobster palaces, restaurants, and bars of almost equal importance dotted Broadway and the side streets from Thirty-fourth street to Columbus Circle and beyond, and there was laughter, music, life and color, where today there is the drabness of orange drink stands and chop suey restaurants, and the dizzy gaudiness of moving picture palaces.

Among the most widely known of the luxurious houses that catered to the gambling proclivities of the gay throngs which nightly promenaded Broadway were the establishments of Honest John Kelly, William Busteed, Sam Emery, Davy Johnson, Dinky Davis, and John Daly; while across town beyond Fifth avenue, at No. 5 East Forty-fourth street and next door to Delmonico's famous restaurant, was Richard Canfield's. Canfield also owned the resort at Saratoga Springs which had been established by John Morrissey in 1867, and had enhanced its great natural beauty by the addition of a restaurant, Italian gardens and an art gallery, the most celebrated feature of which was a portrait of Canfield by his friend James McNeill Whistler. Canfield's place in Forty-fourth street was the most famous gambling house in the United States, and was operated without molestation until the fall of 1902, when a member of the Vanderbilt family was reputed to have lost one hundred thousand dollars in a single night's play. Naturally, there was vast indignation, and a few days later, on December 1, 1902, the place was raided by William Travers Jerome, District Attorney, who had started a war against gambling which resulted in the closing of many noted houses. For a year after the raid Canfield's doors were barred and his windows shuttered, but thereafter it opened for short periods until late in 1904, when it was again invaded and an indictment procured against Canfield, charging him with being a common gambler. He pleaded guilty and paid a fine of one thousand dollars, and then retired from business, closing his Saratoga house also. During the next ten years the Forty-fourth street place was occasionally used as a gambling resort, but Canfield had no connection with it after his indictment. He lived quietly until 1914, when he died following a fall in the subway. He left an estate appraised by the Tax Department at $841,485.

Honest John Kelly acquired his sobriquet in 1888, when as a baseball umpire he refused a bribe of ten thousand dollars to make decisions favoring Boston in a game with Providence. He came to New York in the late nineties and opened a gambling house, and as his prosperity increased he operated in various parts of the city. But his most celebrated place was the brownstone building at No. 156 West Forty-fourth street, which is still pointed out to tourists by the guides of the sight-seeing wagons. Throughout his long career Kelly was notoriously at odds with the police, and often boasted that his persistent refusal to pay for protection compelled him to purchase many new doors and windows to replace fixtures wrecked by indignant detectives. The most destructive of the raids upon Kelly's occurred in 1912, when the doors, windows and furniture were smashed by a squad of policemen armed with axes, fire hatchets, and crow bars. Kelly then abandoned his Forty-fourth street establishment and opened the Vendome Club in West 141st street, but he retained ownership of the former property, and the police always suspected that he continued to use it for gambling purposes. From 1918 to 1922, while Richard E. Enright was Police Commissioner, a uniformed policeman paced back and forth in front of the building day and night. Kelly finally sold the structure to a Republican political organization. During the last years of his life he operated a place at Palm Beach, Florida, but without notable success. He died on March 28, 1926, at the age of seventy.

No proof was ever produced that Big Jack Zelig numbered such houses as Canfield's, Kelly's, and Busteed's among his clients, although it was often reported that Monk Eastman had received commissions from Canfield and that Zelig was paid a considerable sum to keep his gunmen out of Honest John's. The major portion of Zelig's gambling house business came from such second-rate places as those operated by Bald Jack Rose, Harry Vallon, Bridgie Webber, Sam Schepps, and Herman, otherwise Beansy, Rosenthal, all of whom were more or less prominently connected with the Becker-Rosenthal case. Rosenthal's connection, indeed, was extremely prominent: he was murdered. In seeking such gang business as bombing, raiding, shooting, and stabbing from houses of this class Big Jack Zelig had considerable competition from no less a personage than Paul Kelly, who had moved down from Harlem about 1910 and opened the New Englander Social and Dramatic Club in Seventh avenue, just north of the Roaring Forties. There he had established a headquarters for the remnants of his gang, and for the next two years his gunmen were notable figures of the theatrical district, and responsibility for many shootings and stabbings was laid at their door by the police. Detectives often raided Kelly's resort at the behest of the District Attorney and the few honest officials of the police department, but never found evidence sufficient to warrant closing the place. Kelly, indeed, was of great aid to the raiding officers; he appeared always to know when a visit was in prospect, and met the detectives at the front door or on the sidewalk, and ceremoniously conducted them through the establishment. But they never found anything more immoral than a dozen of his henchmen playing checkers or dominoes.

Herman Rosenthal was always in trouble, either with the police or with his fellow gamblers. He first appeared in the underworld as a bookmaker at the race tracks, and in 1910 opened a gambling house near Kuhloff's place at Far Rockaway, on Long Island. But he was soon raided, for Kuhloff possessed great influence and resented Rosenthal's efforts to capture his clientele. Rosenthal then became interested in the Hesper Club in Second avenue, and was almost immediately embroiled in a dispute with Bridgie Webber and Sam Paul, who were having great success with the Sans Souci Music Hall in Third avenue near Thirteenth street, not far from Rosenthal's place. The trouble was intensified when two of Big Jack Zelig's gangsters waylaid Webber and gave him a terrible beating, and thereafter for several years Rosenthal found the hands of practically every policeman, politician, and gambler in the city turned against him.

He opened a house in West 116th street which was soon closed by the police, and then started a more elaborate establishment in West Forty-fifth street near Broadway, which was frequently raided and twice wrecked by bombs. But according to the testimony of Bald Jack Rose during the Becker-Rosenthal trials, the gambler finally made his peace with the police by accepting Lieutenant Charles Becker, head of the Gambling Squad, as a partner. For a few months Rosenthal prospered, but in March, 1912, he incurred the enmity of Becker by refusing to pay five hundred dollars for the defense of the policeman's press agent, who had been charged with killing a man during a raid on a dice game.

Lieutenant Becker retaliated by raiding Rosenthal's house in West Forty-fifth street on April 15, and Rosenthal publicly threatened to reveal to the District Attorney, Charles S. Whitman, the extensive ramification of the system under which the gamblers obtained protection. Rosenthal's enemies then determined to put him out of the way, for the notoriety which he was receiving threatened the extinction of gambling and the loss of vast fortunes by both policemen and gamblers. In June, 1912, Big Jack Zelig was approached while under arrest in the Tombs, and as the

Police Lieutenant Charles Becker

Herman Rosenthal

Lefty Louie and Gyp the Blood

Whitey Lewis

Dago Frank

Big Jack Zelig

price of freedom agreed to furnish gunmen to murder Rosenthal, and to see that the killing was properly carried out. He was provided with a fund of two thousand dollars, and gave the commission to Gyp the Blood, Lefty Louie, Dago Frank, and Whitey Lewis. A few days later, in the early part of July, the four gunmen went to the Garden Café in Seventh avenue with the intention of killing Rosenthal as he sat at dinner with his wife, but their nerve failed them and they retreated without firing a shot.

On July 13, Rosenthal made an affidavit which was published in *The World* next morning, in which he swore that Lieutenant Becker was his partner and had received twenty per cent. of the profits of the West Forty-fifth street gambling house. These disclosures caused a tremendous sensation, and District Attorney Whitman promptly summoned Rosenthal to the Criminal Courts building. The gambler agreed to make his long delayed revelations, and on the evening of July 15, 1912, was in conference with the District Attorney for several hours. About midnight he walked into the dining-room of the Hotel Metropole in West Forty-third street just east of Broadway, and was still at supper some two hours later when a man came in from the street and told him he was wanted outside. Rosenthal stepped to the sidewalk, and was shot through the heart by the four gunmen who were waiting for him in an automobile. The murderers escaped, but all were captured within the next few weeks, and Lieutenant Becker was arrested on July 29. Gyp the Blood, Dago Frank, Lefty Louie, and Whitey Lewis were brought to trial in the early fall, and Big Jack Zelig was expected to be one of the state's star witnesses, for he had testified before the Grand Jury that he had furnished the gunmen at the behest of Becker and Bald Jack Rose. But on October 5, 1912, the day before he was to have appeared in court, Zelig was shot and killed by Red Phil Davidson as he stepped aboard a Second avenue trolley car at Thirteenth street.

But even without Zelig's testimony the four gunmen were convicted, and on April 13, 1914, were put to death in the electric chair at Sing Sing Prison. Lieutenant Becker was also found guilty of murder in the first degree, and his appeal for clemency came before Charles S. Whitman, who had meanwhile been elected

Governor. Whitman refused to commute the sentence, and Becker was electrocuted on July 30, 1915. His friends insisted that he had been jobbed, and when his body was prepared for burial his wife attached to the top of the coffin a silver plate with this inscription:

CHARLES BECKER.
MURDERED JULY 30, 1915
BY GOVERNOR WHITMAN.

The plate was not removed until Police Inspector Joseph A. Faurot had convinced Mrs. Becker that she was liable to prosecution for criminal libel.

CHAPTER XVI

THE PASSING OF THE GANGSTER

1

THE POLICE made a gallant gesture late in 1910 against several of the gangs which had incurred their displeasure, or had operated with such boldness that public sentiment made even the politicians fearful of protecting them; and when the smoke of battle cleared away half a score of the most noted figures of the underworld had been imprisoned. Among the eminent heroes who thus passed from the scene were Newburgh Gallagher and Marty Brennan, of the Gophers; Willie Jones, of the Gas Housers; Al Rooney, of the Fourteenth Street Gang, and Itsky Joe Hickman, who had proclaimed himself ruler of the remnant of Paul Kelly's old Five Pointers. And, as we have recorded, Kid Dropper, Johnny Spanish and Biff Ellison. The police believed that Dropper and

Spanish had become joint captains of the same gang when Paul
Kelly moved uptown, but later it became clear that they controlled separate groups. However, until a woman came between
them they were boon companions, and engaged in many joint
enterprises.

There was much shooting and clubbing in Hell's Kitchen
before Gallagher and Brennan were safely on their way to Sing
Sing, and the police were not loath to end their foray against the
ferocious Gophers. But the capture of their leaders had demoralized the gangsters, and within a few months a campaign was
begun which resulted in their dispersal, though not in their complete submission. For many years the Gophers, and the earlier
Hell's Kitchen gangs before them, had found the freight cars and
depots of the New York Central Railroad, along Eleventh avenue,
a fruitful source of plunder, and at length, unable to obtain relief
by ordinary process of law, the railroad organized a special police
force which had no other duties than to stop the depredations of
the Gophers. Many of its members were former policemen who
had suffered grievously at the hands of the gangsters, and they
welcomed the opportunity for revenge; unhampered by the politicians they went joyfully into the West Side and clubbed the
Gophers from one end of Hell's Kitchen to the other, or, as an
admiring patrolman phrased it, from hell to breakfast. And when
the gangsters resorted to firearms the private watchmen beat
them at their own game and shot straighter and faster. Many
thugs were wounded and several sent to prison, and there was
scarcely a Gopher who did not receive a sound thumping. Within
a few months the new force had devastated Hell's Kitchen with
clubs and blackjacks, and thereafter the Gophers avoided railroad
property as they would a plague. To this day a New York Central
watchman is regarded as the natural enemy of the Hell's Kitchen
hoodlum.

As a result of these activities, the Gophers split into three factions, the most important of which came under the domination of
Buck O'Brien and Owen Madden, who was widely known in the
underworld as Owney the Killer. The third group, small in numbers, called itself the Sullivans and swore allegiance to a leader of

that name. But Sullivan was ineffectual and accomplished little, and when the time came for the partition of the Gopher kingdom he was left out of the reckoning. Buck O'Brien formally assumed the overlordship of the area from Forty-second street north to Fifty-ninth, and from Ninth avenue to the Hudson River, and maintained his supremacy therein against occasional attacks by the Parlor Mob, which roared down from the sixties and attempted to drive the O'Briens below Fiftieth street. Owney the Killer occupied the territory below Forty-second street, and ranged southward as far as the domains of the Hudson Dusters and the Marginals commanded by Tanner Smith. Madden was on friendly terms with Smith, and for all practical purposes their gangs were one. But he was a bitter enemy of the Dusters, and his gang frequently engaged them in bloody combat.

Madden was almost the exact antithesis of Monk Eastman; he was sleek, slim and dapper, with the gentle smile of a cherub and the cunning and cruelty of a devil. He was born in England, but came to the United States at the age of eleven and was only seventeen when he acquired his nickname of Owney the Killer. He was but a year older when he assumed command of one of the Gopher factions, and had scarcely passed his twenty-third birthday, with five murders chalked against him by the police, when he was imprisoned. He was a crack shot with a revolver, and an accomplished artist with a slung-shot, a blackjack, and a pair of brass knuckles, not to mention a piece of lead pipe wrapped in a newspaper, always a favorite weapon of the thug. The police regarded him as a typical gangster of his time—crafty, cruel, bold, and lazy. Until he went to jail he had never worked a day in his life, and often boasted that he never would. Once when a Headquarters detective, at the request of a newspaper reporter, asked him how he spent his time, Owney the Killer obligingly wrote this record of his activities over a period of four days, carefully omitting anything which might incriminate him.

Thursday—Went to a dance in the afternoon. Went to a dance at night and then to a cabaret. Took some girls home. Went to a restaurant and stayed there until seven o'clock Friday morning.

Friday—Spent the day with Freda Horner. Looked at some fancy pigeons. Met some friends in a saloon early in the evening and stayed with them until five o'clock in the morning.

Saturday—Slept all day. Went to a dance in the Bronx late in the afternoon, and to a dance on Park avenue at night.

Sunday—Slept until three o'clock. Went to a dance in the afternoon and to another in the same place at night. After that I went to a cabaret and stayed there almost all night.

Soon after the breakup of the Gophers, Owney the Killer was accused by the police of murdering an Italian for no other reason than to celebrate his accession to the throne, but several important witnesses found it convenient to disappear, and detectives could not find sufficient evidence to justify a trial. A year later William Henshaw, a clerk, was killed on a trolley car at Ninth avenue and Sixteenth street after he had quarrelled with Madden over a girl, and before he died in New York Hospital gasped that Owney the Killer had shot him. Ten days later three detectives found Madden skulking in the doorway of a Hell's Kitchen tenement, and captured him after a chase over the housetops along Tenth avenue. But he was not convicted, for again the witnesses vanished. Nevertheless, the successive arrests frightened him, and for several months he was careful to give the police little cause for offense, and temporarily checked the cop fighting which so delighted the heart of the true Gopher. During this period of quiescence Madden and Tanner Smith organized the Winona Club, designed to serve as a joint rendezvous, and engaged rooms in a house owned by Dennis J. Keating, an honest horseshoer, who knew nothing of what manner of men he had accepted as tenants. The gangsters soon made the Winona Club a blot upon an otherwise fair neighborhood; they engaged in drunken revels and made the night hideous with the sound of their bickerings and brawlings. Less than a week after they had moved in Keating, whose own home was on the ground floor, climbed the stairs to tell them that the neighbors were complaining, and that unless they were quieter he would evict them. He found Owney the Killer and Tanner Smith at a table discussing affairs of state over a bottle of

Dopey Benny

Owney Madden

Kid Dropper

Little Augie

whiskey, while half a dozen members of both gangs lounged about the room listening to the music of a piano thumped by a gifted thug.

"You'll have to keep quiet up here," said Keating, "or I'll put you out of my house."

"You'll put *me* out of your house?" said Madden, smiling gently. "Mister, did you ever hear of Owney Madden? Yes? Well, Mister, I am Owney Madden!"

Keating stared at the celebrated gang chieftain for a moment, and then turned and went downstairs. Thereafter he was afraid to tell even the police about the gangsters and their doings, for he knew they would hold him responsible for whatever happened— and the Gophers were noted for the quickness and inventiveness with which they obtained revenge; the least Keating could expect was a bomb under his house. But finally a tenant of a neighboring house complained, and Patrolman Sindt was dispatched to investigate. He departed in haste as soon as he learned with whom he had to deal, and appealed to the captain of his precinct for aid. Sergeant O'Connell and a squad of reserves were sent to the house, but Madden's spies had given him word of their coming, and they found the gangsters behind barricaded doors, against which the furniture had been piled. The demand of the police for admittance was greeted with threats and curses, and when Sergeant O'Connell began to thump the door with his nightstick a bullet crashed through a window and grazed a policeman's skull.

"We'll shoot the gizzard out of any cop that tries to get in here!" cried Owney the Killer.

Sergeant O'Connell and his men withdrew around a corner, and two of the patrolmen were told off to gain entrance through the rear of the house, while the remainder of the attacking force marched across the street in full view of the gangsters who watched from windows. Sergeant O'Connell then approached the door and engaged Madden and Smith in argument, while the thugs crowded round to hear their lords bait the police. They thus left a rear window unguarded, and the two patrolmen crawled into the house and reached the room where the gangsters had congregated. The first intimation Madden and his henchmen had of their presence was when they rushed into the room and fell upon the gangsters with their clubs. Bewildered by the sudden onslaught, the thugs fell back, whereupon Sergeant O'Connell and the reserves swarmed across the street, battered down the door and rushed into the building. Fifteen minutes later the gangsters, handcuffed and bleeding, were driven none too gently into the street and hauled in a patrol wagon to the police station. But in court next morning Owney the Killer, being a minor, was lectured by a benevolent judge and placed under bond of five hundred dollars to keep the peace for six months. Tanner Smith also received only nominal punishment, and immediately hastened to City Hall, where he obtained an audience with Mayor William J. Gaynor and displayed the bruises which he had received during the battle. He complained that the police had made a wanton attack upon himself and his friends while they were playing cards. The Mayor publicly reprimanded the police, and the result of the agitation was the famous Order No. 7, which prohibited a patrolman from using his club unless he was prepared to prove that it was in defense of his life, and left nothing to the discretion of an Inspector or a Captain if a citizen, honest or otherwise, complained that he had been clubbed. Nothing could have more effectively tied the hands of the few policemen who were attempting to rid the city of gangsters; and until the order was rescinded some two years later by Mayor John Purroy Mitchel, it was an important factor in maintaining the power of the gangs. A great chortle of glee went up from the underworld when Mayor Gaynor's action became known, and for a little while Tanner Smith strutted in the limelight, as congratulations on his foresight poured in upon him. But within another year he was arrested and sent to prison to serve a year for carrying a revolver, and when he was released the gangs were on the run. So, late in 1914, Tanner Smith proclaimed his reformation and went into business as a boss stevedore and contractor. He was very successful and apparently lived uprightly, but early in 1919 he reverted to his old habits and established the Marginal Club above a saloon at No. 129 Eighth avenue. There he was shot through the heart a few months later by a man who approached him as he sat at a table with his back to the door. He left an estate of about one hundred thousand dollars.

2

MADDEN'S principal lieutenants were Eddie Egan, Bill Tammany, and Chick Hyland, none of whom made much of a splash in the underworld. Tammany was arrested and sent to Sing Sing for fifteen years before he could fairly show his mettle; Chick Hyland was imprisoned for four years, and Egan dropped out of sight after his chief had been convicted. Madden's sources of revenue were much the same as those of other gang chieftains, although he does not appear to have been a rival of Big Jack Zelig in the protection and raiding of gambling houses. He thrived principally upon sneak thievery, stickups, loft burglaries, intimidation of merchants and saloon-keepers, and collections from shady politicians. He made enemies by the score, for he was ambitious and domineering, and frequently let it be known that he aspired to be the acknowledged king of all the gangs. Many attempts were made to kill him, but none even approached success until the night of November 6, 1912, when he went to a dance given by the Dave Hyson Association in the Arbor Dance Hall, once the old Eldorado dive, in Fifty-second street near Seventh avenue, now the heart of the theatrical district. The Dave Hyson Association was merely a device to beat the excise laws and enable the management of the Hall to comply with the provision which permitted liquor to be sold after hours at a dance given by a legitimate social organization. Each of the waiters organized an association and gave dances in turn throughout the winter.

The merriment was at its height when Owney the Killer stepped into the Hall and strode to the middle of the dance floor, where he stood with folded arms and glared menacingly about him. Almost instantly the music stopped, the women began to crowd toward the exits and the men backed into the corners, looking to their artillery. But the Killer waved a lordly hand.

"Go on and have your fun!" he shouted. "I won't bump any-body off here tonight!"

He beckoned to Dave Hyson and graciously shook the trembling waiter's hand.

"Let 'em dance, Dave," he commanded. "I don't want to spoil youse guys' party!"

He then retired to the balcony, where he took a seat from which he could see and be seen. For several hours he sat alone, drinking whiskey and preening himself, enjoying the coy glances of the women and the envious glares of other and less famous gangsters. Soon after midnight a woman climbed the stairs and sat at his table. She was pretty and she prattled charmingly in obvious hero worship, and the gang chieftain was so interested in her that he relaxed and paid no attention to the eleven men who came up one by one and unostentatiously took seats near him. But finally the woman went downstairs, and Owney the Killer glanced lazily downward to the dance floor. Then his idle gaze swept the balcony. He saw enemies on three sides of him, eleven men who stared at him out of cold eyes. He knew that they intended to kill him, and would shoot before he could even so much as make a movement toward his pocket. Nevertheless, he slowly rose to his feet and faced them, for Owney the Killer was no coward.

"Come on, youse guys!" he cried. "Youse wouldn't shoot nobody! Who did youse ever bump off?"

One of the eleven men cursed. That broke the tension. Guns blazed and Owney the Killer went down, and while he lay unconscious on the floor his enemies went calmly down the stairs and into the street; and no hand was raised to stop them. Patrolmen pushed their way through the crowd after a while, and sent the gangster to a hospital. Later a detective asked who had shot him.

"Nothin' doin'," said Madden. "The boys'll get 'em. It's nobody's business but mine who put these slugs into me."

Surgeons dug half a dozen bullets out of the gangster's body, and he recovered after a long time. And in less than a week after the shooting three of the eleven men had been murdered.

While Madden was recuperating from his wounds Little Patsy Doyle, an obscure member of the old Gophers who had spent much of his time along Broadway, suddenly appeared in Hell's Kitchen and for no apparent reason blackjacked a policeman. Encouraged by the favorable comment which greeted this exploit, he endeavored to gain control of the gang, industriously spreading a report that Madden had been permanently crippled. Little Patsy was not alone ambitious; he nursed a grievance because his girl, Freda Horner, had cast him out and announced that she was going to marry Owney the Killer, or at least live with him, which in the underworld amounted to the same thing. Little Patsy acquired a small following of disgruntled thugs, but before he could make any considerable progress Madden was discharged from the hospital and immediately took steps to suppress the insurrection. He had scarcely returned to the Kitchen when Little Patsy was slugged with a piece of lead pipe and almost killed; but with the courage of desperation himself embarked upon a slugging spree and blackjacked several of Madden's favorite henchmen. And he not only slugged Tony Romanello, one of Owney the Killer's friends, but stabbed and shot him as well, for Romanello had taunted him with the fact that Madden had appropriated his girl.

Little Patsy became increasingly obnoxious, and Madden marked him for the sacrifice. Ugly rumors that Little Patsy was a stool-pigeon and a snitch began to circulate in Hell's Kitchen, and one by one the rebel's adherents deserted him and again swore fealty to Owney the Killer. At length the time came for direct action. Madden went into conference with two of his best gunmen, Art Biedler and Johnny McArdle, and commissioned them to attend to the job of permanently silencing Little Patsy. Freda Horner was instructed to have speech with Margaret Everdeane, a warm friend of many Gophers and the current sweetheart of Willie the Sailor, otherwise William Mott, and devise a scheme whereby Little Patsy could be lured within range of the guns. So it happened that on the night of November 28, 1914, Margaret Everdeane telephoned to Little Patsy that Freda Horner was pining away for love of him and desired mightily to be reconciled.

"The poor kid's all busted up over the way she treated you, Patsy," said Margaret Everdeane. "She wants to see you, Patsy. I'll have her with me an' Willie, an' you can talk to her."

An appointment was made, and shortly before midnight Little Patsy entered a saloon at Eighth avenue and Forty-first street. He was too much occupied with thoughts of Freda Horner to observe three men who lurked in the shadows across the street, or to notice that two pushed through the swinging doors not three minutes after he had entered the saloon. He strode hurriedly past the bar and into the back room, where he found Margaret Everdeane sitting at a table with Willie the Sailor. But Freda Horner was not there.

"Where's Freda?" demanded Little Patsy, suspiciously.

"She's gone out a minute, Patsy," said Margaret Everdeane. "She'll be right back. Sit down, Patsy."

A moment later a bartender came in and said that a man outside wanted to see Little Patsy. The gangster entered the bar-room, but saw no one he knew.

"Who wanted to see me?" he asked.

"I did," said a voice.

Little Patsy turned to face the speaker, and was greeted with a bullet in his lung. He reeled, and two more shots ploughed through his body, and he collapsed to the floor. He scrambled painfully to his feet and attempted to draw his revolver, but lacked the strength to pull it from his pocket. Lurching drunkenly, his face as white as the thin blanket of snow which covered the pavement, Little Patsy staggered out of the saloon and fell dead in the street.

Owney the Killer was arrested two or three days later, and at his trial Freda Horner and Margaret Everdeane turned state's evidence. Crying and raving that he had been jobbed, Madden was sent to Sing Sing for ten to twenty years, while Johnny McArdle was given a sentence of thirteen years and Art Biedler one of eighteen. And at Police Headquarters the detectives drew a breath of relief and scratched the name of Owney the Killer from their list of dangerous gangsters. But in January, 1923, after having served less than his minimum term, Madden was released on parole, and went to work for a taxicab company, the officials of which said that he had been hired to protect their drivers from unfair competition. In plain language, that meant blackjack the opposition. But this job lasted only a few months, and the next heard of the gang leader he and five other men were arrested near White Plains, in Westchester county, while riding on a truck which contained twenty-five thousand dollars worth of stolen liquor. The police said that Madden had been actively engaged as a hi-jacker, but the charges against him were dismissed when he told the court that he had merely begged a ride and did not know what was in the truck. Since then he has more or less dropped out of sight, but is said to have backed several night clubs in Harlem and mid-Manhattan.

3

WHILE Big Jack Zelig was leading his gangsters in the wars against Chick Tricker and Jack Sirocco, and Owney Madden was welding a faction of the old Gophers into a formidable organization, scores of other gangs were in process of formation throughout the city, for the sympathy with which the police and politicians regarded the activities of Zelig and his contemporary chieftains had vastly encouraged every ambitious young thug in New York. Early in 1911 Terrible John Torrio appeared along the East River water front, in the old Fourth Ward, and as chieftain of the James street gang terrorized a large area for almost five years, when he removed to the west and soon became a conspicuous figure in the underworld of Chicago. The gangs captained by Joe Baker and Joe Morello struggled fiercely for supremacy along the upper East Side; five men were killed in a great battle at 114th street and Third avenue on April 17, 1912, and eventually they simply shot each other to pieces. The Red Peppers and Duffy Hills continued their nightly brawling in East 102nd street in the vicinity of Third and Second avenues, while the Pearl Buttons, ancient enemies of the Hudson Dusters, moved uptown late in 1910 and became lords of the area around West 100th street from Broadway to Central Park. The Parlor Mob, hitherto a vassal organization of the Gophers, abandoned Hell's Kitchen when the special police of the New York Central Railroad went into action, and assumed control of the Central Park district around Sixty-sixth street, wherein were many low class tenements.

Late in 1911 the Car Barn Gang came into existence, and soon became one of the most feared collections of criminals and brawlers in the city. Its members were recruited principally from the young hoodlums who loafed around the East River docks, fighting, stealing, and rolling lushes. But as members of the gang they became gunmen and highwaymen, and the Car Barn area, roughly from Ninetieth to One Hundredth streets and from Third avenue to the East River, became as dangerous for respectable people as Hell's Kitchen. The first intimation that the police had that the thugs of this district had formally organized was when the following placard suddenly appeared on a lamp-post near the old car barns at Second avenue and Ninety-seventh street:

Notice
COPS KEEP OUT!
NO POLICEMAN WILL HEREAFTER
BE ALLOWED IN THIS BLOCK. BY ORDER OF
THE CAR BARN GANG.

The police soon found that the Car Barners were prepared and eager to enforce their proclamation. Half a dozen patrolmen who ventured into the forbidden area were stabbed or beaten with slung-shot and blackjack, and thereafter they patrolled the district in fours and fives. After Mayor Gaynor's Order No. 7 had been revoked the Strong Arm Squad made frequent excursions into the the domain of the Car Barners and clubbed the gangsters unmercifully, but it was not until two of their principal captains had been sent to the electric chair that the gang was smashed. These martyrs were Big Bill Lingley and Freddie Muehfeldt, better known as The Kid. Lingley was reputed to have been one of the organizers of the Car Barn Gang; he was a widely known desperado and burglar, and habitually carried two revolvers, a blackjack and a slung shot, which he was very keen to use, either on the police or an inoffensive citizen. Freddie Muehfeldt came of a good family, and in his early boyhood was prominent in Sunday School work, so much so, indeed, that his good mother expressed the hope that he might in time become a clergyman. But in his late teens the boy acquired an aversion to work and took to loafing on the docks, where he conceived a tremendous admiration for Big Bill Lingley, whose swagger was imitated by the boys of the neighborhood. Big Bill saw possibilities in young Muehfeldt and took the lad under his wing, and together they set out to bring honor to the Car Barners and glory to their own names. Accompanied by half a dozen satellites, they began a series of raids upon saloons from Fourteenth street northward to the Bronx, meeting with much success and filling their pockets with gold. But at length a liquor dealer in the Bronx, just across the Harlem River, fought back in defense of his till, and Big Bill and Freddie Muehfeldt promptly killed him. Both paid the penalty for murder, and the career of The Kid was ended before he was twenty-one years old.

South of the Car Barn kingdom, around Fifty-ninth street, the Bridge Twisters prowled the darkened streets under the approaches to the Queensboro Bridge over the East River. At Fortieth street and the River, and as far inland as Third avenue, there was constant fighting between the Tunnel Gang, the Terry Reilleys and the Corcoran's Roosters led by Tommy Corcoran; and the Gas House Gang continued to flourish along Eighteenth street and as far west as Fourth avenue, although these thugs were not so successful as during the days of Monk Eastman and Paul Kelly. The Gas Housers vanished from the scene early in 1914, when their last great chieftain, Tommy Lynch, was killed in a fierce battle with the Jimmy Curley gang captained by Gold Mine Jimmy Carrigio. A little farther south were the Carpenters, small in numbers but murderous of habit; and the lower East Side fairly swarmed with gangs of all degrees of importance. Among them were the Little Doggies, the Neighbors' Sons, the Dock Rats, the Chisel Gang, the Folly Gang; and the Frog Hollows, who operated uptown as well, and specialized in white slavery. They were finally dispersed late in 1913 when three of their principal thugs were sent to prison for a total of more than forty-two years. And in this

area, also, were the gangs captained by Dopey Benny Fein; Joe the
Greaser, otherwise Joseph Rosensweig; Billy Lustig, Pinchey Paul,
Little Rhody; Punk Madden, who was no relation to Owney the
Killer; Pickles Laydon; Ralph the Barber, whose real name was
Ralph Daniello; Yoske Nigger, born Joseph Toplinsky; Johnny
Levinsky, and Charles Vitoffsky, called Charley the Cripple. Along
the lower West Side north of the Battery there were innumerable
small gangs which preyed upon the produce and chicken markets,
and found the rivalry between men engaged in these lines of business greatly to their advantage. The most notable exploit of these
thugs was the murder of Barnett Baff, a chicken dealer, in 1914.
This job was reputed to have cost its instigators forty-two hundred dollars, which was divided among several gang leaders, while
the man who actually fired the death shot received but fifty dollars. The police always believed that Baff's death was procured by
his business rivals, for competition was very keen and it was not
uncommon for a man whose affairs were threatened by the enterprise of a rival to hire gangsters to wreck the enemy's establishment and, if necessary, kill him.

Yoske Nigger, Charley the Cripple, and Johnny Levinsky specialized in stealing and poisoning horses; and by the end of 1913
the invariable satisfaction which their work afforded had given
them practically a monopoly of the business. They thereupon
shrewdly divided the field and worked in harmony for some two
years, on occasion lending thugs to each other to help carry out a
particularly ticklish assignment. Yoske Nigger catered exclusively
to the produce markets, truckmen and livery stables, while Levinsky
confined his activities to the ice cream trade, and Charley the
Cripple handled such commissions as developed from the rivalry
between the seltzer and soda water dealers and manufacturers.
Their fees varied according to the magnitude and danger of the
task, but usually were as high as the traffic would bear. A gangster who finally divulged their methods of operations to the
police said that these were the average rates:

Shooting, fatal $500
Shooting, not fatal 100

Poisoning a team 50
Poisoning one horse 35
Stealing a horse and rig 25

The shooting items, the gangster explained, referred to human beings. However, these prices were extremely high; the chieftains of many of the East Side gangs were prepared to commit murder for as low as twenty dollars, while lower New York fairly swarmed with thugs who guaranteed a neat and workmanlike job, with no entangling consequences, for from two to ten dollars, depending upon the prominence of the victim and the state of their own finances when they received the commission.

These groups formed a very small minority of the gangs which sprinkled Manhattan Island during the final years of the gangsters' rule. By the latter part of 1913, about a year after Big Jack Zelig had passed to his reward, it is likely that there were more gangs in New York than at any other period in the history of the metropolis; their number and the ramifications of their alliances were so bewildering that of hundreds there now exists no more than a trace; they flashed into the ken of the policeman and the reporter and flashed out again like comets, leaving a gaseous trail of blood and graft. But it is improbable that the total number of gangsters was any greater than during the reign of Monk Eastman, for the gangs were smaller; the time when a chieftain could muster from five hundred to a thousand men under his banner had passed with the dispersal of such groups as the Eastmans, the Gophers and the Five Pointers, and there were few gang leaders who could take the field with more than thirty or forty thugs. Consequently an area which in former years had been plundered exclusively by a single great gang became the haunt of innumerable small groups, which constantly fought each other, frequently strayed beyond their own domains, and robbed and murdered whenever the opportunity for gain presented itself. Moreover, their organization was more elastic; there no longer existed the undying loyalty to the captain which had been such a distinguishing characteristic of the old-time gangs, and it was not unusual for a gangster to owe allegiance to three or four leaders at the same time, performing a different sort of thuggery for each. Throughout the city there were also a far greater number of independent thugs who bound themselves to a chieftain only for a definite campaign or for a specific blackjacking, stabbing or shooting assignment. The number of gangsters of this type continued to increase as decency invaded politics, and as the police became more honest and efficient and waged clubbing campaigns against the organized gangs.

4

THE gangs which flourished throughout the eastern part of Manhattan during the few years that followed the death of Big Jack Zelig performed any sort of criminal work which their clients required, but their opportunities for enrichment were far fewer than in the old days. The disclosures which followed the murder of Herman Rosenthal had resulted in the closing of most of the gambling houses, and had compelled the remainder to operate with a minimum of police protection; and the gangsters had become such a stench in the public nostril that the politicians dared not employ them to the extent of former years. Consequently it became necessary to develop new sources of revenue, and the gang chieftains found a rich harvest awaiting them in the constant industrial strife with which the East Side was afflicted, especially among the needle and allied trades. Late in 1911 the labor unions began the practice of hiring thugs to murder and blackjack strike breakers and intimidate workmen who refused to be organized, while the employers engaged other gangsters to slug union pickets and raid union meetings. The thugs seldom became strike breakers, for actual physical labor was repugnant to them, but they acted as guards to the workmen who were recruited from the hordes of casual labor which haunted the Bowery and Sixth avenue employment agencies. In time a distinct class of men arose who refused to perform any other sort of work, and went from city to city earning high wages as strike breakers. They were called finks, while the gunmen who protected them were known as nobles. For the most part they are now provided by private detective agencies.

Within a few months slugging, stabbing and shooting were accepted concomitants of industrial troubles throughout the East Side, and the bulk of the labor union business was carried on by the gangs captained by Dopey Benny, Joe the Greaser, Little Rhody, Pinchey Paul and Billy Lustig, while the employers were compelled to content themselves with the services of less efficient combinations. The chieftains of the important gangs were regularly on the payrolls of the local unions at from twenty-five to fifty dollars a week, and for each gangster assigned to blackjack strike breakers or frighten obstinate workmen they received ten dollars a day, of which they retained two and a half dollars. The remaining seven and a half dollars was the wages of the thug. The union officials also bound themselves to pay all fines, provide bail, engage lawyers and arrange for as much protection as possible through their political and police connections. Dopey Benny further safeguarded himself by retaining a lawyer on an annual fee; and the legal luminary drew up contracts without too much mention of the character of the work involved, but specifying that the gang leader's salary was to continue if he went to prison. For several years Dopey Benny was constantly attended by a professional bondsman, who not only arranged bail for the chieftain when required, but for his henchmen as well.

Dopey Benny began his criminal career at the age of ten, when he prowled the streets of the East Side stealing packages from express wagons and delivery carts. From this lowly beginning he became a lush worker and a footpad, then a pickpocket of distinction, and at length the greatest, or at any rate the most successful, gang captain of his time, however unworthy he may have been to wear the mantle of Monk Eastman. Dopey Benny was not a drug addict, but adenoidal and nasal troubles from infancy gave him a sullen, sleepy appearance from which his nickname was derived. As a leader he was far superior to his contemporaries, and in time commanded the allegiance of half a dozen smaller gangs, among them the Little Doggies, the remnant of the Hudson Dusters, a few Gophers who had wandered into the East

Side after the private police force of the New York Central had swept through Hell's Kitchen, and the groups led by Porkie Flaherty and Abie Fisher. Dopey Benny districted the lower half of Manhattan Island, and to each area assigned one of his vassal gangs, which wielded pistol, blackjack and slung-shot for the benefit of whichever side first spoke for its services, although in the main the thugs worked for labor unions. However, it was not uncommon for Dopey Benny to slug and stab for the unions in one district, and against them in another. For some three years there was scarcely a strike in New York in which these gangsters were not employed, and during this period Dopey Benny's annual income averaged between fifteen and twenty thousand dollars. So widely was he feared that a group of employers once offered him fifteen thousand dollars if he would remain neutral during a threatened strike. But Dopey Benny indignantly refused, saying that his heart was naturally with the working man, and that he would continue to hold himself and his gangsters at the disposal of the union officials. His methods were thus described in a confession which he made to the District Attorney after he had finally been brought to book:

My first job was to go to a shop and beat up some workmen there. The men that employed me gave me ten dollars for every man that I had to use and one hundred dollars for myself. I picked out about fifteen men, and later met the man that employed me and told him that I couldn't do the job for the money that he wanted to pay—that it took more men than I had calculated on, and that I wouldn't touch it unless I was paid more money.

Finally he agreed to pay me six hundred dollars for the job. I got my men together, divided them up into squads and saw that they were armed with pieces of gas pipe and with clubs, but this time not with pistols, and when the workmen came from work the men I had got set on them and beat them up. I wasn't right there when this was going on. I told the men what to do, and I was near by, but I didn't do any of it myself. After the job was over I saw the man I had made the agreement with and asked him how he liked the way the job was done. He said that it was fine and paid me the six hundred dollars in cash.

From this time on one fellow would hear from another that I did these jobs, and would come to get me to do a job, and so I was kept busy all the time. Some of the jobs were just individual jobs. I would be told there was a certain fellow whom they wanted beaten up, and they would take me where I could get a look at him, and then when I got a chance I would follow him and beat him up, and afterwards get my pay.

One time when we were doing a job in a place where there were some girls, who blew police whistles, and policemen came before we could get away. I was caught and got thirty days, and three of the other fellows got fifteen days apiece. All the time I was serving my thirty days my wages of fifteen dollars a day, which I was getting then for doing these jobs, kept on just the same, though some of it wasn't paid until later.

After this I did a number of jobs for which I didn't get any special pay—just my regular payroll, which was then twenty-five dollars a week. At this time I was getting that regularly and wasn't charging any more for the jobs I did. Afterward I got to doing jobs again as so much a job. I got three hundred and fifty dollars for doing one job. That was in addition to the regular twenty-five dollars a week which I was getting. I had thirty men on this job, and a lot of the employes were hurt.

In January, 1914, I was tried and convicted of assault, and sentenced to state prison for five years, but afterward the conviction was reversed and so I got out. All the time I was in the state prison I continued on the payroll and did several more jobs. Some of them were quiet work, without any weapons at all—just scaring people and threatening them—and some of them were violent work.

Attracted by almost constant opportunity to display their skill, some of the most ferocious of the independent thugs enlisted under Dopey Benny's banner, and his cohorts were further augmented by desertions from rival gang leaders. Even Joe the Greaser lost many of his best men, but that astute chieftain prevented his utter downfall by forming an alliance with Dopey Benny, and thereafter accepted the latter as generalissimo of all the gangs, although he continued to operate his own group as an independent unit. Through this alliance Dopey Benny and Joe the Greaser practically controlled the situation, and Little Rhody, Pinchey Paul and Billy Lustig, as well as a score of other minor captains, were ignored by the union officials who assigned the jobs. In desperation the smaller gangs combined, and late in 1913 declared war against Dopey Benny and Joe the Greaser, opening hostilities with a gun battle at Grand and Forsyth streets. But the gangsters were notoriously poor marksmen and no one was wounded, although the indiscriminate shooting smashed several store windows and caused a great scurrying in the crowded thoroughfares. One of the principal instigators of the war, and a constant schemer against the power of Dopey Benny and Joe the Greaser, was a man known as Jewbach, who finally became so obnoxious that Nigger Benny Snyder, a local henchman of Joe the Greaser, was dispatched to silence him. Nigger Benny attacked Jewbach with a knife at Rivington and Norfolk streets, but could only slash his enemy twice before he was arrested. Jewbach loudly proclaimed that he would prosecute Nigger Benny and send him to prison, whereupon Joe the Greaser called upon him with half a dozen of his thugs. While the gangsters held Jewbach down, Joe the Greaser cut a large piece out of his lower lip.

"Let that learn you," said Joe the Greaser, "not to talk so much."

Jewbach was unable to speak for several weeks, and had been so thoroughly cowed by Joe the Greaser that he failed to appear for the trial, and Nigger Benny was discharged. Subsequently, when Pinchey Paul was found dead, Nigger Benny was accused of the murder, and found himself in such a tight place that he promptly confessed to the District Attorney, shifting responsibility for the killing to the shoulders of Joe the Greaser, who he said gave him five dollars for the job. Nigger Benny was sent to prison for twenty years. Joe the Greaser pleaded guilty to manslaughter, and in December, 1915, was sentenced to ten years in Sing Sing.

It was this war, though trivial in comparison to those of earlier days, which brought about the final smashing of the gangs. In November, 1913, the rival thugs clashed in front of a hat factory in Greenwich street, where the Dopey Benny gangsters were waiting to assault workmen who had refused to strike, and in December the six-day bicycle race in Madison Square Garden was enlivened by a fight in which one of the gangsters opposing Dopey Benny was shot. Less than a month later, early in January, 1914, some thirty thugs came together in front of Arlington Hall in St. Mark's Place, where a ball was in progress under the auspices of the Lenny & Dyke Association, of which the leading spirit was Tommy Dyke, manager of Chick Tricker's Bowery dive. For almost half an hour the gangsters fired at each other from the shelter of tenement doorways, and while none was wounded one of their bullets killed Frederick Strauss, a court clerk who was passing on his way to a lodge meeting. Strauss was a substantial citizen with important fraternal and political connections, and his murder aroused such a commotion that Mayor John Purroy Mitchel, who had only recently assumed office after defeating the Tammany Hall candidate, ordered Police Commissioner Douglas I. McKay to suppress the gangs at all costs. At the same time he revoked Mayor Gaynor's order against the use of nightsticks, and assured the patrolmen that they would not be brought up on charges if they found it necessary to club a gangster.

Commissioner McKay promptly suspended the police captain in whose precinct the battle had occurred, and within twenty-four hours the uniformed force, aided by a large squad of detectives under command of Deputy Commissioner George S. Dougherty, had arrested more than a hundred thugs. Many were subsequently sent to prison, for the Tammany Hall district organizations had been temporarily demoralized and discredited by the result of the election which had put Mitchel and a reform administration in City Hall, and the Wigwam politicians were unable to protect their hereditary allies. Arthur Woods, who had been the Mayor's secretary, succeeded McKay as Police Commissioner in April, and prosecuted the war against the gangsters with even greater vigor, while District Attorney Charles A. Perkins started an investigation of the part the labor unions had played in gang activities. Officials of the United Hebrew Trades Union began to raise a defense fund by levying an assessment of seven cents a week upon its sixty thousand members, and increased this amount to forty cents when the District Attorney's inquiry developed new and damaging evidence. Late in 1914 Dopey Benny was arrested, and the following May, after he had waited patiently for his political and union friends to procure his release, he became convinced that they intended to sacrifice him. He thereupon struck a bargain with the District Attorney, and in return for slight punishment prepared a confession in which he detailed at great length his connections and activities over a period of some five years. Eleven gangsters and twenty-three union officials were indicted upon the basis of this information, but none of the latter ever went to prison; and in June, 1917, the indictments were dismissed when District Attorney Edward Swann, who had succeeded Perkins, informed the Court of General Sessions that he did not have sufficient evidence to obtain convictions. Six months after his confession Dopey Benny was again arrested, and was tried for the murder of Frederick Strauss in St. Mark's Place, but the jury disagreed, and in May, 1917, the courts dismissed the indictment. But his successive encounters with the police had broken Dopey Benny's hold upon the East Side, and he was never able to regain his former power, for his gangsters had been scattered and the labor unions refused to have further dealing with him.

During the first year of his administration Commissioner Woods procured the imprisonment of more than two hundred of the most eminent thugs in the city; and the gangsters against whom conclusive evidence could not be obtained were fiercely clubbed by the uniformed patrolmen and closely watched by the detectives. By the middle of 1916 the police had completed the smashing of the Hudson Dusters and all of the other gangs which had roamed Manhattan Island from the Battery to Spuyten Duyvil, and as their organizations lost all cohesion the gangsters engaged in honest occupations or became commonplace criminals operating in small groups. A few continued to find employment from the labor unions, although most of the union officials had been badly frightened by the activity of the police and the determination of Mayor Mitchel to put an end to the wholesale stabbing, slugging, and shooting which had kept the city in a ferment for so many years, and had found other means to settle industrial disputes. But there were no organized gangs of any consequence in New York until late in 1917, when Johnny Spanish and Kid Dropper were released from Sing Sing Prison and returned immediately to the East Side, where they attempted to revive their ancient glories, and renewed the feud which had begun when both were members of the old Five Pointers under Paul Kelly. They enlisted followings of perhaps thirty men each, and clashed in several minor affrays, but without doing much damage or attracting much attention from the police. Finally, on July 29, 1919, Johnny Spanish was murdered in front of a restaurant at No. 19 Second avenue by three men who came up behind him and emptied their revolvers into his body.

Kid Dropper was promptly arrested, but was discharged for lack of evidence, although his enmity toward Spanish was common knowledge, and it was shown that they had been at loggerheads over the little union business that was available, and had led their gangs on opposite sides in a garment strike. During the days of Monk Eastman and Paul Kelly, Kid Dropper had not been a thug of the first rank, but with the death of Johnny Spanish he became the most imposing figure in the underworld. In the old days, too, he had been slovenly in appearance and slouchy in gait, but he now undertook to dress according to his position, and appeared along Broadway and throughout the East Side in a belted check suit of extreme cut, narrow, pointed shoes, and shirts and neckties of weird design and color combination, while his pudge face, pasty gray from his long imprisonment, was surmounted by a stylish derby pulled rakishly over one eye. In the summer months he wore a straw hat with an extremely narrow brim and a brightly colored band. He also let it be known that he preferred to be called Jack, and named his gang the Rough Riders of Jack the Dropper.

For some three years after he got out of prison Kid Dropper operated with considerable success around Madison, Monroe, and Rutgers streets, with occasional forays into the Broadway theatrical district and other areas, and appeared to possess a singular immunity. During this period the police implicated him in twenty murders, but were never able to obtain evidence sufficient to bring him to trial. Encouraged by the success of Kid Dropper, who was earning large sums by various criminal operations and by lending his sluggers to the few labor unions which still followed the practice of slugging their opponents, Jacob Orgen, otherwise Little Augie, who had been an obscure member of the Dopey Benny gang, emerged from retirement and organized a small group which he called the Little Augies. And Solomon Schapiro, who had been operating independently, appeared in the field with another small gang. The Rough Riders and the Little Augies were all Jewish gunmen and sluggers, while Schapiro's men were Italians.

Little Augie and Solomon Schapiro combined against Kid Dropper during a strike of wet wash laundry workers in 1923, and in August of that year the gangs fought a gun battle in Essex street, during which two innocent pedestrians were killed before they could scurry to safety, although none of the gangsters was wounded. Four days later Kid Dropper and fifteen of his thugs were arrested at Broadway and Forty-third street, but there was scant evidence to connect them with the murders, and they were discharged upon arraignment before a Magistrate in Essex Market Court. The police then prepared to take Kid Dropper to the West Side Court, where a charge of carrying a concealed weapon had been made against him. Reports had reached Headquarters that the Rough Riders would attempt to rescue their chieftain, and half a dozen patrolmen and detectives were stationed in and about the building, under the command of Captain Cornelius Willemse, who had been active in the suppression of the East Side gangs. When Kid Dropper was led from the court room he was surrounded by policemen, all of whom had loosened their pistol holsters and were ready for trouble.

Meanwhile a great throng had gathered in the street to see the famous gang leader, and Kid Dropper was escorted down a narrow lane through the crowd toward a taxicab which had been drawn up at the curb. The detectives saw the baleful eyes of Little Augie glaring at his enemy, but they did not see Louis Kushner, known in gang circles as Louis Cohen, for Louis lurked in a tenement house doorway across the street, a hand on his revolver, waiting for an opportunity to kill the chief of the Rough Riders. Kushner was a very minor follower of Little Augie, and heretofore had been entrusted only with the most menial of missions, even though he nursed an ambition to be a killer and see his name in the newspapers as a great gangster and a tough man. Likewise he nursed a great bitterness toward Kid Dropper because that eminent captain had only recently attempted to blackmail him out of five hundred dollars, having acquired damaging information respecting the slugging of a strike breaker. So Kushner had come to the Essex Market Court, not to see Kid Dropper, but to kill him, both for revenge and for glory.

When Kid Dropper and the group of accompanying policemen reached the taxicab Detective Jesse Joseph opened the door and climbed in, followed by the gang chieftain, while Detective La Battaglia and Captain Willemse stood beside the door and delayed the departure of the cab for a moment to give instructions to the driver. In that moment Louis Kushner crept across the street, and unnoticed by the police gained the shelter of another taxicab alongside the vehicle through which the head of Kid Dropper could be seen against the small pane of glass in the rear. With the rapidity of a snake Kushner darted from behind the cab, pressed the muzzle of his revolver against the glass and pulled the trigger. The bullet crashed through the window and into Kid Dropper's brain, and the gang leader collapsed with his head against Detective Joseph's chest. Kushner fired again, and the chauffer screamed and clapped his hand to his ear. Two more shots roared from Kushner's revolver, and Captain Willemse leaped toward him, thinking that Detective Joseph had been hit. Kushner twisted his arm and fired again, and a bullet whirled Captain Willemse's hat from his head. But the next instant detectives had flung themselves upon Kushner and wrenched the revolver from his hand. He offered no further resistance; pale and with his eyes glittering wildly he faced the circle of policemen and sighed deeply:

"I got him!" he said, simply. "I'd like a cigarette."

Little Augie and one of his principal henchmen, Sammy Weiss, were immediately arrested, but were soon discharged, for Kushner insisted that the murder of Kid Dropper was his own scheme and that Little Augie had given him no instructions. In the course of time the young killer was sent to Sing Sing to serve from twenty years to life. Dropper's gangsters quickly dispersed after the death of their leader, and a few weeks after the shooting the police had a serious talk with Solomon Schapiro and Little Augie. Just what they were told is unknown, but both immediately retired from business. Schapiro dropped out of sight, while Little Augie, by far the more dangerous of the pair, was ordered to report twice a week to the Clinton street police station. And what a spectacle that must have been for the shades of Monk Eastman and Mose the Bowery Boy—Little Augie, the last of the gang captains, fat, flashy and addicted to fawn colored spats, standing meekly before a police sergeant and recounting his doings, refreshing his memory from entries in a notebook!

The police relieved Little Augie of this onerous obligation after two years, but detectives continued to keep him under more or less strict surveillance, and for several years he perforce lived quietly. Then, late in 1925, he began bootlegging along Broadway, supplying liquor to speakeasies and night clubs. Great success attended his new enterprise, and within a year he told his friends that he would soon be able to retire. But liquor peddlers whose customers he had appropriated had marked him for death, and on October 16, 1927, Little Augie was killed in front of No. 103 Norfolk street, between Delancey and Rivington, while talking to his bodyguard, Legs Diamond. Four men drove up in a black touring car, and when Little Augie turned in response to a hail, one of them shot him in the back of the head. He was buried in a massive cherry-red coffin lined with white satin, and on the lid gleamed a silver plate:

JACOB ORGEN
Age 25 Years.

His real age was thirty-three. But it had been eight years since he had assumed active leadership of his gang, and on that day his father had proclaimed him dead.

SLANG OF
THE EARLY GANGSTERS

THE FOLLOWING slang terms are from *"Vocabulum, or, The Rogue's Lexicon,"* by George W. Matsell, Special Justice and Chief of the New York Police. It was first published in 1859 by George W. Matsell & Company, proprietors of the *National Police Gazette*. It is interesting to note that of the words and phrases which are still in use, the meaning of many has entirely changed. Others, however, retain their ancient meanings, and have been appropriated by the modern wise-cracker:

Ace of Spades. A widow.
Active citizen. A louse.
Addle-cove. A foolish man.
Alamort. Confounded; struck dumb; unable to say or do anything.
Ankle. The mother of a child born out of wedlock.
Anointed. Flogged.
Autum. A church.
Autum bawler. A parson.

Baby paps. Caps.
Ballum-rancum. A ball where all the dancers are thieves and prostitutes.
Balsam. Money.
Bandog. A civil officer.
Baptized. Liquor that has been watered.
Barking irons. Pistols.
Barrel fever. Delirium tremens.

Bat. A prostitute who walks the street only at night.
Beak. A magistrate; a judge.
Beans. Five dollar gold pieces.
Ben. A vest.
Benjamin. A coat.
Bens. Fools.
Billy Noodle. A soft fellow who believes all the girls are in love with him.
Bingo. Liquor.
Bingo-boy. A drunken man.
Bingo-mort. A drunken woman.
Black-box. A lawyer.
Black ointment. Raw meat.
Bleak. Handsome. "The moll is bleak"; the girl is handsome.
Bleak mort. A pretty girl.
Bloke. A man.
Blowen. The mistress of a thief.
Bludget. A female thief.
Blue ruin. Bad gin.

Blunt. Money.

Boke. The nose.

Boodle. A quantity of bad money.

Booly dog. A policeman.

Bouncer. A fellow who robs while bargaining with the storekeeper.

Brads. Money.

Brass. Money.

Broads. Cards.

Broken leg. A woman who has a child out of marriage.

Bucks-face. A cuckold.

Bull. A locomotive.

Bully. A lump of lead tied in the corner of a kerchief.

Buzz. To search for and steal.

Cab moll. A woman who keeps a bad house.

Cad. A baggage smasher; a railroad conductor.

Cain and Abel. A table.

Can. A dollar.

Canary bird. A convict.

Captain Heeman. A blustering fellow.

Captain Toper. A smart highwayman.

Caravan. Plenty of money.

Casa. A house.

Case. A dollar.

Castor. A hat.

Cat. A prostitute; a cross old woman.

Century. One hundred dollars.

Charley. A gold watch.

Charley Prescot. A vest.

Chink. Money.

Chips. Money.

Church. A place where the markings on stolen jewelry are changed.

City College. The Tombs.

Clout. A handkerchief.

Conk. The nose.

Cove or covey. A man.

Cow. A dilapidated prostitute.

Cows and kisses. The ladies.

Crib. A house.

Crokus. A doctor.

Crusher. A policeman.

Cull. A man; sometimes a partner.

Cymbal. A watch.

Dace. Two cents.

Daddles. Hands.

Dangler. A seducer.

Devil books. Cards.

Dews. Ten dollars.

Diddle. Liquor.

Diddle cove. A landlord.

Dimber mort. A handsome girl.

Diver. A pickpocket.

Diving Bell. A rum shop in a basement.

Dopey. A thief's mistress.

Dots. Money.

Emperor. A drunken man.

Eriffs. Young thieves.

Evil. A wife.

Fag. A lawyer's clerk.

Faker. A jeweller.

Fams. Hands.

Fan. A waistcoat.

Fanny Blair. The hair.

Fawney. A ring.

Fenced. Sold.

Fibbing. Striking with the fist.

Figure dancer. One who alters the numbers or figures on bank bills.

Finniff. Five dollars.

Flappers. Hands.

Flash panny. A house frequented by rogues of both sexes.

Flat. A man not acquainted with the tricks of rogues.

Flimp. To tussle or wrestle.

Fork. A pickpocket.

Friday face. A dismal countenance.

Frog. A policeman.

Frog and Toe. The city of New York.

Gadding the hoof. Going without shoes.

Gagers. Eyes.

Gan. The mouth or lips.

Gander. A married man not living with his wife.

Gelter. Money.

German flute. A pair of boots.

Gigg. The nose. "Snitchel the bloke's gigg": smash the man's nose.

Gip. A thief.

Gob. The mouth.

Gonnoff. A thief who has attained the higher walks of his profession.

Gooh. A prostitute.

Gooseberry pudding. A woman.

Goosing slum. A brothel.

Governor's stiff. A governor's pardon.

Ground sweat. A grave.

Gun. A thief.

Gutter lane. The throat.

Guy. A dark lantern.

Hackum. A bravado; a slasher.

Hamlet. A captain of police.

Handle. Nose. "The cove flashed a rare handle to his physog": the fellow has a very large nose.

Harp. A woman.

High pads. Highway robbers.

High tobers. Gonnoffs.

High toby. A highway robber.

Hob or nob? What will you drink?

Hockey. Drunk.

Hogg. A ten cent piece.

Hoister. A shoplifter.

Huey. The *National Police Gazette.*

Idea pot. A man's head.

Intimate. A shirt.

Jack. A small coin; money.

Jack Cove. A mean, low fellow.

Jacob. A ladder.

Jaw coves. Lawyers.

Jew's-eye. A pleasant sight.

Jomer. A mistress.

Joseph. A coat that's patched; a sheepish, bashful fellow.

Joseph's coat. Guarded against temptation. "I say, my bene blowen, can't you kiddy the bloke?" "It's no use trying, he wears a Joseph coat." I say, my good girl, can't you seduce the fellow? It's no use trying, he is guarded against temptation.

Joskin. A countryman.

Ken. A house. "Bite the ken," rob the house.

Kiddies. Young thieves.

Kirkbuzzer. A fellow who picks pockets in churches.

Kitchen physic. Food.

Laced mutton. A common woman.

Lady. A humpbacked female.

Lady bird. A kept mistress.

Leaf. Autumn.

Left handed wife. A concubine.
Lib. Sleep.
Life preserver. A slung-shot.

Mab. A harlot.
Magg. A half cent.
Marking. Observing.
Moll. A woman.
Moll buzzer. A thief who picks women's pockets.
Moon. One month.
Mort. A woman.
Moses. A man who fathers another's child for a consideration.
Mow. To kiss. "The bloke was mowing the molly": the man was kissing the girl.
Muck. Money.
Mush. An umbrella.
My Uncle. A pawnbroker.
Music. A verdict of not guilty.

Ned. A ten dollar gold piece.
Neddy. A slung-shot.
Nickey. The devil.
Nope. A blow.
Nose. A spy, an informer.

Ochre. Money.
Ogles. The eyes.
O.K. All right. "Oll kerect."
Oliver. The moon.
Owls. Women who walk the streets at night.
O Yes. To cry out.

Pad. A street; a highway.
Pad the hoof. Walk the street.
Padding ken. A lodging house.
Panny. A house.
Panzy. A burglar.
Picture frame. The gallows.

Pig. A policeman.
Pigeon. An informer.
Ponce. A man who is kept by a woman.
Pop. To pawn.
Pops. Pistols.
Popshop. Pawnbroker's shop.

Rabbit. A rowdy. "Dead Rabbit," a very athletic, rowdy fellow.
Rabbit suckers. Young spendthrifts.
Rag. A dollar.
Rap. To take a false oath.
Reader. A pocketbook.
Red. Gold.
Red Super. A gold watch.
Regulars. Share or portion.
Rhino. Money.
Rub. Run.
Rub us to whit. Send us to prison.
Ruffian. The devil.
Rumbeak. A judge who can be bribed.

Saint Giles Buzzman. A handkerchief thief.
Saint Terra. A churchyard.
Sam. A stupid fellow.
Sawney. Bacon; fat pork.
Scandal soup. Tea.
Screw. A key.
Screwsman. A burglar who works with keys.
Shakester. A lady.
Sheeney. A Jew thief.
Sheriff's ball. An execution.
Shines. Gold coin.
Sky blue. Gin.
Slum. A package of bank bills.
Slumming. Stealing packages of bank bills.

Snafflers. Highwaymen.
Spark. A diamond.
Stretch. One year.

To break a leg. To seduce a girl.
Toby. The highway.
Tombstones. Teeth.
To bounce him. To get one's property and refuse to pay for it.
Turkey merchants. Purchasers of stolen silks.

Upper Benjamin. An overcoat.

Vamp. To pledge.

Vampire. A man who lives by extorting money from men or women seen coming from a house of assignation.
Velvet. The tongue.
Venus' curse. Venereal disease.

Wattles. The ears.
Whit. A prison.
Wife. A fetter fixed to one leg.
Wire. A pickpocket.

Yack. A watch.
Yam. To eat.

An Example

Tim Sullivan buzzed a bloke and a shakester of a reader. His jomer stalled. Johnny Miller, who was to have his regulars, called out "copbung," for as you see, a fly-cop was marking. Jack speeled to the crib, where he found Johnny Doyle had been pulling down sawney for grub. He cracked a casa last night, and fenced the swag. He told Jack as how Bill had flimped a yack, and pinched a swell of a spark fawney, and had sent the yack to church, and got half a century and a finniff for the fawney.

BIBLIOGRAPHY

MOST OF the material in this book was obtained from the newspapers and magazines, from police and court records, and from personal interviews with criminals and police officials. In addition, more than two hundred books and pamphlets were consulted, including standard histories and works of reference; reports of reform agencies; reminiscences of criminals and police and court officials; handbooks, guide-books, etc. Following are a few of the outstanding volumes:

Professional Criminals of America. Inspector Thomas Byrnes.
    1886–1895.
Recollections of a New York Chief of Police. George W. Walling. 1888.
The American Metropolis, From Knickerbocker Days to the Present Time.
    Three Volumes. Frank Moss, LL.D. 1897.
History of Tammany Hall. Gustavus Myers. 1917.
Secrets of the Great City; The Virtues and the Vices, the Mysteries,
    Miseries and Crimes of New York City. Edward Winslow Martin. 1868.
Nation-Famous New York Murders. Alfred Henry Lewis. 1914.
The Apaches of New York. Alfred Henry Lewis. 1912.
Danger! A True History of a Great City's Wiles and Temptations.
    William F. Howe and Abraham Hummel. 1886.
The Dangerous Classes of New York. Charles Loring Brace. 1880.
The Great Riots of New York. J. T. Headley. 1873.
Hot Corn. Anonymous. 1854.
A Week in New York. Ernest Ingersoll. 1892.
Asmodeus in New York. Anonymous. 1868.
The Old Brewery and the New Mission House at the Five Points. Ladies
    of the Mission. 1854.
Forty Years at the Five Points. William F. Barnard. 1893.

The New York Tombs; Its Secrets and Mysteries. Warden Charles Sutton. 1874.

The Volcano Under the City. By A Volunteer Special. 1887.

The Metropolitan Police. David Barnes. 1864.

Our Police Protectors; a History of the New York Police. A. E. Costello. 1885.

Account of the Terrific and Fatal Riot at the New York Astor Place Opera House. Anonymous. 1849.

London and New York: Their Crime and Police. J. A. Gerard. 1853.

Report of Gambling in New York. J. H. Green. 1851.

Our Fight with Tammany. Rev. Charles H. Parkhurst. 1923.

My Forty Years in New York. Rev. Charles H. Parkhurst. 1923.

The New York of Yesterday; a Descriptive Narrative of Old Bloomingdale. Hopper Striker Mott. 1908.

History of Lower Wall Street and Vicinity. Abram Wakeman. 1914.

The Old Merchants of New York City. Walter Barrett. 1885.

History of New York City. William L. Stone. 1872.

Valentine's Manual of Old New York City. 1866 to 1927.

King's Handbook of New York City. Moses King. 1892.

Rider's New York City. Edited by Fremont Rider. 1924.

The Gang. Frederic M. Thrasher, Ph.D. 1927.

INDEX